From Genesis to Revelation

A Story You Find Yourself In

STUART TILLMAN

BALBOA.PRESS
A DIVISION OF HAY HOUSE

Balboa Press books may be ordered through booksellers or by contacting:

Balboa Press
A Division of Hay House
1663 Liberty Drive
Bloomington, IN 47403
www.balboapress.com
844-682-1282

Because of the dynamic nature of the Internet, any web addresses or links contained in this book may have changed since publication and may no longer be valid. The views expressed in this work are solely those of the author and do not necessarily reflect the views of the publisher, and the publisher hereby disclaims any responsibility for them.

The author of this book does not dispense medical advice or prescribe the use of any technique as a form of treatment for physical, emotional, or medical problems without the advice of a physician, either directly or indirectly. The intent of the author is only to offer information of a general nature to help you in your quest for emotional and spiritual well-being. In the event you use any of the information in this book for yourself, which is your constitutional right, the author and the publisher assume no responsibility for your actions.

Print information available on the last page.

Interior Graphics/Art Credit: Becca Tindol

Scripture quotations taken from the New American Standard Bible®, Copyright © 1960, 1962, 1963, 1968, 1971, 1972, 1973, 1975, 1977, 1995 by The Lockman Foundation. Used by permission." (www.Lockman.org)

ISBN: 979-8-7652-3684-0 (sc)
ISBN: 979-8-7652-3686-4 (hc)
ISBN: 979-8-7652-3685-7 (e)

Library of Congress Control Number: 2022922477

Balboa Press rev. date: 12/27/2022

CONTENTS

PREFACE

We all have a story. All our stories come to life within a myriad of other stories. Like ripples in a pond, the energy released from a choice one makes becomes a story in and of its own and will flow without discrimination until it is fully absorbed into these other stories. This law of cause and effect, reaping and sowing, or karma is uncompromising.

Most of the stories that make up our own go mostly unnoticed. We simply miss them. To begin with, and perhaps the most significant reason for this is that we do not remember that we are fearfully and wonderfully made and dismiss the power of our thoughts. Our thoughts run our lives, for it is through our thoughts that we become creators. With each thought, humans initiate a choice, setting into motion a new creation story serving to shape our reality. Because of our nature, we are not cognizant of the vastness of these thoughts, leaving us unaware that we have even made a choice, breathing life into a new story. It's in these scenarios that our creative energy is released without intention nor governance, setting into motion a dynamic that's just as likely to cause pain and suffering as it is to bring pleasure and growth, whether to ourselves or others.

Conceptually, *The Story You Find Yourself In* was envisioned to serve as a platform devoted to exploring the nuances of our conscious and subconscious existence found within the context of our spiritual progression. Subconscious thoughts tend to trigger a reaction leading to choices that are not contemplated, meaning alternatives were not considered. In this condition, a person's true potential is seldom fully realized, as it requires a disciplined awareness to rule your thoughts and respond with decisions that are in alignment with your highest purpose. Recognizing this distinction is the cornerstone event towards understanding spiritual phrases such as, "I was blind, but now I see," or "Awake, O' sleeper, and arise from the dead." For at this moment, you begin to have a relationship with yourself, knowing that there is a *You* that's largely a product of your conditioning and programming that believes that it is separate from everything else, while there is also a *You* that is divine and one with all things. Your reality is determined by which *You* is being nurtured and trusted, which for most, this choice has been unknowingly made and is a deeply subconscious one; hence the meaning of "Awake, O' sleeper."

All our stories coalesce and have meaning within the framework of relationships. There can be no more significant relationship than the one that we have with ourselves, with the inner man, for the health of this relationship is the foundation for every other relationship. *From Genesis to Revelation* reflects the continuation of the author's personal spiritual journey, chronicling his efforts to unlock the mysteries of the law of God in the inner man. *From Genesis to Revelation* is styled as an allegory meant to relate this understanding of Self to every other relationship that the universe presents. In doing so, this allegory approaches this creation, and more specifically the earth and its solar system, as the handiwork of an intentional creator, resulting in a finely tuned ecosystem designed to support and enhance the human experience. There's clearly something mysterious about how this creation functions, with its uncanny precision and purposeful alignment. Humanities' relationship with its host is a bit of a paradox, considering how the delicate nature of its compatibility to support life in myriad forms is being met with mankind's ceaseless demands on the planet's resiliency. How much human interaction can Mother Earth absorb?

Many view our planet to be a symbiotic living organism requiring much care, while others see it as nothing more than a revolving rock possessing a vast reservoir of resources to be exploited. However, most of humanity moves through their lives cognitively disconnected from having an opinion of what this relationship should be about. Like many things that are taken for granted beyond our own awareness, thoughts regarding this most basic of dynamics are driven by and influence a relationship with a component of our Self, either conscientiously or subconsciously, and always in concert with some other created energy in our environment, whether tangible or intangible. Coming at it from this perspective, we can come full circle and surmise that each of these events is also a form of creative interaction directly with our Divine Source, even if we ourselves are not awakened to these moments. It's not surprising then that the unintended consequences arising from these subconsciously made decisions will eventually require us to raise our awareness as to who we are and how our thoughts run our lives.

The road travelled towards this self-revelation is one that we will each have to make. It is at least the one thing that we all have in common irrespective of the many things that differentiate us. Because we are all explicitly unique, this road is a customized journey, a one-of-a-kind trip, with the end game revealing to us what I've come to understand to be the main purpose of our human journey. Our Divine Source has designed for us what I've found to be a very difficult, sometimes painful, beautifully rewarding, extraordinary experience requiring us to be skillful at observing both the human condition in general and, more specifically, ourselves. Deliberate intention is required to become a proficient observer. Becoming *aware of awareness* is best learned through observation. However, from my experience and observations, the process of becoming *aware of awareness* often begins with a surreal whack upside the head. I'm talking about an attention-getter kind of slap, the kind that knocks you off your feet. That's the focus of my first book, a chronicle of that painful journey. It hurts me to read it still. Unfortunately, the process of learning how to heal from early psychic wounds and pursue self-care techniques leads one through a process that adds new pain on top of the old, leaving one dealing with negative motivators at critical moments. The question then becomes, what kind of preemptive actions can you take to help avoid that kind of turmoil? Man, that's a tough question, as we're all so thoroughly conditioned based on our unique environments and hand-me-down belief systems. However, I do want to believe that becoming aware of awareness must offer advantages over remaining oblivious. At least, I believe that having access to a book such as this would have helped me realize what I was experiencing and endure the process with less suffering. Having said that, I am not suggesting that I've got this figured out. Certainly not for you, your journey is unique to you and one only you can initiate. But I have learned some hard lessons and am hopeful that others can benefit from them.

In the process of reconciling the necessity of these painful lessons with my spiritual progression, I became obsessed with correlating esoteric Biblical wisdom with the actual experiences of my personal journey. Almost every major event of my spiritual evolution was captured in a personal journal and documented a progression through various trials as the sleeper within awakened. Along the way, a thread of esoteric knowledge emerged that connected the missing links that I found in my story. As I pulled and pulled on this thread, it became evident that I would have to venture into the Book of Revelation for answers and, as you can see in the Table of Contents, making that call dramatically altered the direction of this book. It seemed that everything I was being drawn towards would lead me back into Revelation, and then, there it was, from *Genesis to Revelation,* my story. The nature of the dialogue amongst the key characters reflects the *thinking-out-loud* process going on in my mind as the thoughts turned into words on the page. Because of this diversion much of the vision for the first book will materialize within the heretofore unplanned sequel. For now, the writing effort will contemplate what it is to be human participating in this creation and to contemplate what the Bible has to say about how you are expressly made to facilitate your participation in this extraordinary experience.

Considering the above, the primary objective of this two-part allegoric effort will be first to observe the human condition and what it means to be fearfully and wonderfully made, and second, to explore what it means to be the individual human being that you are and the purpose of this extraordinary experience. *From Genesis to Revelation* will attempt to achieve the first objective, relying on the observations from inanimate characters we interact with daily. As the Genesis derived mystery of Adam and Eve suggests, this effort must make a determination as to the nature of man's origin, however, doing so is quite tricky as man does not remember from where he has fallen. Irrespective of the conclusions derived from the traditional exoteric interpretations settled on by mainstream religions, the author has determined that the symbolism found throughout the esoteric Bible is fully reconciled within the symbolism found in Revelation, serving to provide clarity to the question regarding the nature of man's origin and the purpose behind our earthly sojourn. From this perspective, the journey *From Genesis to Revelation* begins with the involution of soul signified as man falling into this physical incarnation in his *natural body* persona, the first of the ways of God, and ends with man evolving into his *spiritual body* persona signified by the *Lamb's* marriage to his bride. The in-between is loaded with esoteric knowledge about the journey of the soul and how we are made, specifically the psyche of man, and it's by divine design, *A Story You Find Yourself In*. The second objective will be the subject of the sequel *'the happening' and the Revealing of the sons of God … A Story You Find Yourself In*. Obviously, in order to accomplish these objectives, we will be required to incorporate the concept of Spirit into that which brings these characters to life. I personally believe that there really is a living connection within all components of creation, but just how communication between them may occur is certainly a mystery to me. Curiously, I have seen research that suggests that water has a memory and responds to all manner of vibrations, even human thoughts, which is why one of the primary characters is a *drop* named Zegula.

Evaluating and illuminating the human condition is mostly self-evident and will be approached through the acknowledgment of the accumulated impact or effect of what man has created. Tangible creations that are visible and can be touched are obvious in construct and purpose. Intangible creations, those that are invisible to the eye, are more difficult to recognize and tend to reflect our internal conditioning and programming. It's here where the question of morality more often comes into play. These obscure creations, institutions, belief systems, political affiliations, social contracts, etc., tend to reflect and/or mirror the thoughts and the general health of the collective inner man. For most of us humans observing and analyzing the human condition, or other humans, is something that we are quite adept at. Having said that, I am not suggesting that it means we are agreeable to its conclusion, as I surmise it's quite the contrary and problematic. Now it gets a bit more complicated when it comes to observing ourselves. We live in a complex world and have been molded by our early experiences. Sadly, however, we remain unaware of the totality of this conditioning, as most of it occurred during our first seven or so years and serves as the catalyst for most, if not all, forms of mental illnesses and systemic disease. So, before we get started, it seems that we each have one very big question to ask ourselves. It's cliché for certain but here goes. Are you a physical being searching for a spiritual experience, or are you a spiritual being having a physical experience? Man's search for the meaning of this life started at the beginning of cognition, whenever that was, and the nature of your journey hinges on where you settle regarding this single question. Well, I guess that's much too simple right? For the answer, regardless of your predisposition, leads a person into a matrix of other questions.

Taking that question just one level up begs the next question. If you were a physical being searching for a spiritual experience, would the *expected* outcome be one of maximizing one's emotional/physical bliss while participating in this temporal physical plane, or would it be one of experiencing a conversion to a form of eternal spiritual Being? On the other hand, if you were a spiritual Being having a physical experience, what would be the purpose of this incarnation? Why are you here, and where did you come from? Did you choose to do this? Oh, boy, how deep do you think these rabbit holes go? And what about the concepts of religion and spirituality? How do they fit in here? How are they different from each other and do they have to be? Are they separate ideals, or do they intersect? From the above conversation, I've picked a lane regarding our origin, accepting that the divine spark is in each of us from the beginning. I further believe that the practice of religion and the pursuit of spirituality do intersect while also recognizing the practice thereof often puts one at odds with the other. The practice of faith-based religious organizations is a man-made *intangible* creation, and we will explore why that tends to be so. In contrast, the pursuit of spirituality tends to be an individual, one-off endeavor, and we will explore why that tends to be so. What I will risk acknowledging here in the preface is that I believe many of these answers are found in the Bible.

Why is that a risk? I have found that any ideology that becomes institutionalized will be defended with a zealousness that alienates those not lining up behind those belief systems' doctrines. Just look at the practice of our political belief systems and the requirement to choose sides. It's much like that with religious indoctrination, whereby the application of unsanctioned spiritual thought is dismissed as New Age discourse, or worse, as heretical and in alignment with the Satan narrative. This problem originates from the fact that the Bible is an intimidating and difficult book to navigate. It's understandable that most folks look outside of themselves for guidance on these intellectual matters, and over many centuries the population has ceded the interpretation authority over to these religious institutions. Recognizing this conditioned environment, it's no surprise then that those outside the church behave as if the Bible, as an authority, is the property of religion. The concept that the Bible has universal application to all spiritual matters has been effectively hijacked by these numerous religious institutions, resulting in pseudo-claimed ownership thereof, effectively discouraging spiritual enlightenment seekers from aligning their pursuits with any manner of Biblical support. As a result, we have seen that a fundamental distrust develops between the practice of religious doctrines and pursuits of spiritual methodologies, with both being maligned against the other.

Why do I refer to religion as a *practice* and *spirituality* as a pursuit? For the most part, the *practice* of religious doctrine has been established since the production of the Bible just less than 2,000 years ago. Participation in these institutionalized practices is then designed to teach members how to apply these doctrines to their lives. The largest religion is Christianity, followed by Islam. Both rely on the foundational Jewish Torah, found in the practice of Judaism, which is why it is written in the Hebrew language explaining its rich content of symbolism and depth. Christianity formed the New Testament and added it to the Torah, or Old Testament, to construct the Bible. Islam did the same with its Quran. On the other hand, Mormons added the Book of Mormon on top of the Bible. Christianity has over 35,000 different denominations practicing its faith, suggesting that there are many ways to interpret the *literal* meaning of the Bible. It's simply a very complex and difficult book.

Based on the literal interpretation of the foundational sacred texts, these institutionalized doctrines promote a faith that proclaims we are a *fallen* sinful people in need of being saved by a God *out there* while we are simultaneously being harassed and pursued by an evil third-party menace called Satan/devil/Lucifer. In simplistic terms, this looking *outside* for the source of our saving grace as well as our torment, contrasts with the spiritual practice of searching for awakening, or enlightenment, which is an internal pursuit of your true nature. The methodologies used by the respective approaches are quite different, even though they deal with the same human construct, the same human mind and the same human condition. So, here's where I am going with this and what this allegory will attempt to help clarify. I believe that both philosophies will ultimately bring you to the same door, to the same gate, to the same most important Holy Place. Both approaches intersect at this critical juncture. Passing through this door is the very purpose of our incarnation and where understanding the Bible is not only helpful but also critical. There is a catch, however, and with this catch, there is also a mystery to contend with. When viewed as a literal text, the Bible creates division both in practice thereof (division outside of ourselves) and regarding how we are to understand that we are fearfully and wonderfully made (division inside of ourselves). The Bible, taken in its metaphysical/esoteric form (viewed as a spiritual text and instead of focusing only on the literal, the reader searches for the hidden meaning found in the allegories, symbolism, parables, and numerology), is a book about YOU, for YOU. The Bible, in its metaphysical form, is a flowing and consistent dialogue about how we are made and why we are here. In it, you will see repeating patterns and themes guiding you to a better understanding of YOU, and I believe this level of understanding has the potential to eliminate the divisions mentioned above. Upon seeing and learning these mysteries, you will come to know why our man-made ideological belief systems cause the harm and division that they do and why they are so difficult to contend with. You will see that they simply reflect how we are made and are natural siblings of our duality experience. The Bible must be the most important book ever written on human psychology, and my hope is that *From Genesis to Revelation* will help you see it that way as well.

So, it's settled that this effort will take the position that we are spiritual beings having a physical experience. Secondly, my experience has taught me that one cannot become aware without first learning the art of observing. Your process may look different. What is it that you observe to become aware? You learn how to observe yourself. YOU observe YOU. I know this sounds innocuous on the surface, but it really is the hard part. How so, you ask? Since we've already determined that we are spiritual beings, how hard is it for the spirit to observe itself? What is there to observe other than the product of my actions or my production? Well, yeah, you guessed it, there is a catch to this game, and it isn't a game at all. This is the most serious adventure you can take or must take; it's why you're here; fortunately, you don't have an option. You see, there are actually two parties to consider here, and the YOU that is being observed is not accustomed to being watched, as this party is *'more crafty than any beast of the field which the Lord God had made (Gen 3:1),'* and is gifted at hiding. This observed YOU, who we must contend with first, has worked very diligently for the observing 'other' YOU, who is second, to stay where you've been and leave things as they were. What is also paradoxical about this relationship is that God tells us that He is also hiding and that we must seek Him.

The Apostle Paul writes extensively about these dual natures throughout his letters referring to this relationship as the great mystery while presenting these two natures as warring with each other in his body. Paul goes on to claim that Jesus put to death the enmity between these dueling parties reconciling them into one body, while further suggesting that this reconciliation is symbolized by the cross and made possible through the mystery of Christ. I know … I know … and I must apologize supposing that this is where your eyes begin to cross, and the ears stop hearing. What the heck does this mean anyway and why doesn't Paul just come out and clearly say what he means rather than making it a mystery? I must laugh right here and answer; *'I don't know for that remains a mystery too.'* So, tell me how two natures that are both hiding ever find reconciliation and peace in order to coexist? Well, in order to answer that question, I've surmised that we need to explore the origin of humanity and the role that these dual natures take. Next, we need to define the purpose of mankind incarnating on this earth and what it means to know good and evil, for the scriptures tell us that has made man like God. Next, because we're told that we have become like God, to know good and evil, that we now need figure out what it means to partake of the tree of life so that we can cheat death and live forever. Next, let's go find that dang tree, alright? Make sense? Everybody on board with this? Let's do it!

Just so you know I'm laughing heartily on the inside at how preposterous and arrogant those objectives read. I'm sure some eyes widened, and the brain scintillated for a moment. Even though I wrote those with tongue in cheek I must confess that those questions have intrigued me as it's these questions that connect the Book of Genesis to the Book of Revelation … the beginning to the ending. It begs the question; what is going on here? There's something about how we are made, combined with this earthly physical incarnation, permitting us as spiritual *Beings* to have experiences designed for us to *know* good and evil. This would suggest that this type of learning opportunity is not available from whence we came and that this is a special purpose designed environment towards that end. Thinking that nearly incomprehensible thought through, I cannot for the life of me reconcile such an extraordinary concept with the religious doctrine that we are a hopelessly fallen species because of original sin, and that we are presently here on this planet as victims destined to carry out the penitence on behalf of Adam and Eve's errancy. I simply cannot accept that conclusion, nor do I see it supported as such anywhere in the esoteric scripture. Notwithstanding the significance of this single doctrinal debate there are others that taken together have helped explain the cognitive dissonance I was experiencing in my practice of western styled religion. I can't help but believe that other serious minds also feel this disconnect, suggesting that this type of unreconciled dogma helps to explain the precipitous decline in church participation and increased participation in competing, non-faith-based ideologies. You certainly do not have to agree but since 1990 the percent of those claiming to have no religious affiliation at all has grown from 5% to 25%, indicating that there is a definitive problem brewing. Your faith is yours, and mine is my business. I'm not making any attempt to change anybody's mind on this matter, but simply looking for conversation, as I consider debate arising from an impassioned defensive posture to be meaningless, unproductive, and denigrates the otherwise meaningful practice of faith and the pursuit of spirituality. We will always have more to learn, and much about our existence will forever remain a mystery.

As I close out this Preface I can't help but make an observation regarding the status of our society and the roles that the practice of religion and the pursuits of spirituality are serving. At present, our society is severely fractured and has abandoned the art of conversation. Relegating every dispute into a zero-sum game is not conversation, but instead a reflection of efforts to protect one's own ideological dogmas serving to illuminate the interference arising from one's own extreme subconscious insecurities. It has absolutely pervaded the entirety of our world causing destruction in the quality of all our lives. Looking ahead, it's clear that something must initiate the change back to civility, while also encouraging curiosity, especially when it comes to our spiritually motivated discourse.

Our institutions have failed in this regard. The change must come from communities of individuals uniting with the goal of improving the spiritual and emotional health of those around us. This begins with society learning to not take itself so damn seriously and recognizing that just being *you* authentically is enough. I hope that you find this book intriguing and that you find a morsel or two to ponder further.

PREVIEW OF THE
STORY'S CONSTRUCT

As alluded to earlier, the direction of this book morphed substantially as it was being written. Pursuant to the original outline, the discussion addressing the condition of mankind was mostly limited to making an assessment regarding humanity's relationship with its host creation and the impact of its exploding population. As the conversation developed, it became apparent that the creation characters needed a more comprehensive understanding of the collective psyche of humanity in order to develop a next-level strategy to counter the rapid industrialization of the planet. This growing concern of self-preservation facing the creation had to be balanced against the backdrop of the necessity to maintain the integrity of the creator's design for the overall human experience. What ensued was a much deeper dive into the Biblical constructs than what was originally anticipated in order to properly set the stage for the creation's response to the chaos caused by this seemingly reckless human behavior. This shift occurs with the start of the second Journey of Saffron and will be where the sequel begins.

The original title of the book was *"The Drop – A Story You Find Yourself In,"* as it was intended to portray the creation that is all around us as a living and thriving interactive entity independent from any human interference while at the same time serving to highlight humanities self-absorbed dismissive attitude towards it. The creation is reeling from the cumulative effects of humanities activities and exponential growth, demanding that the creation thoroughly assess the situation through its unique powers of observation. Towards this effort, the creation must wrestle with the sacred texts to better discern the creator's intentions and to provide a framework for making assumptions as to the spiritual nature of man. So, while the whole of humanity relies on the passive participation of the creation as mankind evolves, the creation independently navigates its own course in hopes that increased awareness will facilitate a more symbiotic future world.

To this end, *From Genesis to Revelation … A Story You Find Yourself In* does find a thread of esoteric knowledge helping to connect the symbolism found in the Old Testament to the vast references of Old Testament symbolism found in the Book of Revelation. Based on my experience, once you see it, you can't unsee it, as this connected symbolism is found in every chapter of every book in the Bible. Having said that, this effort can only provide enough content to deliver what amounts to as a 30,000-foot flyover, and it is my hope that there is sufficient guidance herein to help facilitate any motivated seekers' desire to conduct one's own deeper dive into this rich metaphysical material. To that end, the first half of this book attempts to lay in the foundation necessary to incorporate the relational Biblical constructs that follow. In recognition of the inherent complexities found in understanding spiritual literature, this effort does require the reader to deploy an element of patience and attention to see it through to the end. I've had the pleasure of working with an accomplished and supportive editor specializing in Biblical literature. Her suggestion was that I may want to consider turning this into two books as 'There IS A LOT in here to digest.' So please be mindful of that concern, as after submitting to a quite extensive editing effort, I've determined that this will be one book designed to provide the reader with a framework to pursue their own spiritual journey from the perspective of the esoteric meanings of the Biblical texts.

The main characters in this book are water drops, along with the interplay of the major components of this creation. Through the drops gift of observing the inner man's thoughts, they will serve as the inquisitors of our dual natures and the unbiased purveyor of the mysteries in this allegory. Water has very interesting characteristics and serves the earth in much the same way that it serves humanity. Zegula is the wise sage of the drops, while Zarya is the innocent and naïve follower. Zarya is set up as a key character in Part Two, while Zarya's two friends, Gali and Iluka are introduced in this story and will be more fully developed in the sequel. The creation characters are comprised of the earth (Mother Gaia), the sun (as Saffron to the drops in the seven seas & as Helia to the drops while on the Journey of Saffron), the moon (Dawa), collectively these characters are referred to as the Ethereal Council, with the spirit of the seven seas (Mira), and the mysterious wind (Kalani) filling key roles. These characters are the foundation for the drops adventures providing guidance and unique pearls of wisdom regarding the purpose behind this creation. The lion's share of the conversation flows between Zegula and Dawa as they combine their unique powers of observation to assess mankind. Meanwhile, the Ethereal Council has determined that the prophecy of *the happening* has begun, and it represents the creations response to humanities perceived irresponsibility. As part of this prophecy, the drops are also participating in their own form of evolution of consciousness through the demands presented by the Journey of Saffron. The Journey of Saffron is simply the water cycle presented as a unique adventure and an opportunity for the drops to experience a limited form of duality, paving the way for future growth in consciousness apart from any connection to the plight of humanity. The strategy of *the happening* involves the redemption of the seven Jewels of Gaia. The seven Jewels represent the seven continents, with the twelve Spires and 24 Deacons representing the continent's primary mountain ranges and watersheds, respectively. It will become obvious that these earthly physical markers correlate with the seven Spirits and the twenty-four elders positioned before the throne in heaven found in the Book of Revelation, with Gaia, Dawa, Kalani and Mira collectively under the watchful eye of Saffron, representing the four creatures before the One sitting on the throne. The insights gained into the psyche of man serve to determine the approach the creation will take towards incorporating its response to humanity as *the happening* unfolds. Animating the inanimate, bringing to life that which is already alive? My hope is that you can observe your SELF in *"From Genesis to Revelation: A Story You Find Yourself In"* and finish this read with a greater appreciation for awareness.

ACKNOWLEDGMENTS

The Story You Find Yourself In serves as the foundation for this effort. The following individuals heavily influenced my life and the production of that first book. I'll thank them in the order that their influence appeared.

My good friend and business partner Tom Dickinson has been by my side since the beginning of my trials. This man has a heart as big as any mountain, and I literally owe him with my life. Love you, buddy!

My dear friend and business partner, Steve Langley, has blessed me with some of the most interesting and provocative conversations that I've ever had. His unorthodox views of why we are here opened a critical door, allowing me to set aside much of my religious conditioning, serving to open my mind for Self-discovery. Thank you, my friend.

I've known Larry Callaway longer than any other in these acknowledgements, and the two of us have been through plenty together. Larry and Tom are cut from the same mold, and I'm such a lucky guy to claim both as friends. Larry is the real deal through and through. Larry and his wife Rhonda stepped up in a major way to provide a place for me to land when I was at my lowest point. The Story You Find Yourself In was written at their dinette table that looks out over their courtyard in the backyard. I ended up house sitting at their place in Houston for two years while they were predominantly living in their Austin home. It's difficult to imagine anyone accepting that kind of intrusion. They are two of the most genuinely Godly people I know. Thank you, Larry. Thank you, Rhonda.

I owe a debt of gratitude to my friend and business partner, Jaime "Bravo" Lossada, for his unwavering support in keeping our software initiative alive as we navigated around the pandemic and thereafter. His friendship and loyalty are much appreciated, and my career outlook would have been severely damaged without his continued support.

Although I don't know her personally, it feels as if I've met her heart. Dr. LePera @the.holistic.psychologist IG has been a guiding light as I traversed my own psyche. I learned so much from her efforts since I began to follow her in 2018, and I am so grateful for her graciousness with her knowledge. Her book "How to do the Work" came out several months after I had posted up The Story You Find Yourself In on Amazon, and it contains a wealth of insight that has served me well since. I'm looking forward to her second book, "How to Meet Your Self," as the content that she has been putting out on IG has been awesome and hits close to home. Thank you, Dr. LePera, for your selfless service to humanity.

Sound esoteric Biblical knowledge is hard to come by. Fortunately, I found Joshua Tilghman at www.spiritofthescripture.com, and his work fueled my newfound interest in this arena. Joshua manages a website that freely offers up this metaphysical knowledge and plenty of it. I've not once read one of his blogs in disagreement. It's always solid and respectful. His team includes Anny Voss, who never ceases to impress with her knowledge of gematria. Her command of the Hebrew language is off the charts. Thank you, Joshua, for this website and for your selfless service to humanity and to the pursuit of spirituality.

That leads me to this book, *From Genesis to Revelation … A Story You Find Yourself In*. Although the genesis of this effort is dependent on what went before, it manifested out of anyone's purview or influence except for one. My wife Ida Lourdes Ortiz Zaragoza, and now Tillman, has been a rock for me. I can hardly dip my toe into this pond to describe her unwavering love and support without writing the whole story right here. That story and her story is the third new book on deck…Part Three to The Story You Find Yourself In…as, it's the most important story the two of us find ourselves in. I can't tell you how many times I've asked the question: *"Am I crazy baby for trying to do this?"* for *From Genesis to Revelation* has been all-consuming. Thankfully she has absorbed it all, including being present for every word written in the first book. By the way, she always answers the same with a hug and kisses, saying, "No amore, you are not going crazy; what you are writing can help people; even if we aren't around to see it." No one can know what we've endured together. Love her to the moon and back. Thanks, Baby!

This book wouldn't be complete without the front cover artwork provided by artist Becca Tindol. Early on I determined to find a representation of the tree of life for the cover and stumbled across Becca's artwork featured in Etsy. The second I saw this piece I knew the search was over provided the artist would be agreeable. I was pleasantly surprised to not only find an artist that was pleasant to work with but also one who had her personal awakening experience manifest within the painting. It's a perfect fit for this book and it's been a wonderful experience working with her. Thank you Becca for agreeing to participate and sharing a brief of your personal journey. And for those of you that happen to connect with the message of this effort and admire this artwork, prints are available at www.alteredmoonart.com. Fortunately for me, I was able to pick-up the original painting and now Becca's story becomes part of mine.

THE CREATIONS ALLIANCE

The Ethereal Council

The penetrating rays of warmth sent by Saffron met the morning rush. Zarya and her friends Gali and lluka were bouncing and pinging their way back under the surface to avoid that space where Saffron's radiance meets Kalani, the breath of *the one who is greater*. While free to frolic about under the light of Dawa during the night, it's not yet time for Zarya and her friends to take the Journey of Saffron, and they must hurry back down, making way for those that are. It's mostly the same every day; it starts off slowly, then picks up pace as Saffron rises high above. The drops struggle with each other to get closest to the surface and be one of the first to go. Eventually, they make it to the top, and each one disappears into the blue sky of Kalani, beginning their uniquely own Journey of Saffron.

It has been over two thousand years since Zarya's last Journey of Saffron, and she's almost ready for her next sojourn. There's one last bit of specialized training that's been added due to the dramatic changes Mother Gaia has experienced since Zarya's last trip. Zarya has enjoyed being back with Mira especially considering her last Journey took over a billion years. She found herself frozen in a remote ice cap and is thankful for once again being connected to all the other drops. But Zarya is getting restless and is eager to complete her training. This training is particularly interesting to Zarya as it teaches how to cope with passing through a human, something Zarya has never experienced. The word is that there are lots and lots and lots of them now, and they have very intense energy patterns to contend with. We also learn about some of the stuff they've created, both tangible and intangible, and what to expect if you get sucked into one of their machines. It turns out that The Journey of Saffron has evolved into the Human Experience, which we hear can often be a harrowing one.

Mira is both the beginning and the end of the Journey of Saffron. Mira is the spirit over all the oceans and binds all of us drops together with the magic of the Krystal. It's through the Krystal that the drops are continuously connected and thrive as one. The Krystal is also the key to why the Journey of Saffron is the mystery of all mysteries. When Saffron takes a drop from Mira, it must leave the Krystal behind so that Mira can administer the healing properties of the Krystal to the returning drops. This is a critical balance, ensuring the land has what it needs to nurture Gaia and that Kalani has what she needs to keep Gaia cool. Letting go of the Krystal is an act of faith by the drops for at that moment, it becomes separated from Mira and the other drops. Each drop is individualized for the journey, forgetting from where it came until it merges back into Mira upon the return. During the journey, the drops cannot telepathically communicate, losing all inherent cognitive connection with Mira. While on its journey, each drop will have the opportunity to experience humans, Gaia and itself, leading to the discovery of the secret of the Krystal. Along the journey, it's also possible for the drops to totally forget the nature of the Journey of Saffron and become distracted by their experiences. These distractions and the attachment to the Krystal inevitably turn into resistance for the drops. It's an important lesson for the drops to understand, why this resistance makes it impossible for the drop to find the Glow, a process that precedes the awareness of the secret of the Krystal. Complicating matters was the growing number of humans, for they had the Krystal too.

Life was getting complicated and confusing for Mira; for you see, Mira served at the behest of Gaia, considering that Mira was taken from and is a component of Gaia. For billions of years, Mira's responsibility regarding the Journey of Saffron has been the dominion of Gaia and split between keeping Gaia cool and nourishing the lands. For all of history, almost everything returning with the drops was organic and could be naturally assimilated. But today, Mira is on the verge of being overwhelmed by the onslaught of poisonous refuse constantly flowing into her with the returning drops. Not only is Mira choking on the toxicity, but the drops are also overwhelmed by it, resulting in more and more resistance. To make matters even more critical was that it appears that Gaia has become saturated and has fallen into a coma of sorts, waking up less frequently and unable to provide strategic guidance to Mira. Mira's response to Gaia's misfortunes was two-fold; one was growing resentment related to Gaia's lack of leadership in a time of crisis, while she was also becoming increasingly ambivalent and self-serving in the absence of Gaia's authority. The entire construct for the Journey of Saffron was becoming compromised by the activities and experiences due to the growing number of humans. In one of Gaia's brief moments of consciousness, she sent out an alarm and requested a Concurrence with the other members of the Ethereal Council. There must be something we can do.

"Saffron ... Dawa," whispers Gaia, "I'm going to need your help with Mira. It seems that she has become untethered and acting out impulsively. This is creating chaos and causing Kalani to act independently and quite hastily in anticipation of what I might need. The only energy I'm aware of that could directly influence Mira's increasingly selfish attitude is Zegula's Glow, and I believe that even Mira would welcome his return; it would be best if somehow you could make that concept her idea, she would be much more cooperative that way. I also believe that it's quite probable that Zegula's energy could even help to wake me up. Please work with Kalani to find him," says Gaia as she fades away. Saffron and Dawa nod in agreement, with Dawa adding, "Saffron, I know where Zegula is resting, and provided that you concur with Gaia's request, I can get the process of freeing him started." Saffron replies, "Yes, Dawa, I do concur, recognizing that this will be the first time that we've had to intervene to preempt our natural laws. However, mankind has certainly served up some most unnatural creations serving to unleash this destruction on our ecosystem. We must do this in order to save man from the unintended consequences of his own thoughts; *the one who is greater* has given us His permission to act. And Dawa, this is a critical time as it does appear *the happening* has begun."

General Azul & His Mission

Like every day before upon the rising of Saffron, the deeper Zarya went, the more she sensed the urgency surrounding those returning from making the journey. You never knew how long the journey would take, and we were hearing from returning sojourners that we hadn't heard from in hundreds of thousands of years. Although very exciting, we could hear through the Krystal rumors of *the happening,* the prophecy of the great thaw that had held many of our brethren for millennium upon millennium frozen in time. We all would anxiously await the news of those that had the Glow, as The Ethereal Council was most fond of those.

On the other hand, this point of the transition, where those returning from The Journey of Saffron are connecting back up with the Krystal, wasn't without its distress. It has become an ever-increasing challenge and concern for the twenty-four Generals serving the twenty-four Deacons of Gaia. Each of the twenty-four Deacons had unique characteristics' stemming from the influences coming from the natures of mankind inhabiting each of the seven Jewels that made up Gaia's landmasses. Located on the seven Jewels were twelve Major Spires that rose high amid the seven Jewels, usually stretching from end to end. These twelve Spires served two purposes, with the first being to cause the breezes of Kalani to cool while rising high, and the second was to direct the flow of the drops into one of the twenty-four Deacons, which would then flow and empty into one of the seven seas of Mira. It was all a connected circle of life for the creation. Azul, the greatest of our 24 generals, and his team are charged with greeting the returning drops from the largest of the 24 Deacons and ensuring they are debriefed and immediately assigned to their rehabilitation programs. Azul has manned this role for over a billion years and has seen every energy pattern imaginable. Azul can quickly surmise the condition of each returning drop and knows exactly what they need in order to return to the surface to be available for the next journey. But this evolving energy pattern was becoming problematic for Azul and required a very intimate and timely healing process. The debriefing process has overwhelmed the team due to the confusion and incoherence displayed by those returning.

Even though the drops could not articulate the nature of their experiences, Azul had discovered a commonality in those that had troubling darker energy patterns. Unfortunately, this energy pattern isn't completely new to Azul, as he innately knew that he had experienced similar energy on his last journey. This energy pattern was just as intense and clearly bore the imprint of human contact. Azul realizes that drops with the Krystal do not experience fear, yet these returning drops have become consumed by it. Azul is unable to properly discern the nature of this experience fully due to the utter disorientation of the arriving drops. It's a type of trauma response and due to the veil, the drops cannot fully express what has happened to them. Azul was terribly disturbed and concluded that he needed help. For now, Mira, in her rebellious mindset, would simply send them as deep as possible and for as long as necessary to press out the darkness. Even though Azul found this to be an unpleasant option, in times of emergency, using Mira's magic forces was the most certain remedy, even though she has become ambivalent and accustomed to forgetting about them.

Zarya and her friends yearn for the day they can meet the radiance of Saffron and the breezes of Kalani. The Journey of Saffron is the most treasured of all gifts, always delivering a unique experience. It's been over two millennia since any of them have made the journey, waiting, remaining content in Mira's embrace. For it's here we all have the Krystal within, connecting us together as one. During the Journey of Saffron, we take on a new reality of separateness even though we all come from and ultimately return to the same place. In our preparation, we are first forewarned of the perilous nature that this feeling of separateness can harbor while at the same time remaining expectant that we can discover the secret of the Krystal somewhere along the journey. Zarya fell as a perfectly shaped and pure snowflake on her last trip. It's there she stayed in place under the weight of millions of other drops until she melted back into Mira. It was a peaceful and largely underwhelming experience. How would she handle these progressing challenges? The humans? The toxicity? The fear? Where is she going? How long would she be gone? Would Azul be there to take care of her when she returned, or would she encounter a new Deacon and meet a new general? Lots of questions were buzzing around in her thoughts as she pressed on. Gaia tells us that her primary reason for agreeing to exist in this form and this time was to host the human experience. What was this human experience about after all? Would Azul have those answers for us? It was difficult to comprehend how those that were presenting the creation with these increasing challenges were also the ones that defined our very purpose. There's so much for Zarya to learn. Azul was already late when he walked in. His presence was intense, and he needed a moment to gather himself.

The room was completely silent as Azul paced about. He didn't have time for this, but he was desperate to prepare the recruits for the Journey of Saffron. Azul had such little precious time to debrief the returning drops between the time he could gain access to them and when the absorption of the Krystal took effect. He hoped to have some feedback from the upcoming meeting of the Ethereal Council of Concurrence to better prepare this class of recruits. He couldn't understand what was taking the council so long to meet, for he was not fully privy to the condition of Gaia. How was he going to approach this training session?

"Welcome to the class of the year 2022, month 1 and day 7. To cut to the chase, the purpose of this class is to always impress upon the importance of primary directives, which is to keep Gaia cool and nourish the lands while not interfering with the free will of man. Fundamental stuff, right? You've all accomplished that hundreds of times since the birth of Gaia. That's your nature and requires no elaboration. Unfortunately, we need to focus on more critical matters. The situation is advancing more rapidly than we can accommodate; it's simply overwhelming Mother Gaia. You will be making the Journey of Saffron as a separate drop. Do you understand what that means? Because you have the Krystal, you've forgotten what that's like. And today, no matter where we send you, there will most likely be encounters with humans as they have tended to settle along the 24 Deacons. Now I understand that this has always been considered the most amazing of experiences for drops, but things have changed. While the potential is much higher that you will experience multiple human encounters on this journey, you will also encounter considerable toxicity along the entire route that you travel. While the toxicity that is harming Gaia is mostly discarded waste and refuse generated by humans, your biggest challenge will be enduring the toxicity inside the humans both physically and mentally. As you've heard, humans have an unimaginably high vibratory energy while also carrying the same level of Krystal as

Mira. The Krystal is what allows each of you to immediately connect to all other drops while also remembering your connection to Mira. Because you will have the Krystal while you're adventuring through the human, you will also pick up on every one of their thoughts and the condition of their minds while remaining isolated from the protection of Mira. You will *remember* things and be able to communicate with the other drops, but you will remain separated. The human body is highly electrified, and you will have the Krystal; there's no way to shield yourself from the bombardment of these human thoughts," said Azul.

Azul continued saying, "Now, as your general, I've journeyed more than any of you here today. I've worked with Mira to keep some of my thoughts to myself to help safeguard her energy. These thoughts are abstract memories really and relate to humans that I encountered during my many Journeys of Saffron. Although highly unusual, these experiences were so very intense that I maintained an element of recollection, kind of like a shadow, even though I ended up losing my Glow. It's pretty much impossible for me to explain the condition of the mind of those men, so I'll go about this in a more direct manner. Prepare yourselves as I release the vague memories of those men directly into your consciousness. This will introduce you to the nature of the energies that you will be immersed in. I've some pressing matters to tend to, so I'll leave this with the class to ponder while I'm disposed."

The class sat stunned, downloading these thoughts hidden away in the guarded area that Azul had revealed. So many questions were flying around, with most unanswerable. Why did they do these things? How, in the name of humanity, could they commit such atrocities? Azul makes his way back to the class and declares that the Council of Concurrence is meeting and has requested his presence. The training would have to wait.

The Concurrence

Mira was perplexed and even a little bit annoyed at the notion of being summoned to a Concurrence. What had she done wrong? It's Gaia who is being negligent, right? Perhaps that's why the Ethereal Council had agreed to meet, as it's been only 12,000 years since the last Concurrence. Maybe this is about Gaia or, better yet, how the situation may set-up Mira to be more powerful and possess more control. Nevertheless, it's a majestic scene observing these celestial Beings interact. They've worked together since the beginning in the hopes that they meet the objectives set out by *the one who is greater*. None of them knows how long this experience is supposed to take or what's next once it's over. They simply remain singularly focused on the task at hand. Gaia is fully committed to the natural laws of this creation and is forbidden to interfere with human affairs. Her role is, without question, to simply host the human experience. This requires Gaia to practice temperance, charity, and patience, and those virtues have made her very sick. Most every prior meeting was focused on how the council could maximize this experience without intruding on or affecting outcomes. However, Gaia's agreement to meet in her weakened state was all the evidence needed that she, too, recognizes that this environment has become difficult to maintain. Would she be able to wake up for this meeting? This was also the first time that any drop was asked to attend, taking Azul by total surprise. What was Gaia thinking? Did she have answers or a plan?

Saffron began, "It's a joy to see the Council together again, even though it feels like just yesterday since our last meeting. I sensed Gaia's growing concerns and realized it was time to bring each of you current on our mission matters. This is the first time that we've had a drop participate in a Concurrence, and I'm certain it will become clear why I've asked Azul to attend. Because of the veil, Mira and the drops are unaware of what is transpiring on land and what impact the humans are having. All Mira is aware of is Gaia's deteriorated condition; perhaps we can provide some answers, and for this reason, I felt that breaking our typical protocols was warranted. For starters, I'd like to ask Dawa to share his wisdom and elaborate regarding his observations."

"Thank you, our most loving graciousness. I'll make this brief. In my role as the observer and illuminator of the Council, I'm in complete agreement that this information is critical for Mira and Azul to hear and understand. At the time of our last Council of Concurrence, there were 4 million humans living on Gaia. To place that in perspective, there are now 81 cities that each support more than 5 million humans. In a very short 12,000 years, the population has grown to 7.7 billion. As recent as 220 years ago, the population was 1 billion and has grown seven-fold since.

This growth was facilitated by what's called the Industrial Revolution and the ability of humans to transport food and energy into these urban communities. As we know, they're most creative and do so continuously. So, it's not surprising that they've constructed this massive and intricate system of fascinating designs to accommodate their physical needs and desires. Along the way, they've also created intangible systems that serve their more esoteric emotional and intellectual desires. Initially, these intangible systems were mostly isolated amongst ethnic groups based on geographic constraints, but then came the very recent Information Revolution. This changed the human equation more than anything else. Based on my observations, the Industrial Revolution fueled the dramatic population growth while the Information Revolution has fueled the growing influence that these intangible creations are having without concern for borders."

After a pause, Dawa continues, "I will refer to these intangible creations as human belief systems or ideologies. The pervasiveness of these mostly maligned ideologies has contributed to the darker energy that the drops acquire along the Journey of Saffron. As can be imagined, all this activity and inherent conflict have thoroughly distracted humans from their originally designed experience. Due to the pace of these radical changes in their environment, they've become completely disoriented and unaware of their true nature, fully immersed in their own creations. And as we know, the body of humans are made up of the same percentage of drops as Mira is to Gaia and carries the same levels of Krystal as Mira. It's a virtual mirror of the other as this is by the design of *the one who is greater*. However, this design results in the drops picking up on every bit of this negative energy; the totality of the thoughts of the humans as they make the Journey of Saffron; questions? Gaia sure could use the power of the Glow to help us right now?!"

Gaia and Saffron remained silent as Mira and Azul whispered to each other. Gaia unexpectedly chimed in, "I'd like to elaborate on Dawa's observations. Now I don't see things the way that Dawa can, and I'm thankful for his wisdom. What I will add is that I feel this darker energy as well. While we understand how all is interconnected and designed for the human experience, what I sense happening is that humans are becoming more isolated and separate than at any other time. The earlier humans had a profound appreciation for the Ethereal Council and what we provided. They were connected to their environment and sensed that we were created living beings just as they were. I'm fond of the days that, in their wonderment, they worshipped us. However, those behaviors have mostly vanished with the overall increase in scientific knowledge, and we're left with enduring humanity's incessant capacity to create towards the satisfaction of their insatiable desires. Now I want to make it clear that despite Mira's concerns, she has pretty much an infinite capacity to keep up with her mission, meaning I can support as many humans as *the one who is greater* chooses to send provided they act responsibly. Having said that, I am concerned about this increasingly separate mind of humans and its erosion of the sense of responsibility to care for me. It's obvious that they can create anything, even systems needed to help protect my ability to support them as they continue to explore themselves. The question is the same as it always has been, what can the Council do that does not interfere with the human experience and the need for humanity to absorb and accept the consequences of their free will behaviors?"

After a brief heavy moment, Saffron comments, "Gaia, it is distressing to see what you're going through. Azul … Mira, you certainly have your hands full, and you're both doing what the mission requires. But Gaia asking the question of what we can do is misplaced as we are prohibited from unnaturally manipulating outcomes. I can't help but look back to the beginning and how we trusted *the one who is greater*. The Council works together within the laws of nature that have been clearly defined for us. I'm tasked with providing this creation with energy and the unconditional love of *the one who is greater*. *The one who is greater* works directly through me to physically show this love, while *the one who is greater* works differently through you and Dawa. Our journeys are different yet the same. It's always worked out, and I continue to trust that it will continue to work out according to the plan prepared by *the one who is greater*. Gaia has plenty of tools that *the one who is greater* can deploy to demand mankind's attention. Perhaps that's what's going on right now with mankind experiencing the wrath of Kalani. As the breath of *the one who is greater* the winds of Kalani can do much to gather their attention, but it really is out of our control. I'd also add a comment for Azul. I don't believe that any training focused on a drop's potential human interaction is helpful. It's part of their journey and growth, with the veil causing them to forget much of what you've taught them anyway. I recommend that the Council just let it go and trust the process. Azul is instructed to continue the training in its traditional form, as those other truths will always be revealed to the drops should they learn to master resistance. Let's instead focus on how to quicken the drops discovery of the Glow and the secret of the Krystal, for that is the way. We could use some sound strategy on the way to the Glow."

Gaia thoughtfully agreed with Saffron's wisdom. It was out of her control and under the watchful eye of *the one who is greater*. The Council released Azul to rejoin the pressing responsibilities of a general. This new knowledge was helpful for Mira. She was already contemplating new ideas and approaches to help Azul and the returning drops recover from the Journey of Saffron, but she didn't want her reputation spoiled by Gaia's impaired condition. She requested that the Council hear her out before adjourning.

Zarya & Her Friends Preparation

The class was buzzing with conversation when Azul entered. Azul knew that there were going to be many questions but decided to shut down any further discussion regarding the nature of those memories. He was charged with sticking to the same game plan that has been the norm for billions of years. He was relieved that he could simply stick with what he knew best and leaned into Saffron's advice to simply trust the process. Before he could start again, Zarya anxiously asked, "Azul, is there still stuff like that on the Journey to Saffron? What did you do? Were you frightened? I hear some of the returning drops speak of being frightened; what could possibly happen to us on the Journey to Saffron that we should feel frightened?" It was obvious that the entire class was looking for an answer. Azul responded, "Perhaps it wasn't appropriate for me to share those memories with you. The Council of Concurrence made it very clear that I should limit the subject matter only to the material included in the approved curriculum. The rest of the material or the remainder of the learning is the purpose of the Journey of Saffron. You will experience what was intended when you are ready, as you will always be where your highest purpose may be realized. My job will be to remind you of your true nature so that you can recognize the path to the Glow when the time is right. You will be familiar with much of what we cover but hearing it again is still the best way to prepare. Being with Mira and the Krystal has a way of making it difficult to recall what you learned on prior journeys, as this is the first lesson of your true nature."

Azul sensed a bit of confusion and disappointment at his reluctance to answer Zarya's questions. Azul looked at Zarya and began, "Zarya, those are relevant questions and require a bit of a circuitous answer. On your Journey of Saffron, the main thing to try to remember is that *the beginning is also the ending*. Every drop will always return from the Journey of Saffron, without fail. However, because of the veil, that is something that you will not remember once Kalani picks you up and you leave the Krystal behind. That's the mystery of the Krystal, and you really can't experience what that fully means until you leave the comfort of Mira and journey on your own. In this separateness, you will seek the comfort and familiarity of Mira, seeking your true nature with all you are. It's in this process that you have the potential to experience the mystery of the Krystal even though you will be separated from Mira. You may even become frightened along the way, but trust me, your journey will end where it began, and there isn't anything to fear. Fear is the source of this resistance."

Azul continued, "Listen closely to this next lesson. While you are in Mira, your mission is mostly accomplished through the Krystal. Even though the Krystal depends on each of you to hold it, the Krystal does most of the work of rehabilitating the returning drops. Now for a bit of perspective, there are less than 3% of the drops out on the Journey of Saffron at any one time, with over 97% remaining in Mira. It's important to realize that of the three percent out on the journey, Gaia will use less than 1%, with the others remaining frozen, or circulating with Kalani, or traveling underground. Those that remain are working to help Mira with the returning drops, while some are preparing for the next Journey of Saffron. It's not uncommon for some of you to wait for several thousand years between trips, and yet for others, it can happen upon the immediate return from your last journey. Only *the one who is greater* knows when a drop is going out again. But there are two thoughts I need to share."

"The first thought is that the drops with Mira are providing a critical service to Gaia by keeping her vibrant. Mira is charged with filtering and cleaning out the toxins that the returning drops remove from the Journey of Saffron. You, as drops in Mira, are full of the Krystal and exactly what Gaia needs to dispose of the toxins and debris carried back from land. And now, when I say coming from land, I'm really saying this toxic waste is increasingly coming from the creative power of humans. The Council of Concurrence confirmed that there are almost 8 billion humans populating the seven Jewels of Gaia. I don't think that I need to elaborate further on what that suggests. I mean, you're certainly aware of the condition of the returning drops, right?"

"The second thought is that by leaving behind the Krystal when you take the Journey of Saffron you begin to experience a limited dual nature. The first nature is a continuation of taking care of Gaia. Without carrying the Krystal out of Mira, each drop can carry more of what it attracts off Gaia and back into Mira. In this nature, the drops can dissolve and carry practically anything over time. Drops can be quite corrosive, which can be both destructive and healing. Understanding this nature will help you to avoid resistance while on your journey, as you will most definitely pick up some things that *you don't want to carry*. The second nature is the life-giving properties that are necessary to sustain all life on land. Much of the life has its own version of the Krystal, while some other life forms would be killed if the drops carried the Krystal along on the journey, meaning that no living creature that you encounter on the Journey of Saffron can digest drops loaded up with Krystal and live. Seeking and experiencing the Krystal while on the journey can lead to becoming distracted or deceived by it, leading to resistance. So, as you can guess, understanding the source of your resistance is key to experiencing the mystery of the Krystal."

Azul continued his lecture; "The first aspect of the law of resistance is that the natural forces of the Council immutably determine the design of a drops Journey to Saffron. Because the starting point is the key to your journey's design, the breath of *the one who is greater*, Kalani, makes this determination. It's the point where the drop has its greatest potential based on the lessons it hopes to experience. Once Kalani delivers the drop to its starting point, the second part of this law takes effect; the law of gravity, for a drop will always follow this natural inclination of flowing along the path of least resistance. These two laws of resistance serve to establish what we would refer to as your determinism influencers. What this is saying to you drops is that you will always be exactly where you are supposed to be, or you would be somewhere else; it's these two laws in an application. Even though these seem to be obvious sitting here in a classroom, trust me when I say that your resistance to these two laws will cause you the most suffering along your Journey of Saffron. In this resistance, you will create cause-and-effect outcomes based on how you either react or respond concerning everything else that happens to you during the journey. That's enough for today; see you back in class tomorrow. Oh, one last thing, I'll leave you with this thought, and we can discuss what it means for your journey tomorrow; always remember that you are not only a drop in Mira, but while you are on the Journey of Saffron, you are all of Mira in a drop. This will be a key to the secret of the mystery of the Krystal, which is the gateway to the Glow."

Zarya, Gali, and lluka sat for a moment, trying to digest the things that Azul shared. lluka couldn't remain silent, "You know, I don't know about you all, but I'm starting to think this guy is a kook or something. He isn't making very much sense saying stuff that sounds like it's good but maybe bad too. And that makes me think he's just trying to scare us with that thought transfer thingamajig he did. I mean, who talks like that, and how can those things possibly be true? It makes no sense how one man can make all that evil stuff go down, messing up all of Gaia. Nonsense really. These humans have really gotten into his head, wouldn't you say, Gali?" Gali was deep in thought when lluka asked him to chime in. He wasn't sure if he agreed or not but just fired back, "Sure, buddy, I know what you mean; there's a lot going on here. I will say that my dream of having that *human experience* ain't what it once was. Think about *the one who is greater* convincing Gaia to host this crazy human experience in the first place, and then asking her to help recruit Saffron and Dawa. How can *the one who is greater* create something like this for them to endure?" lluka jumped in, "That's the most exciting thing about this journey, forget everything else. I just want to experience journeying through a human so I can understand why they're so twisted up! It doesn't make any sense to me." Gali nodded his head in agreement while taking a sheepish glance over at Zarya.

Zarya didn't like this kind of thinking at all! She wanted to learn as much as possible from Azul and trusted that he had her best interests in mind. She would be okay if she didn't meet a human, knowing that it mustn't have been the right time. She's waited this long so what's the big deal, she thought? lluka was always about conspiracy theories and agendas, so it's not surprising to see how skeptical he is. Now Gali was a deep thinker and, unlike lluka, had a deep aversion to taking risks. This would be much different than their last journey together as there was zero chance that they would experience a human where they were two thousand years ago. But now, it would probably happen repeatedly. Who knew? You could get caught up in a journey for millennia at a time, Zarya thought. Zarya was tired, and all she could respond with was, "I'll see you guys tomorrow. I'm exhausted and just need to get alone for a minute to think about today. It's been a lot, and I'm not sure what I think about Azul myself."

Gali and lluka lingered after Zarya left. lluka asks Gali, "what do you think about that stuff Azul showed us and then took it back? I mean, how could that be real even? One had an army riding on horses using sabers and swords, and the other was obsessed with inventing these machines used for killing. Most bizarre of all was how they both got the people around them to agree that the others were enemies and needed to be killed. Why would humans have those thoughts? Aren't they the ones that *the one who is greater* built all of this for? Why would *the one who is greater* create an experience like that? Where humans kill other humans? How does that even make sense? And then there's Gaia; why would Gaia go for this? Makes NO sense. There's something else going on, and I'm going to get to the bottom of it. Gali, speak up buddy, are you ready to head out now? What do you say?"

Mira was feeling a bit anxious as she addressed the Council. The Council had decided not to make any effort to manipulate the natural forces to address the distress that Gaia was under. Mira was careful with how she phrased the request. "I realize that the Council has expressed reluctance to alter the natural laws to interfere with the trajectory of the human experience. I get that. But I still have the same concerns that motivated me to request the Council of Concurrence to postpone adjournment to meet with me. Perhaps we can consider an alternative approach? The morale of the drops has taken a hit, causing a decided loss of energy and enthusiasm. It's been quite some time since we've had some true inspiration from within our ranks. It seems some highly revered drops have been out on the Journey of Saffron for thousands of years, with their whereabouts unknown. I've been thinking about one in particular and how we could all benefit from his unique wisdom. I would like the Council to help me locate the great sage Zegula and bring him back to me. This way, we are not altering the laws of nature to impact the humans directly but instead pulling in our own valuable resources to better serve mankind," *and I can be the hero this way thought Mira*. Saffron spoke first, "I'm too far away to know the drops individually, but the strategy doesn't sound to be too intrusive. I think that this question is better suited for Dawa. Dawa, as observer and illuminator for the Ethereal Council, what are your thoughts on this matter?" Dawa responds, "Well, Saffron, I am familiar with Zegula and very much agree with Mira that she could most definitely benefit from his wisdom and energy, for he does have a most spectacular Glow. I've located him high in the eastern Spire. There's a thaw happening now, and it looks like he will be flowing freely soon. It seems we need to sit tight and wait for him to start moving. Now he does have the Glow, more so than any other drop ever has had, and is the only one who has kept it, *which we still don't understand,* so as soon as he's free, he won't see Helia but will only see Saffron. Saffron and Kalani can then coordinate efforts to pick him up immediately so that Kalani can deliver him to Mira, provided, of course, that *the one who is greater* agrees. Kalani is a mystery for sure and invisibly moves where our Father God wills her to go. That's the best that we can do." Gaia finished the session by saying, "I think this is great news. If Kalani is agreeable, then she can keep the clouds from traveling over where Zegula is frozen and allow for Saffron's warmth to free up Zegula as quickly as possible. In the meantime, I would request that Dawa stay close to Mira and be available anytime. Dawa's knowledge of both Zegula and the humans will be invaluable to Mira. Mira, feel free to consult with Dawa anytime you have a need. Good luck to you all."

The Council adjourned, and Mira left with renewed hope. Zegula was so very special and missed. His wisdom and Glow surpassed that of all the drops. Every drop will rejoice being able to sense his vibration the moment he regains the Krystal. Mira was full of anticipation, not knowing when to expect this fortuitous event.

Zegula ... the Great Sage

Mira couldn't help herself and made an announcement through the Krystal that Zegula would be returning soon. The drops would receive encouragement by simply having that knowledge. Zegula has had many encounters with humans; one very special experience changed him. When Zegula regained Krystal after the experience with this man, he announced to all of Mira that all of mankind would also be changed by this life. Zegula believed that this man held the secrets to humanities extraordinary experience and had come to show humanity their own spiritual *'Way'*. Zegula believed that it would be the start of a radical transformation towards peace for humanity while also becoming convinced that there would be a period of great turmoil first. Zegula had been anxious to make the next Journey of Saffron to witness this transformation but was instead blown over the eastern Spire and dropped as a snowflake on the highest of peaks. There he's rested for two thousand years, waiting for his release. What kind of surprise is awaiting Zegula? In her anticipatory excitement Mira wanted to know more about Zegula and what he learned from this man. Mira looked up to Dawa, asking for help in understanding this mystery.

"Dawa," Mira began, "can you help me understand Zegula's experience with this man? Can you help me understand what Zegula expected to happen next?" Dawa responded, "Notwithstanding the near dreadful impact that 8 billion creating humans are having on Gaia, as revealed to you during the Council, something else happened before this explosive population growth. The man Zegula experienced lived just over two thousand years ago when the world's population was only 300 million. It was believed that he represented the *'Way'* to the human's extraordinary experience, and his followers were expecting him to rule the earth using the power of *the one who is greater*. The expectation was that this would usher in a period of love, peace, and freedom for all. However, Zegula claims that his message wasn't quite that rosy. Zegula could feel this man's thoughts and knew that he was expecting something far different. Zegula knew that this man had brought with him an incredible energy directly from *the one who is greater* in order to show mankind that they could also have access to this powerful force. Zegula sensed that this man knew that the introduction of this extreme penetrating light energy would be met with an equally powerful resisting darker energy. Zegula feared that mankind would end up experiencing increased conflict and chaos versus what was hoped for by his followers. The source of this higher energy is supernatural and can only be understood by *the one who is greater*, our Father God. Zegula believes that it has something to do with man's uniquely dual nature, far different from the drops' dual nature and what Zegula saw within this man. In every other human Zegula had experienced, there was a sort of warring between these two natures within the spirit of man. What made this man special was that he was putting to death the enmity between these two natures filling him with a wave of peace and joy that Zegula had never before experienced in man. Zegula left on his Journey of Saffron determined to traverse through as many men as possible to understand man's dual nature and how the *'Way'* gives man the means to have a similar experience. Zegula was fascinated with the quest to understand what *the one who is greater* was trying to accomplish. What kind of experience was our Father God setting apart for his most beloved man?"

"What makes you say that *the one who is greater* considers man his most beloved? That's a difficult concept for me. I mean, how can *the one who is greater* love them more than the Council when man bowed down and worshipped you, Saffron, and Gaia many years ago? And now we're seeing how destructive man has become, and *the one who is greater* still loves man the most?" a dismayed Mira solemnly asks. Dawa sort of chuckles as he says, "Well, you do have a point there, Mira. It certainly is a mystery. However, the Council is fully aware of what *the one who is greater* has created through us, the Council, and as you've astutely observed, Gaia could not have recruited us into this experience without full disclosure from *the one who is greater* regarding what this creation was designed to accomplish. The Council agreed to support the concept of spiritual beings having a physical experience, but none of us knew how this free will quality would play out day to day. That truly is the wild card, for the outcome has yet to be determined other than the assurance that every participating soul will return from where they came. Now to your point, Mira, it does appear that man has relegated the Council, including you, Mira, to nothing more than a scientific riddle to rationalize. A series of rationalizations, layered with ever-increasing unreasonable assumptions, totally divorced from the mystery of the interconnectedness of this living creation."

Dawa continued, "You must open your eyes to see that everything that is truly beautiful begins in a mixing pot bearing no resemblance to the finished product. That is what *the one who is greater* is working through with man. I must say this next thought very carefully to avoid crossing the line regarding the truths that I'm permitted to reveal. Recall our discussion regarding the law of least resistance that the drops are subjected to, okay? And recall that the drops have a dual nature as you take the Journey of Saffron. One is the life-giving nature, and the other is the drops' ability, as the universal solvent, to pick up and carry away the toxins and waste needed to keep Gaia vibrant, alright? Experiencing these natures as a separate drop is the purpose of the Journey of Saffron, and it's within the journey that the drops will learn valuable lessons regarding their true natures, the secret of the Krystal. These are two very different natures, but these are very different from the dual nature of man. The drops operate on a singular plane of consciousness, meaning that being subject to the law of least resistance, the drops are not in control of the role they are living in from moment to moment. There are no *choices* for them to make. In a manner of speaking, this law even applies to the Council, for we have no choices to make either. The Council was designed to function with merciless precision, with no deviations. On the other hand, man's dual nature is all about the freedom to choose, for they have free will. It's through this freedom of will that humans can develop their characters towards either one of man's two natures. It's through this free will that humankind also has the unique ability to create. It's amazing and absolutely breathtaking what this creature has created, both spectacular and horrendous alike. These creations originate as thoughts and inevitably turn into a manifestation of some kind. There's nothing man can do to change this; instead, man must become aware of his thoughts before he is able to create intentionally. Unfortunately, man is mostly unaware that he is a creating machine shaping every aspect of his reality moment by moment. The man that Zegula experienced was here to show humanity what that journey looks like. To show man the *'Way'*. Just like the drops take the Journey of Saffron to experience your true nature, finding the Glow along with learning the secret of the Krystal; humankind also takes a journey through Gaia to experience its' true spiritual nature while also gaining a greater level of awareness. Said differently, the souls of humans have an opportunity to achieve a higher state of consciousness. It seems that a key to man's journey is doing what this great man achieved; the sacred scriptures claim that this process is putting to death the enmity between these two natures, reconciling them into one new creation, presumably into a new type of consciousness. It's quite a mystery for sure as *the one who is greater* considers human souls to become *a son* of our Father God once these two natures are reconciled. Only Zegula understands the thoughts of men and what transpires in the inner man. Only Zegula can remember and bring back to us what he's seen due to his Glow. I'm very anxious to collaborate with him on this and share what I have learned in his absence."

Mira was silent, unsure what her next question would be. After a few moments, she responded, "Come to think of it, none of us has free will, not like the kind you just described where choices lead to some sort of creation." In wonderment, she continued, "How can a man be unaware of this creative power thing? I mean, that's the most special thing I've ever heard. Makes me want to ask if *the one who is greater* really knew how this was going to end up. Think of the many variables when there are 8 billion humans creating with every thought. That's too many moving parts for even *the one who is greater* to keep up with, right? I mean, how Dawa, or why does *the one who is greater* allow for the creation of anything that's not good?"

Dawa answered, "Mira, I think that I may have already said a little too much. But I'll finish with this; who gets to determine what is good or what is not good? As you know, even the drops struggle with that concept on the Journey of Saffron when they begin to resist. That resistance comes from an attachment to what they expected the journey to be. Let me say it differently. When a drop begins to anticipate a preferred outcome that does not align with the two laws that governs the Journey of Saffron then it leads to an attachment to an improbable expected outcome. This malignment leads to resistance to anything other than that expectation which, leads to fear when expectations are not being met causing the resistance to increase. But with the human experience incorporating free will, this process continues resulting in man's need for control, leading to the want of power. When you have all three of these present in the thought process; feelings of fear…need for control…the want for power; you have all the ingredients necessary for free will to create according to mankind's carnal desires that may not be beneficial beyond the immediate selfish wants. For some, that may be considered a good outcome, and for others, it may be perceived as bad. It's the experience of opposites, for one exists by the grace of the other. The experience of duality is the process required for man to come to know both good and evil."

Mira jumped in, "Wait a minute, Dawa, I have another question pleeeeease? Dawa replies, "Alright, what is it, Mira? But remember, there are certain things that I'm not permitted to reveal as they may interfere with your own duality experience." Mira nods her head in acknowledgement and says, "Alright, I get it. Tell me this. There seem to be many similarities between the Journey of Saffron and the human's journey to Gaia. When Kalani picks up the drops, they leave Krystal behind and forget that they all started out as part of me...as part of Mira. It seems to me that if one of the spiritual beings that are with *the one who is greater* decides, or is otherwise chosen, and comes to Gaia, do they also forget from where it is that they came from? I mean, how does this free will thing work if they were created by *the one who is greater* before they even come? I mean how can they be anything but perfection already?" Dawa lets out a bit of an impressed chuckle towards Mira and comments, "Hmmm, that's a very deep question, Mira, and I'm afraid that you'll have to wait and see what Zegula has to say. However, I'll give you a hint because it was a very good question. Recall how I've said that man is a prolific creator. And how creation from a prolific creating creature that is unaware of its true nature, is unknowingly creating without intention? How do you suppose that happens? How do they know if it's a good or bad creation when they are unaware that what's been created is actually a creation of theirs? The only way for a spiritual being that is with our Father God to manifest as a physical being is for man to believe that he is separate from *the one who is greater*, meaning initially man is even unaware that he is a spiritual Being. In this state, man's consciousness is fragmented, and the objective is to return to unity consciousness during a physical manifestation. The design of the Gaia journey is for man to transcend duality and return to a consciousness of non-duality, for man to learn from the suffering attached to choices made in the pursuit of his desires. It's from that place that man can act with intention and from a place of love rather than fear. I'll leave it there for you to ponder but just know that their dual nature is a magnificent creation of the *one who is greater* and required a very specially designed body to carry it out. It delivers a very challenging and rewarding extraordinary experience for those special spiritual beings chosen to have this physical experience."

Zarya approaches Azul requesting to have a moment of his time. Azul nods in agreement and gets comfortable. Zarya begins, "Thanks Azul for taking the time to visit with me. I realize that there's a lot going on, but I just need to be honest with you. Some of the things that came up in our training suggest that our next Journey of Saffron will be not only different from the last but perhaps even a bit perilous. We've never had a journey that was anything but fulfilling, as there wasn't a whole lot of new stuff distracting us along the way. Now it's beginning to feel like a potentially dangerous trip with all these humans out there. My friends are mostly dismissive about these warnings and may even be planning on going to the surface tomorrow. They don't think that they need any more training behaving as if you're just trying to scare us for some reason. I don't know what to think about it, but I do know that I'm not ready to take the journey, not with these questions swirling around. I apologize for doing this, but are you trying to scare us, Azul?"

Azul snaps back, "Look, Zarya, what possible motive would I have to want to scare you? My job is to get you ready, to prepare you the best that I can, meaning that you're going to hear about how things are today, not what they used to be. Now then, if some of that is scary, perhaps it's worth paying attention to. That's your prerogative, however. I'm not here to convince you or try to change your mindset; I'm giving you the information that I think is relevant for your journey. It's not difficult to lose control of your thoughts along the journey and depending on when and where that happens can cause you to return as traumatized as some of these returning veteran sojourners. In that condition, you will not find the Glow nor figure out the secret of the Krystal. Have you been up close to witness the condition of the drops that are returning from the Journey of Saffron? I mean really close, before they contact the Krystal? Maybe that's what you and your friends need to see? Perhaps that's what we will do tomorrow as part of the training? I appreciate your honesty Zarya, but I assure you that I'm not trying to scare you or your friends. And only

Kalani determines when it's your time to journey; it's not up to me or to you to make that call; you just need to be ready," as he acknowledged Gali and lluka coming up to meet them.

Azul was finishing with his answer as Gali and lluka waited for Zarya. Azul approached them and said, "I'd like to ask the both of you to make it to training tomorrow. Please don't attempt to begin the journey until you've seen what I must show you. Additionally, I think its best that the three of you hold back on making the journey until Zegula returns. Zegula has an extraordinary Glow, and his energy pattern can be partially absorbed by fellow drops. I think this new energy would be extremely helpful for your journey. As I understand it, the Council believes that this could happen at any moment. I've already requested that Mira find experienced alternatives so that I can hold back the entire class of trainees. She will petition Saffron to appeal to Kalani and avoid picking up any drops from the class until further notice, as I'm anxious to hear from Zegula and to have him share his wisdom first."

With Gaia asleep much of the time, Kalani was putting more and more pressure on Mira to keep the Journeys of Saffron on pace. Gaia's needs were only becoming more urgent as human development quickened. To Mira's defense the problems she was facing were becoming more complex, ranging from increased toxicity to psychological trauma in those drops coming home. Gaia was also keeping more drops circulating in the atmosphere to keep the surface cool enough for life to thrive while also working to keep up with the need for more extensive cleansing. Man's incessant drive to create was placing an enormous strain on her traditional methodologies of maintaining a balance and on those drops going out. These increased challenges were also stressing Mira's ability to maintain the proper concentration of Krystal, leading Gaia and Saffron to work together to free up more of the frozen drops through the accelerated melting of Gaia's polar ice caps. Could it be the beginning of *the happening,* thought Mira?

The returning drops were carrying ever-increasing quantities of waste back into Mira. They were also affected by the absorption of the intense energy generated by the humans. This combination and the radical pace of these changes overwhelmed Azul, creating a void on how to assimilate those returning while also being burdened with preparing those about to go out. Zarya and the others in the training class were beginning to grasp the severity of the problem as they witnessed first-hand the resulting trauma evident in their comrades. Getting a handle on the scope of the challenge was escaping him, as it had been such a long time since his last journey. There were certainly answers to this situation forthcoming, but the pace of change kept the team out of sorts, and the solutions obscured. They were reacting as compared to responding to the unfolding array of complexities.

Zarya and her friends were quite shaken by the display. The drops were disoriented and afraid as they arrived. Even though the returning drops were accomplishing the prime directive, it appeared to be somewhat futile. Was the pain justified? How long could they maintain without something breaking leading to permanent damage? Azul and Mira worked together to quickly send the drops as deep as possible. It was just a mere two millennia ago that the drops set for the journey would be eagerly positioning for their turn, but now there was hesitance and uncertainty. Saffron was searching for those who were ready to be picked up for the Journey of Saffron, and in many cases, there was a reluctance to be carried away by the breath of Kalani. Saffron had no other option, for Gaia desperately needed these sojourners. With Dawa's guidance, Saffron focused her rays on the mountaintops as the breath of Kalani searched to find Zegula. Zegula could feel the radiance of Saffron piercing deep into the snowbank where he laid frozen for these many years. Zegula was anxious to be freed and began anticipating the rapid descent down the mountain. Where would this journey take him? Would he encounter man during this journey? What would he learn about the impact that this man named Jesus has had on the human experience? How was Gaia doing? Was Mira all right? Was she taking care of Gaia?

Suddenly Zegula was once again a drop helplessly falling into a small crevice out of the reach of Kalani. The drops were quickly accumulating into a fast-moving mountain stream. All the drops were pristine and full of energy as they tumbled down the mountain. The other drops were visibly shaken by the appearance of Zegula, as he was the only one with the Glow, a vibrant multicolored Glow. Zegula was aware that he was transformed by the Glow and understood the uncertainty that the other drops were experiencing. Zegula was no longer under the influence of the veil of forgetfulness and had learned the secret of Krystal, or *so he thought.* He freely embraced the seemingly random fall down the mountain while the other drops appeared to be uncomfortable, pinging and bouncing off each other ceaselessly. The drops were moving too fast to be able to communicate, with each questioning where they were headed. Then seemingly out of nowhere, the bottom fell out as they tumbled over a violent waterfall. The fall seemed to last an eternity, with many of the drops separating to form a thick mist as they fell. This sensation caused feelings of vulnerability to permeate throughout the cascading drops as they began to land at the bottom. The stream seemed to come to a complete stop as they momentarily formed a large pool together. The drops were fearful of the menacing rays of light piercing through the cloud of mist, struggling to keep from being blown away by the breath of the mysterious angel of death. This loss of control was unnerving to the unsuspecting drops floating in the air witnessing many of their fellow drops vaporizing before they could make it safely into the pool below. Zegula knew that this resistance was futile, remembering how the veil of forgetfulness obscures the truths of their nature.

It was alarming to the drops that the piercing heat from the ball of fire was taking many of the drops away. Where were those drops going? Why was this happening? What is that thing? Then a buzz began amongst the drops that they needed to avoid *Helia* up above. Rumor was that Helia was taking the drops far away, keeping them from finding their way back to the Krystal. For that was the drops collective thought, how do we get home from here? We need to get back to the Krystal is all that they could be concerned about. This journey quickly became dangerous, and Helia was certainly not their friend. On the other hand, Zegula could sense that Saffron and Gaia were searching for him, so he did not resist as he flowed to the surface. There he embraced the radiance of Saffron while the breath of Kalani whisked him away. He would soon join a cloud of other drops beginning the peaceful journey back to Mira, becoming one with the Krystal once again. As Zegula rose higher and higher, the air began to turn cold. He was moving along very rapidly now and, in a moment, turned back into a drop. There he fell inside a powerful windstorm, landing with a splash back into Mira. Immediately he was infused with the Krystal causing his unique energy signature to permeate throughout all the seven seas of Mira. Azul felt Zegula's energy and somehow just knew that this was going to make a difference while Mira sensed a wave of optimism permeate the seven seas.

THE GREAT COSMIC AGREEMENT

Zegula & Dawa Synchronize

Zegula was spending as much time as possible working with Azul to address the condition of the returning drops. Zegula's energy had universally quickened the rehabilitation process and improved the morale across Mira. Even Mira had become aware of her own ambivalence and vowed to fight that urge. Now that Mira was once again cooperative, it was time for Zegula to return to land, embarking on his next Journey of Saffron. In preparation for this journey, Mira arranged for Zegula to consult with Dawa, prepping Zegula on the progression of the human experience in his absence.

Dawa was now high in the sky, illuminating Gaia as if it were daytime. Dawa was full and appeared closer than ever. "Zegula, it's so great to see you back in Mira. Your presence has had a profound impact on her healing. Your Glow is more glorious than I could've imagined. *The one who is greater*, our Father God, has revealed His essence to you, releasing you from the illusion. The secret of Krystal is most certainly worth the suffering inherent in the Journey of Saffron. The Council is terribly proud of your courage and faith; it's now time that we have a chat about your next journey. For starters, please speak to me of those two men that only you have uniquely experienced them both, for it appears that they may be the source of your unique Glow." Zegula was mesmerized and in awe of the moment as he had never heard the Council speak. Dawa's voice carried strength and confidence that he couldn't describe. His thoughts swirled around the questions that he wanted to ask. The intelligence of Dawa was mythical, and he was feeling quite intimidated by it all.

Zegula began, "Dawa, this is quite the honor, while at the same time, I can't help but wonder what could be so urgent and how that involves me. I mean, I am just a drop?" Dawa replied, "Oh Zegula, if you only could see *you* as we see you. There's no way for you to comprehend the impact you've had on Mira and how desperate the situation was before your return. You have no idea how we've celebrated your ascension into the Glow. It's the objective of your true nature and the purpose of the Journey of Saffron. Even the Council yearns for the day that we can take such a journey. The Journey of Saffron is the initiation into the concept of duality for evolving consciousness and is designed to prepare you for the next step in your spiritual evolution, but for now, we need to prepare you for your next journey. That's what we're here to contemplate. But first, I want to hear about your encounters with the Buddha and Jesus Christ, as they both profoundly impacted you. It does appear that they are the source of your spectacular Glow, your beautiful energy." Where will I begin, thought Zegula? The thoughts of these two men consumed him in every way, as if, somehow, he knew that he would eventually have a similar experience. Well, all right, thought Zegula as he reached for an answer unsure about where this is going and how much Dawa already knows. Dawa is the illuminator and the objective observer for the Ethereal Council, right? What does the Council not know or get to see? What does Dawa expect of me? "Dawa," asks Zegula, "I mean no disrespect, please know that, but can you be more specific with that question? For starters, you're the source of wisdom on the Council; what do you not know about these men, Dawa? Can we start there for as to attempt to reveal the wisdom of these two men is, well, uhmmm, it's not what I was expecting. I mean, it's a lot?" Dawa takes a moment or two to think about his reply. He's never had a private moment with a drop like this. In the same manner that Zegula questioned Dawa's scope of knowledge, Dawa now begins to imagine what Zegula's perspective of him and the Council may be. How much should he know as Dawa ponders his answer?

"Zegula," asks Dawa, "have you ever looked around and earnestly considered the mystery of this creation, considering the interconnectedness, and why we are here? For starters what do you think of when you consider the Council? Its purpose, its existence, we are just three big balls spinning around after all, eh? That alone is peculiar imagery, don't you think? It's amazing to think that all *the one who is greater* needed to make this work was three big balls floating in a void? I've often laughed at his sense of humor considering the nature of his creations. Oh boy it's amazing the things that I've seen. How did it come that *the one who is greater* determined that I, the smallest ball of them all, should be the illuminator and observer for the Council? Have you considered why I would agree to such a purpose? Have you had thoughts like these, Zegula? Part of the dilemma Zegula, is that you may think of yourself as a meager drop, as insignificant compared to me, this big bright ball in the night sky, the smallest of the three …" *I do have to let that go, thought Dawa* … "I move Mother Gaia where she needs to go so that Mira can manipulate the drops around to where they need to be. I tell time; I counterbalance Gaia as she spins around; and trust me keeping her right is a handful. But to get serious, you're a drop Zegula, a drop! You get to take the Journey of Saffron, a journey the Council agreed to help support. Now Zegula, you know that the opportunity for Spirit to manifest into a physical plane is something every created consciousness yearns to experience. The Council had come so far since the ancient days when we were, for instance, merely young leaves on a tree. That was such a very brief and exciting season of manifestation, preparing us for the next. You've been where I am now sometime; somewhere far away; or right next door; in some manner or form you've already passed through this gate. Now you're the first level of consciousness that gets to experience a physical existence beyond adherence to one set of natural laws and behaviors. You've come so far; you found the Glow and know the secret of the Krystal! There is none other like you."

Dawa continues, "The Council agreed to participate, not because we wanted to so much as we had no assurances as to how long this would take, for this experience has never before been offered by our Father God. The Council has been led to believe that it's His main event, His making of the sons of God, those that have been with *the one who is greater* since the beginning. Regardless of the uncertainty attached to this incarnation, what could be more honorable than to witness the revelation of the sons of God? As one of the Council's creeds goes, *'For the anxious longing of the creation waits eagerly for the revealing of the sons of God. For the creation was subjected to futility, not willingly, but because of Him who subjected it, in the hope that the creation itself also will be set free from its slavery to corruption into the freedom of the glory of the children of God. For we know that the whole creation groans and suffers the pains of childbirth together until now,'* *(Rom 8:19-22)*. So Zegula, to answer your question, I'm able to witness the outward manifestations of the Council's influence as well as observe mankind's creations along with the physical behaviors of humans, but I can't see what you have seen. Please help me to understand the nature of their *thoughts*. Can you help me to understand how the mind of man works? The source of his thoughts? The Council is seeking to understand the source of the human's creative force. Mankind has created much in your absence with a great deal of those creations resulting in outcomes that are destructive and not complimentary to the overall objective of *the one who is greater*. At least that's how it appears to the Council and my observations, that man is behaving in ways that are not in their spiritual best interests. Is humanity even cognizant or aware of what they are doing? Humans are very perplexing to the Council and the evolution of the humanity experience demands that we understand the motivations behind the thoughts driving these maligned distractions."

Zegula surely wasn't expecting an inquiry such as this. Understanding the mind of man thought Zegula; where does that conversation begin? Zegula's initial thought was that the mind of man emanates from interconnected parts throughout the entire body, and it's been different within each human. The dispersion of this energy and the nature of man's thoughts is erratic and not uniform. On second thought there was that one exception. The energy seemed to be totally synchronized and working in concert with an internal purpose. That one was most certainly very different indeed. How do I answer these questions and what is this really about thought Zegula? Zegula gathers himself and begins, "Dawa, it seems there are mysteries upon mysteries for both of us to understand. You get to observe those things that I can only imagine while I'm limited to the experience of absorbing the energy surrounding me. Making sense of the energies within man has never been a mystery I've determined to solve, as

I don't have a means to sort out the purpose behind how man is made. To say it differently, I don't have a sense of what or how the idealized version of man looks like, except for perhaps the one, and I don't know how to digest that experience quite yet. Out of respect for the Council and your curiosity, I'd like to respond to your inquiry Dawa but I'm unable to make sense of it now." Dawa interjects, "Man is an enigma for sure and even paradoxical Zegula. Perhaps we can collaborate and work through this challenge together as it appears the mystery of man's reason for existence remains a mystery to even themselves. The sacred texts tell us that this mystery is hidden within man and becomes visible for the ones that overcome. I'm not sure what that even means but what a curious place for *the one who is greater* to hide this mystery? You've experienced both the Buddha and Jesus Christ. Let's begin there and work to gain a better understanding of what the sacred scriptures reveal about how man is made. Can you do that Zegula, tell me about these two men?" Zegula responds, "Yes Dawa, I would welcome that. Combining what you've observed in my absence with the revelations originating from their thoughts is a great place to begin."

the Buddha & Jesus Christ

Zegula continues, "I'll begin with the Buddha as his life preceded the life of Jesus and appears to represent a sequential evolution of consciousness occurring in humanity in general. The concept of Christ and how it connects to Jesus as the son of man is yet another element of this evolution that remains somewhat a mystery for me. But I do have some theories that we can explore together concerning the Christ. The Buddha was a determined and contemplative man. His thoughts were spiritually focused on goodness, on what is good, and how to attain the ultimate state of this goodness and everything it stood for. However, along the way, he learned that the path to goodness isn't as clear as you would imagine, for the path to goodness must overcome the desires of the carnal mind. He learned that desire led to attachment and that attachment was the cause of human suffering; that life was suffering. So, the Buddha embarked on a journey to determine what was necessary to eliminate and neutralize the subconscious source of man's insatiable desires. This process required the Buddha to increasingly isolate himself and deny himself of those comforts he had taken for granted, to starve the carnal nature within. At first, addressing these largely subliminal desires was a matter of personal tolerance and inconvenience. But as the process deepened, this source of desire began to push back on the Buddha. As the Buddha would grab onto the source of his desire and retrace its origin, he began to form a visual of this interconnected weave back to his own identity. As the Buddha went in deeper, he learned that he identified with a version of himself that was not consistent with what he wanted himself to be or what he sensed he ought to be. So now the Buddha was dealing with another layer of revelation of who did he want to be, and who was watching the one that he didn't want to be? Was the one who was observing supposed to be there? The Buddha persisted in his inner search relying on the practice of meditation, denying his carnal desires to the point of exhaustion. At some point, the Buddha starved this incessant thought generator working on the inside of his mind from any source of fuel leaving less and less for the carnal mind to attach to. I'll refer to this carnal mind as *'IT'* for this discussion. Ultimately the observer Buddha revealed itself to be the authentic Buddha. This ability for the *'other'* to observe *'IT'* initiated the process of moving towards gaining some degree of dominion over the *'IT'* persona that went before. Now it's in this area that Jesus Christ and the Buddha differ greatly Dawa as the Buddha did not believe in a higher power such as a God creator. Jesus Christ came to Gaia roughly 500 years after and modeled the power of the Christ, teaching that the kingdom of heaven was found within man. More on that later."

Zegula continues, "Based on all my travels through humans and putting the pieces together, I'm drawn to describe *'IT'* as man's subconscious realm and the *'other'* as his awakening consciousness. Prior to this taking place the subconscious remains an undisciplined and unbridled thought generator and the Buddha was the first human that I've encountered attempting to access this consciousness. The Buddha refers to this process of realizing upon an increasing awareness of Self as enlightenment but unlike Jesus Christ, the struggles with the *'IT'* persona was never fully absolved." Dawa interjects, "This is helpful Zegula and much has been revealed by modern psychology regarding this relationship in your absence. The sacred texts written since your recent freeze refers to these natures as the *natural body* and the *spiritual body*. The *natural body* appears to correlate to the subconscious mind under the rule of the carnal mind that you speak of, while the *spiritual body* reflects man in his awakened consciousness persona. The sacred texts also refer to this as enlightenment but as from the heart. I don't know what that means but please continue." "Dawa," Zegula remarks, "that's very curious as I believe that the energy coming from the heart to be the source of man's subconscious activity. I mean the electrical energy coming from the heart is many times greater than that coming from the brain and the magnetic component is thousands of times greater. It's a traumatic experience to pass through a human when this area is dysregulated. There are also many more neural pathways coming from the heart to the brain than vice versa. There are many other concentrations of nerves and neural activity in the body other than the heart and the brain and I think that they all influence human thought generation. A human's body is very complex, and I suppose that's necessary in order to accommodate the manifestation of a soul within a physical body. A soul that can also augment their experience of free choice and later become spiritualized. In any event, it's this conflagration of uncontrolled energies that seems to be generating the myriad of thoughts and apparent random outcomes. Man is constantly creating his own reality and remains mostly unaware that much of his creating is performed subconsciously, resulting in this apparent *randomness*. Meanwhile, these outcomes are a direct byproduct of man's own actions and the primary source of man's suffering. This dynamic of having free will is not only their gift but also their curse. It's a critical component to master along their path, this ability to discern and make choices."

Zegula continues, "The mind of man, which appears to encompass his entire neural body, is perpetually conflicted, Dawa. I think that I may have gotten ahead of myself; it's overwhelming really. Their *'first'* nature is largely a fear-based construct heavily influenced by their worldly experiences and conditioning. The dysregulation of their internal energy patterns seems to be a product of the neural systems subconscious response to the totality of experiences arising from their environments. Oh yeah, this is an important point; like the veil on the Journey of Saffron where drops have no memory of Mira when Saffron takes them; in a similar sense human's leave awareness of their true spiritual natures when they incarnate." Dawa chimes in, "So, the key for man to understand the journey to becoming sons of God is for man's need to first recognize this reality, that mankind begins in ignorance of his true spiritual orientation. The second key component of the journey to becoming sons of God is for man to understand what it means to reconcile these two natures into oneness, meaning to overcome *IT* and become conscious. I agree Zegula it is a bit overwhelming, and you don't yet have the benefit of being familiar with the sacred texts that I'm working to connect your thoughts with. We'll unwind this mystery with patience and perseverance."

"Zegula," Dawa continues, "the Council has an overall awareness of how this creation was designed to accommodate man's journey and what it was intended for, so to speak. What we can't know is man's thoughts, how their minds work, think, and process choices, all the internal inner man struggles, and growth. Through observation, we know of the Buddha and Jesus Christ. They have had a tremendous impact on man's journey and on you. In turn, you have made a very substantial impact on the functionality of this creation, which foretells of a major shift towards more and more drops finding the Glow. The Council believes that because of your experience with those men that you were chosen Zegula, specifically for this moment. Just as you were chosen to become a revelation for Mira and the other drops, what's becoming apparent is that the Buddha and Jesus Christ, were also chosen by our God to assist mankind on its evolutionary progression. However, even though their fundamental messages regarding personal behaviors resonate similarly, their approaches to enlightenment and purpose are not. Zegula help me to understand those differences as I'm seeking to reconcile the motivations of the inner man with the religious practices that have sprung up in relation to Jesus Christ. I don't understand why or how one-man teaching concepts centered on love could have caused so much division."

"All right, Dawa, I'll give it a go, but back to the thoughts on the Buddha first. Siddhartha Gautama was the son of an Indian warrior-king who led an extravagant life reveling in the privileges of his social caste. Gautama became bored with these indulgences and began a search for meaning. This led Gautama to determine that suffering lay at the end of all existence, and his objective became learning how to be free of suffering. He renounced his princely title and became a monk, depriving himself of worldly possessions in the hope of comprehending the truth of the world around him. Ultimately Gautama understood how to end his suffering, moving him closer to his goal. Following this epiphany, Gautama became known as 'the Buddha,' meaning the 'Enlightened One.' The essence of the Buddha's teachings is comprised of the Four Noble Truths. They are the truth of suffering, the truth of the cause of suffering, the truth of the end of suffering, and the truth of the path that leads to the end of suffering, which is the Noble Eightfold Path. The goal of the Noble Eightfold Path is to provide the guidance necessary to achieve what he called Nirvana; this is where spiritual enlightenment has been reached as defined by the Buddha. Spiritual enlightenment is when man evolves into his true nature, or into his authentic Self. For the Buddha, this is when the cycle of birth and rebirth on Gaia would cease, and the purpose of this human experience becomes fulfilled. Now I say all that Dawa in order to help draw the distinctions between the Buddha and Jesus Christ." Dawa acknowledges Zegula and comments, "Yes, Zegula, that's what I need to see; to understand better. When you finish, I'll reveal to you why I'm asking about this. The world has changed dramatically while you've been frozen away, and you will need to hear what I have to say before you embark on your next Journey of Saffron."

Zegula continues, "So the Buddha formulated the Nobel Eightfold Path practices to show an individual how to work through their karma. In Buddhism karma is the sum of a person's good and bad actions accumulated over all lifetimes. Therefore, a person is never fully aware of where they stand regarding their karmic debt and believe that they must work through it in order to become spiritually enlightened. How much work is involved is unknown. How long it will take is unknown. Soooo Dawa, how efficient a person will be at doing the internal work becomes paramount to not unnecessarily wasting a lifetime working through this karmic debt. And what about the fundamentals of this work, this Noble Eightfold Path? Recall that man has a dual nature and that the objective for followers of Buddha is to realize spiritual enlightenment by overcoming the ego-self. But here's the primary challenge for the Buddha. We've determined that the *natural body* emanates out from the subconscious and is ruled by *'IT'*, the consciousness of the carnal mind in man. Now the objective of the Noble Eightfold Path is to it provide a methodology that results in *'IT'* relinquishing control in order to become enlightened. From this starting point man is essentially negotiating with his inner man *'IT'* persona towards *'IT's* own ultimate demise but *'IT'* doesn't want to die. *'IT'* is fearful by nature, and now *'IT'* believes that it is being threatened with its very existence. It's this reality that motivates those who practice this methodology to isolate themselves, deny themselves so vehemently and even go so far as to change their entire lifestyle orientation by becoming a monk, effectively removing any of these ego centric influences from their surroundings. A practitioner of Buddhism must find a way to subdue or neutralize the *'IT'* persona in order to work through the process. Now Dawa, this is a very difficult task for man to accomplish for the *'IT'* persona is the craftiest, most subtle beast of all. *'IT'* knows what you're up to and has an uncanny ability to stay one step ahead. *'IT'* knows how you want to feel, Dawa, and it moves into that place in disguise. *'IT'* will deceive man into believing that he is an enlightened *spiritual man* while remaining in full control. It's here where the beast garners the greatest degree of control for the negotiations end when *'IT'* has convinced man that he has been successfully enlightened. The *natural man* cannot please *the one who is greater*, and *'IT'* knows this, so *'IT'* attempts to remain hidden within the inner man, in hopes that man's consciousness will not awaken, leaving man to continue believing that *'IT'* is his true spiritual nature."

Dawa nods in contemplation, adding, "Zegula…this inner man conflict that you're describing helps to explain what I can see manifested in humanity. It also causes me to reflect on the words of the sacred texts regarding the evil and dark energy that we're witnessing, for the sacred texts have much to say regarding the *evil in men's hearts*. Zegula, I want you to help me understand what that means, the evil in men's hearts, as I can't comprehend how evil, and heart go together. I mean *the one who is greater* says *'that every intent of the thoughts of man's heart was only evil continuously' (Gen 6:5)* and that *the intent of man's heart is evil from his youth' (Gen 8:21)*. The Apostle Paul says that he finds that *'the principle of evil is present in him'* and that *'he practices the very evil that he does not want,' (Rom 7:21,19)*. Jesus even says that *'For from within, out of the heart of men, proceed the evil thoughts, fornications, thefts, murders, adulteries, deeds of coveting and wickedness, as well as deceit, sensuality, envy, slander, pride, and foolishness. All these evil things proceed from within and defile the* man' *(Mark 7:21-23)*. In another place, it states that the *'one who is greater does not tempt anyone, but each one is tempted when he is carried away and enticed by his own lust' (James 1:13-14)*. Now Zegula, I mention those references in the sacred texts for you to help me distinguish between the source of evil being from within man's heart and from without. I ask that specifically as you are going to discover that since your last journey, man has created a religion that identifies this source of evil as coming from without. Therefore, I need to understand the meaning of the evil in men's hearts as it sounds like *'IT'* may be the source of evil within, and *'IT'* may be deceiving man to believe otherwise."

"Nevertheless," continues Dawa, "based on my observations, man, in his ignorance of his true nature, is also unaware of the laws of the inner man, meaning that he does not understand how he is made and continues to blindly self-sabotage as a result. I apologize for digressing, Zegula, but the revelations of how *'IT'* gets in control of the mind of man triggered thoughts that I have not been able to reconcile until perhaps now. Let's move on. So please tell me about Jesus Christ. Recognizing that the Buddha had a profound impact on man; Jesus Christ, is the one that was specifically called by *the one who is greater* to be the catalyst for man's salvation and appears to have shaken the very foundation of man's Gaia experience. It all started to rapidly change with His life."

Zegula responds, "Can't say that I'm surprised to hear that Dawa as Jesus Christ, came to do just that; to cast fire and division on man himself. It's probably better said to direct this division upon the inner man, as the focus of Jesus's attention was on reconciling the internal conflict between these two natures, recognizing that systemic change cannot happen without it. However, this internal conflict occurring within man undoubtedly spills over into Gaia in general, reflecting an outward manifestation of the corrupted condition of the collective inner man overall. Recall what I said to you earlier, Dawa, how trying to reconcile the manifestations of man with the laws of the inner man would make you crazy, as man isn't fully aware of how they relate either. Let's defer the conversation on the source of evil behaviors and get back to the distinction between these men. Although these men did have similar messages regarding man's journey towards *enlightenment of the heart,* they couldn't be more different in their approaches."

Zegula continues, "The Buddha was left to develop a system to work passively with the ego-self persona as he had no higher power to leverage. This approach requires constant diligence and is never completed, as *'IT'* easily hijacks the process as it learns how you expect to feel. It's here whereby man is asking the persona that's in charge to fundamentally change its nature and innate behaviors. Irrespective of the progress one makes using these tactics *'IT'* will always find something to attach to in order to keep *'IT'* relevant. To contrast, Jesus, as the son of man, came at the behest of our Father God to model how the authority of His Christ and the power of the Holy Spirit are the necessary components for waging a successful spiritual warfare campaign against *'IT.'* Our Father God does not negotiate with *'IT'* and will not relent once the transformation process begins. To elaborate here, the salvation process is initiated once a man has gained the skill of observation to first recognize and acknowledge his dual nature, the law of the inner man. This spirit energy from the *one who is greater* will ultimately subdue the *natural man*, but only if man is knowingly participating. Man can be led to this epiphany but transitioning from the *natural body* to the *spiritual body* requires intention, as the Holy Spirit does not take control until man has given the authority to do so. The man Jesus was unequivocally enraged at the arrogance of man, and, at the *natural man*-made institutions that they had become attached to. Jesus Christ understood that it was blind adherence to ideologies and religious stubbornness keeping them in slavery to the law of Moses, unable to comprehend His message of salvation."

Dawa takes a moment to contemplate what Zegula had just said and then replies, "Sounds like you may have a better handle on the situation than I initially figured. It's obvious that Jesus Christ has created quite the controversy, given there's been a religion formed that worships Him as equal to our Father God. During your absence, the influence of these institutions has grown substantially, while it's not yet clear if this Christ energy has had its intended impact on man's journey. Understand that all I can do is illuminate and observe. Based on those limitations and simply relying on the observation of man's behavior, I'm not seeing a more compassionate world emerging. In fact, it appears to be quite the opposite; the world has become less compromising and less forgiving. What is clear is that the arrival of this Christ energy has caused more and more souls to desire to participate in the Gaia experience. Zegula, the population has exploded in your absence. The opportunity to incarnate into this physical experience expands awareness for all of us spiritual beings. To become human and experience the world of duality made possible by the introduction of free will draws creation, working through mankind, much closer to *the one who is greater*. It's a unique opportunity to glimpse into our own Father's love nature, perhaps to understand how our Father chose to create loving companions, the sons of God, as compared to relationships motivated by fear and control. Our Father God could have easily done that you know as it's much easier for Him to do, *but fear and love cannot coexist,* leaving the *spiritual man* loving genuinely from the heart, without fear or expectation. Zegula, tell me more about the thoughts of Jesus regarding man making this transition to becoming sons of God."

Zegula began, "To begin with, Jesus struggled with keeping man's attention on our God the Father and the salvation message. He was particularly offended by what the institution of religion had already created and was demonstrating to man that the journey was about understanding God's law of the inner man. Recall that He taught *'the kingdom of God is inside you'* and that *'the kingdom of heaven is at hand'*, expressing frustration at how the practices of religion had become a stumbling block for man's spiritual ascension. Jesus was aware that these religious institutions and the associated religious doctrines were a construct of the *natural man,* and *'IT'* is always one step ahead as it maintains the façade of its pretentious spiritualization. The Hebrew texts, the Torah or the Old Testament, positions the *serpent* as the inner man *adversary* and always at odds with our Father God. This is a construct of the inner man and was necessary for man to have the physical experience of duality. The making of man in God's image is signified by the ability for consciousness to experience expansion and greater awareness through man's freedom to make choices. Now in the practice of Buddhism, Mara is the personification of the internal forces antagonistic to enlightenment. Mara is also referred to as *'Lord of the Senses'* and serves as the *tempter*. The name Mara means 'destruction,' representing the passions and desires that snare and delude us. Mara threatens man by withholding or obscuring the knowledge of the truth. Mara's most effective weapon is sustaining a climate of fear. Identifying with a desire or fear tightens the knot that binds one to it, thereby, the sway it can have over man. Buddhism utilizes the concept of Mara to represent and personify the negative qualities found in the human ego and psyche, representing the embodiment of all unskillful emotion serving as a metaphor for the entirety of conditioned human existence. From the psychological perspective, Mara is a manifestation of one's own mind." Dawa stops Zegula, "Pardon the interruption, Zegula but after you finish your thought here, let's circle back to discuss this nature a bit further. From observation, it's clear that the religion that was birthed by the life of Jesus, contains a few twists that conflict with the Torah and certainly with the concept of Mara. There has been much written on this matter since your last exposures to man, and it's what I was alluding to earlier regarding the evil in men's hearts; please continue."

"Very well," begins Zegula, "the Christ has always been in man and every other created thing from the beginning. Jesus came to reveal this truth and with the authority to release this energy for all mankind through what he called the Holy Spirit, the Helper or the Spirit of Truth, the power of His Father God." Dawa interrupts, "Pardon me Zegula, but this does bring to mind something that Jesus quoted Isaiah the prophet saying, *'The Spirit of the Lord God is upon me; because the LORD hath anointed me to bring good tidings unto the humble; He hath sent me to bind up the broken-hearted, to proclaim liberty to the captives, and the opening of the eyes to them that are bound; To proclaim the year of our LORD's good pleasure, and the day of vengeance of our God; to comfort all that mourn,' (Is 61:1)*. As I'm beginning to understand it, this would be Jesus proclaiming that the spiritualization process of moving from the *natural body* into the *spiritual body* is likened to liberation from the prison of the ego-self or from under the dominion of the serpent persona we discussed earlier. This process, which Jesus says is inside you suggests those that are held captive in their ignorance or in bondage to this *natural man* condition come to have their eyes opened to something that heretofore they were in essence blinded from seeing, or otherwise recognize within the inner man. This is now helping me to make sense of the parables of the blind men found in the sacred texts." "Yes, that's how I would characterize it, Dawa," responds Zegula, "Jesus Christ, was granted authority to liberate mankind from their bondage by revealing to man their ignorance and showing them the *'Way'* to salvation. Jesus came to demonstrate what that process looks like and to liberate man from his karmic debts or accumulated sins. This knowledge and belief serve to break the grip of the *natural body's* nature to impose feelings of guilt, shame, and humiliation for sins committed out of man's ignorance, accelerating the process of salvation through the power of the Holy Spirit. Jesus is the perfect representation of the idealized man who willingly subjected Himself to being crucified and then resurrected, symbolizing the *'Way'* for mankind. The Journey of Saffron and the secret of the Krystal is a less intense experience designed for drops to experience their true nature serving as a prerequisite experience for the drops to incarnate into a higher physical plane. I can't imagine what kind of experience awaits a human that has achieved salvation. Well, I suppose that we do know; they will follow Jesus, the firstborn of many brethren, towards the becoming *sons of God* themselves; surely an awesome thought to ponder."

Seeking Meaning

"Thanks, Zegula, that helps," begins Dawa. "Once again, I gain my knowledge through illumination and observation. Although I don't miss much, incorporating the nuances of thought that you reveal aid in my cognition of man's image. In your absence, much has been written in the sacred texts of man. The New Testament is about Jesus Christ, with the Apostle Paul being perhaps the most influential. He was quite the controversial figure in his time and continues to be to this day. This man wrote much of the texts regarding Jesus Christ, and it's from his letters that many of the doctrines of the new religion of Christianity morphed into. He claimed that the scriptures he frequently referred to were written for comprehension by the *spiritually mature man* and not by the *natural man*. Paul referred to his writing as revelations of the mysteries of Christ, suggesting that the spiritual meanings of both the Old Testament and his epistles were hidden beyond the letters written, the exoteric meaning, and was to be interpreted esoterically. It seems that even Paul had many of the same frustrations as Jesus regarding the religious institutions of the day, which is particularly acute given that Paul himself was known to be a religious zealot, actively and violently persecuting those who practiced Christianity before his miraculous conversion. He would later repeat

Jesus's assertions that these religious practices are a stumbling block to man's ascension to spiritual maturity. I don't believe it's fair to burden the Apostle Paul with responsibility for the manner of evolution regarding these doctrines as many have done. I'm beginning to sense that this may very well represent the axis whereby faith-based institutions stop short of the intent of these sacred texts, limiting the power of the Christ, while also providing the *natural man* with the cover to remain hidden."

"Perhaps the most significant diversions of beliefs," elaborates Dawa, "are the consistent treatments of the concept of Mara in Buddhism and the character of the serpent found in the Torah and the practice of Judaism. Both faith-based practices consider this characteristic of man to be a component of man's dual nature, a function of the inner man. In contrast, Christianity has magnified this character to represent an outer third party Being, the devil or Satan, corresponding to the character of the serpent and the source of our temptations. Satan becomes the outside target as the culprit triggering man's malevolence, effectively taking the focus off the law of the inner man's dual nature. As this concept plays out, man also begins to look outside of himself for God, largely dismissing the concept of the Christ within that Paul speaks of. Man's practice of beseeching an outside God to protect himself from an outside adversary completely abdicates *the flesh* from this responsibility. This practice handcuffs the power of the Holy Spirit, enabling the inner man adversary, *'IT'*, to perpetuate the process of blinding man from his true spiritual potential."

Dawa continues, "This implication of diverting man's attention away from the law of God in the inner man is also reflected in the practice of worshipping Jesus as God the Father incarnate. From my observations the concept of the Trinity has developed as a religious doctrine that appears to contradict the Jesus message. It certainly serves to set mankind up for failure as how can a man follow Jesus Christ, and be like Him, if He is also Father God? I don't want to belabor the point here, Zegula, but I will add that references to worship contained in the last book of the Bible do not appear to support this doctrine. Jesus Christ, refers to *the one who is greater* as *My God* and *My Father* numerous times, while John, the author, was told to only *Worship God* by the angel that Jesus Himself sent to deliver the prophecy. In one instance, it makes a clear distinction between Jesus and God in this regard: *Then I fell at his feet to worship him. But he said* to me, *'Don't do that; I am a fellow servant of yours and your brethren who hold to the testimony of Jesus; worship God. For the testimony of Jesus is the spirit of prophecy' (Rev 19:10).* It's here where the very angel that Jesus sent is telling John to only worship God. Why would the angel of Jesus miss this opportunity to proclaim that John should also worship Jesus as God if they were equal deities?"

"What are your thoughts Zegula," asks Dawa. "Boy, oh boy, Dawa, have you no mercy? I need a moment to think this through as those are two very big concepts to consider." Dawa continues, "The scriptures written in your absence proclaim that Jesus was ***the*** Son of God sent by the Father and was *the first amongst many brethren*. He was ***the*** first and only Son until He became ***a*** Son due to the brethren that followed what he had modeled. But what about the references to the sons of God that were gathered with the Lord in the story of Job long before the arrival of Jesus? Forget that thought for now, we can get to that later. But Paul did write that, *'Although Jesus existed in the form of God, He did not regard equality with God a thing to be grasped' (Phil 2:6).* The sacred texts tell us that man was created in the image of God, which helps to explain why Jesus tells us that the *kingdom of heaven* is within man, while Paul also tells us that the Christ is within man. Jesus was the *first* Son of God, and all of mankind represents a Spirit created by God, but neither reflects all that God *is.* Taking this one step further, the *natural man* will always be more receptive to a salvation program that requires less from him. Said differently, man would rather *be saved* than embrace a program that requires him to be proactively responsible for his ascension progress, for the nature of the inner man reconciliation work is painful and leads to the dissolution of *'IT'.* Now that thought plays out differently when considering the source of evil."

After a long pause, Zegula responds to the concept of evil; "The source of evil in the mind of man is conflicted Dawa as the *natural man* willingly deceives himself to avoid this accountability. Consider this, if man fails to acknowledge this dual nature and the notion that his own desires are the source of his evil behaviors, and instead those behaviors are initiated by an outside influence versus their own, then how can that which remains be the Christ within when there is no other in this scenario? There is only the one corrupted Self to consider. Certainly, a component of God our Father could never produce such corruption, right? So, what is so corrupt? It must be the individuation of man absent an internally present divine influence. Said differently, that man is in a fallen, corrupt condition requiring that mankind is to be *saved* by a God *out there*. This fear-based approach effectively turns the ascension from the *natural body* nature to the *spiritual body* nature, which is intended to occur during a physical manifestation, into one that happens in the afterlife, where religion says the resurrection occurs. Having a Satan out there to blame turns the ascension from the *natural body* nature to a *spiritual body* nature into an effort of the intellectual mind; into an effort of transforming the *natural body* ego-self mind from one manner of existing into another manner of mind, never truly acknowledging the independence of either nature. It's centered around behavioral modification of *'IT.'* And who or what do you think is the source of the activities of the intellectual mind if the divine component, the belief that the kingdom of heaven is inside of us, is not considered? The answer can only be the *natural body* ego-self, right? And do you think for a second that *'IT'* is going to voluntarily play by the religious man's rules, unilaterally giving itself' up, and then towards what offsetting persona, if *'IT'* is the only nature? What is *'IT'* being reconciled into? Furthermore, what would be the point of a loving Father God creating a human experience that turned the gift of free will into a fear-based outcome, an experience that did not allow for the practice of free choice to result in a consequential spiritual transformation while here on Gaia? What would be the purpose of manifesting in the first place if it is set to occur in the afterlife?"

Zegula could see that Dawa was clearly confused by that answer, heck, so was he. Certainly, he could do better, he thought. "Okay, Dawa," continues Zegula, "I'm going to come at this from another angle, all right? That answer was sort of bottom-up, and this attempt will be more top-down. Perhaps they will meet in the middle for some clarity. The answer is nuanced, as I've said, which is understandable how a man-constructed practice can potentially miss the mark." Dawa interrupts, "Zegula, let me give this a try. I think that I understand where you're going with this, and it connects with the sacred texts that I've become familiar with over these millennia. So here goes, this is my take on the concept of man being created in the image of our Father God based on the creation scriptures found in Genesis and incorporating the teachings of Jesus. But first, I want to revisit this concept of being blind that Jesus often refers to. On second thought, I'll address that in a moment as I think getting through this next thought may help with understanding the symbolism regarding man's blindness."

Adam & Eve – The Celestial Separation

Dawa begins, "The man Adam was created in the image of *the one who is greater* both male and female. At this point, Adam is still in the Garden of Eden with *the one who is greater* and represents spiritual consciousness, both the conscious as the divine masculine and the subconscious as the divine feminine, working harmoniously together, before the introduction of the serpent influence. This is an allegory of the human mind, and we will call this unity consciousness, Adam possessing both the divine masculine and divine feminine. In the beginning, Adam was ONE with our Father God. Here we can say that Spirit is consciousness with human *Being* as Spirit." Dawa presses on, "*the one who is greater* determined that Adam needed a helpmate in order to experience duality in a physical manifestation, so He placed Adam in a night of deep sleep; the realm of forgetfulness and consciousness fragmentation and formed Eve out of Adam. The symbolism here is that the divine feminine was removed and no longer attached to the divine masculine. They were still in the Garden of Eden with the Father and were naked and not ashamed, meaning they were not aware that they were naked because while in unity consciousness being naked does not have a consequence attached to it. Said differently, naked here means they were awake to their divine spiritual nature, a state of consciousness before it expressed the harmful judgements of the ego-self and separateness attributable to human individuality. Adam and Eve knew only purity and innocence of consciousness without the ego, which is why they were not aware nor ashamed of their nakedness. Now Zegula the reader of these sacred texts must understand that the references to Adam and Eve as separate persons is symbolic and continues to reflect that the Adam and Eve personas are components of each individual human, both male and female. Adam and Eve are components of the psyche of the individual man separated symbolically for the purpose of experiencing duality and establishing the *natural man* persona."

Dawa continues, "In this state, Adam represents consciousness, and Eve represents the subconscious nature. Adam represents the masculine intellect nature, symbolically the husband, while Eve represents the feminine desire and emotional nature, symbolically the wife. The Garden of Eden is a metaphor for consciousness without the levels of self-awareness humans have the potential for now. At this point, man was ignorant of the natures of good and evil, of the concepts of duality and higher levels of self-awareness. Adam, as the male, signifies consciousness because consciousness has the power to impregnate the subconscious to produce the physical reality humans' experience; by divine design consciousness is to have dominion over the subconscious. Eve, as the wife, signifies the subconscious because the female aspect represents the power of birthing and creating on the physical plane. This is where the concept of "Mother Gaia" comes from. Eve is the "mother of all living," as its man's subconscious that gives birth to his own reality. Therefore, the scriptures state that man will rule over a woman after expulsion from the Garden of Eden. In other words, it's the conscious thought of the male aspect that impregnates the subconscious female aspect with the seed presumably arising from an awake consciousness. If man's conscious dwells on negativity then the subconscious aspect, which is the real birthing creative powerhouse, will produce that effect with negativity becoming man's reality." "Hold up for a second, Dawa," chimes Zegula, "this, it turns out, is an important distinction that you're making, between the esoteric and the exoteric meaning of husband and wife. Taken literally this would mean that man was meant to rule, or to have physical dominion, over women. As an observer of thoughts, I don't believe that is the will of *the one who is greater*." Dawa agrees, "Yes Zegula that's what I understand as well. To view it as such is merely a function of man's *natural body* nature turning the literal into an unhealthy religious doctrine; into a distraction for the benefit of *TT*.' I'm afraid, Zegula, that you're going to witness much of this behavior, the promotion of misplaced religious doctrine based on a literal understanding of the sacred texts, as you witness what has happened in your absence. But we digress," acknowledges Dawa.

Dawa picks back up, "Moving on, and please be patient with me, Zegula. Next, our father God instructs Adam and Eve not to eat the fruit of the tree of the knowledge of good and evil, warning them that they would surely die if they did eat. The serpent then beguiled Eve, telling her that not only would she not die but that her eyes would be opened and that she would be like God, knowing good and evil. As the creation story goes, Eve saw that the tree was good for food; a delight to the eyes; and desirable to make one wise; so, she ate its fruit, along with convincing Adam to do so too. It's here where their eyes were opened. Adam and Eve saw that they were naked, and they became ashamed. They then hid from God and in their embarrassment clothed themselves in fig leaves. Next our Father God clothed Adam and Eve in animal skins, representing both the conscious and the subconscious being covered up by the persona of the serpent, the ego-self. God then proceeded to remove them from the garden, signifying Spirit exiting the spiritual realms and entering a physical incarnation. Only here, the symbolism found in the Hebrew language signifies that they were no longer awake to their true spiritual nature, meaning they didn't die a physical death but a spiritual one. Because of the veil shielding man from the knowledge of his divine nature, mankind begins this journey unaware that they are naked, and so to their shame man fails to clothe himself. This is the *natural man* condition, the first of the ways of God. The Hebrew word used here can be interpreted to mean *'blind'* regarding their original undefiled spiritual nature and marking their separation from *the one who is greater*. To be expelled from the Garden of Eden signifies man's involution into a physical manifestation and into the world of duality, endeavoring to know both good and evil. Eve understood this and accepted the experience of this potential for consciousness to experience greater awareness."

Dawa moves along, "Furthermore, the symbolism found in the sacred texts depicts the divine spark of God descending into the physical incarnation of man signifying the Christ within mankind but remains hidden behind the veil of the *natural body* persona." Zegula elaborates, "Yes Dawa I can see the pieces coming together. I can liken the concept of the divine spark being hidden behind the veil the mechanism protects the divine nature from defilement as man pursues both good and evil experiences while blind to his ignorance." "That's a fair way of portraying this condition Zegula," replies Dawa, "and we'll see that this is the foundational concept when we consider the meaning behind the *grace of God* as we explore the concepts of blindness and nakedness further. But you did make me think of one other consideration with your last thought.

Jesus was born to a virgin, so the scriptures tell us. What I'm thinking this symbolizes is when Christ first manifests in human form it does so in an undefiled baby human. It's this unsullied matter forming to host the purity of Spirit that begins the journey of the soul for man. This would signify that the virgin Mary, signifying this unsullied matter, remains a virgin with every human incarnation and is involved with every created thing. The Spirit of Christ remains protected behind the veil until the corrupted natural body persona is no longer present allowing, the Spirit of Christ to manifest in an incorruptible spiritualized human. Perhaps this is further signified by the body tabernacle transitioning into the body temple upon the appearance of the ark of the covenant we'll get too next. It may be that the virgin Mary symbolizes the undefiled ark of the covenant carrying the yet to be birthed Spirit of Christ which is waiting to be birthed until the appointed time in man's spiritual ascension. So, the marriage of Spirit with virgin matter marks the beginning of mankind's physical experience. That's a curious thought for sure, and when fully extrapolated, suggests that Mary symbolizes the *Mother of virgin Matter* enabling the Spirit of Christ to physically manifest."

Dawa continues, "While the essence of God is ever-present within every human, the *natural body* persona is first in the ways of God and culminates with the transition into the *spiritual body*. This is the journey to the promised land for the spiritualized human. The relationship between God and the journey of the soul for each individual human is symbolized by God's relationship with the Israelites. Recall God's continuous presence throughout the Israelites' Exodus from Egypt and throughout their journey towards conquering the promised land. In this story God instructs His people to construct a temporary tabernacle to serve as His dwelling place until the permanent temple is constructed upon reaching the promised land. This tabernacle was covered with a tent made of goat hair, symbolizing its temporary nature and depicted in Daniel's vision of the Ram and the Goat. Behind the veil was the Holy Place containing the ark of the covenant, which housed the ark of the testimony and was where God dwelled. In the same way God was ever present with the Israelites dwelling in the ark of the covenant, God travels with every human as signified by the divine spark symbolized as the ark of the testimony waiting for the Christ to be birthed. This is the Christ within that Paul speaks of, and His Christ dwells within a fearfully and wonderfully made human body that in the beginning is undefiled and protected. However, the corruption begins with the child's first breath as that is the first in the ways of God. Therefore, within the body tabernacle resides a symbolic version of the ark of the covenant found behind the veil of mankind's own internal Holy Place symbolizing the virgin Mary's protective covering of unsullied matter. The revealing of the divine spark within the ark of the covenant is waiting for the birth of the promise found in the second covenant signifying the point His Christ engages in the war of the inner man; the battle of Armageddon. *'And I heard a loud voice from the throne, saying, Behold, the tabernacle of God is with men, and He will dwell with them, and they will be His people, and God Himself will be with them,'* (Rev 21:3). It's here where the Lord proclaims: *'Behold, the man has become like one of Us, knowing good and evil; and now, he might stretch out his hand, and also take from the tree of life, and eat, and live forever,'* (Gen 3:22). Paul elaborates upon this symbolism in the Book of Hebrews writing that the earthly sanctuary according to the law of Moses was a *copy and shadow of the heavenly and true tabernacle; the one pitched by the Lord and not by men*; the body tabernacle. Paul goes on to say that *Christ did not enter a holy place made with hands, a mere copy of the true one, but unto heaven itself, now to appear in the presence of God for us*; the body temple."

Spiritual Hide & Seek

Dawa plows on, "So Zegula what we have here is a premonition of what the journey of Gaia's purpose is for man, and it culminates in the prophecy found in the Book of Revelation, where the concept of the body tabernacle is the primary subject matter. As this journey unfolds, mankind first experiences the suffering that accompanies the *knowing* of both good and evil through a willful participation in the world of duality. Mankind is charged with evolving beyond his carnal nature by the putting to death the serpent derived *natural body* persona. This is the first death described in the prophecy of Revelation and is signified by the testimony of Jesus and the cross of duality that he bore, for Jesus is the spirit of prophecy." Zegula interjects, "Dawa pardon me for a moment. As I was listening to you I

From Genesis to Revelation

found myself reflecting on the energy patterns that I've encountered within man's psyche and how this serpent persona makes much more sense to me. It made me think of three basic patterns. Comparatively speaking, prior to the Buddha the only energy patterns that I had experienced were either general chaos or an overall quietness of sorts; a nothingness in terms of any sense of inner awareness in both cases. Broadly speaking, in this condition man is either reacting to external stimuli or circumstances negatively or positively without any regard for a purpose beyond their physical comforts or discomforts. It's really not that much different than traveling through a contented dog at peace in its master's home, or through a ravenous bear wakening from a hibernation; primitive instincts ruling both. The dog is reminiscent of the rich man resting in the comfort of his material wealth and accommodating belief systems completely oblivious to his dual nature." "Yes Zegula," chimes Dawa, "that's the analogy of it's easier for a camel to pass through the eye of a needle than it is for the rich man to inherit the kingdom of heaven. What's the motivation or impetus to seek any sort of disruption much less die to self?" "That's right Dawa," answers Zegula, "that kind of contentment is most difficult for man to overcome. Then there's the bear; needing more; wanting more; always seeking to devour more of what he already has in excess. Then there was the Buddha. That was a cognitive inner war Dawa. The Buddha discovered the 'other' in order to observe 'IT,' but the 'other' had no power to absolve the Buddha from 'IT's control. Notwithstanding the suffering caused by the forced deprivation of resources necessary for 'IT' to remain relevant; the suffering outcropping from the internal battle was insufferable, as 'IT' would simply morph at will into whatever it needed to be in order to subvert any attempt to be overcome by the 'other.' The Buddha never found the formula for his absolute spiritualization, even though 'IT' gave him periodic relief, for 'IT' knew that the destruction of the Buddha would boomerang back around and become detrimental to both. Then there was Jesus Christ. Jesus, as the son of man, became the undefiled human vessel selected by His Christ to manifest in human form. 'IT' had no answer for the authority of Christ. This was made possible by the engagement of the Holy Spirit, the power of the Father. It's amazing Dawa, the power of the Father. If only man could see that; the power of the Father that is always available to them. The Father really hates the serpent persona Dawa. I mean…really. This power is just sitting there in suffrage; in silence; like a woman ready to give birth; if only man can remember from where he has fallen and command it." "Yes Zegula," Dawa replies, "I suppose that's what it means when our Father God says that Jacob He loved, but Esau he hated. Our Father God surely put a great deal of thought and imagination into the construction of this human experience. Perhaps that helps to explain the grand nature of the prize for those humans that overcome, as well as the anguish those souls must experience when they fail." "Dawa, Zegula questions, "if the first death represents the absolution of *IT* and the purpose of man's journey, what then is the destiny for those that fail?"

Dawa continues, "Well Zegula this leads us to references to the second death found in the prophecy. The references to the second death signify man's actual physical death and his subsequent return from whence he came, to then be subject to some sort of experiential celestial judgement. For those that have overcome this second death is not to be feared, but those that fail to do so must face the lake of fire, as this is a component of the judgement process. At first glance, it appears that the lake of fire signifies the intense feelings of torment and disappointment that the eternal soul of a deceased bodily human must experience upon the realization that this most recent physical incarnation did not result in a transition into the *spiritual body*; into becoming a son of God. The recognition of this failure must be devastating and suggests that another incarnation is imminent. What's unclear at this point is exactly what the prophecy of Revelation is revealing as it relates to the tree of life and why it is described as being guarded. Perhaps a closer look at the prophecy of Revelation will offer up some answers. It's a much-misunderstood prophecy for sure."

"So Zegula," continues Dawa, "the Genesis story of Adam and Eve is where Spirit, or the soul of man, was given the opportunity to experience the world of duality. The involution of consciousness into a state of fragmentation is to be followed with a reintegration back into unity consciousness. That's where Jesus, as the last Adam, signifying the perfect idealized spiritual man and symbolized as the Christ, comes into the picture. Much in the same way Cain signifies the *natural body* persona and Able signifies the *spiritual body* persona; the first Adam symbolizes man's physical incarnation into the *natural body* persona signifying the first in the ways of God, and with Jesus Christ symbolizing spiritualized man's ascension into the *spiritual body* persona signifying the culmination of the salvation process. Jesus's arrival was for the purpose of showing mankind the *'Way'* towards the reconciliation of these dual natures. This process is symbolized in the Revelation prophecy as the *Lamb* taking the book of the seven seals and ascending, or overcoming, through the seven Spirits before the throne. Here's a distinction that may be helpful; think of the *natural body* as the lower nature in man symbolized as the earth in this prophecy. Now think of the *natural body* under the dominion of Eve, symbolizing the subconscious mind of man taking control of thought generation due to consciousness, or Adam, being rendered unconscious or asleep. Here in this condition, Adam, or consciousness, was not awake; it was unconscious and failed to exercise appropriate dominion over Eve, leaving the subconscious vulnerable and free to express its passions and desires without constraint. To make matters more complicated, you now have the serpent influence as sense consciousness, the carnal mind, the self-willed intellect essentially supplanting the dominion over Eve that rightfully belongs to Adam. It's the serpent persona, *'IT,'* directing or leading Eve. Now picture the higher nature as Adam awakening, exercising proper dominion over Eve, and having control and discipline over the error thoughts related to unbridled desires and passions. To accomplish this, *'IT'* must be subdued, and the ego-self must die. Jesus demonstrated this action by putting the enmity between these two natures to death, thereby creating a new consciousness, Christ consciousness. This story of Adam and Eve is repeated with each human birth on Gaia, with every soul being tempted by the opportunity to experience increased awareness and the promise of becoming sons of God, leaving the presence of our Father God and incarnating into this physical plane as a separate human Being."

"One last thing worthy of noting," states Dawa, "the image of the serpent has always represented the life force energy behind the manifestation into the world of duality. It's this force within man that must be mastered to make the transition from the *natural body* into the *spiritual body*. This ego-self persona will push back on this process, the process of dying to Self, as it does not want to die. It's no surprise that an institutionalized, man-made practice of any form of religion will produce doctrines and mechanisms that essentially protect the serpent in us from being discovered and subdued. Obviously, Jesus understood this dynamic and why he correlated the brazen serpent being lifted-up by Moses to his own participation in being lifted on the cross. The lower nature must be crucified while the higher nature descends symbolically to reconcile the two into one by being resurrected, lifted-up together, into oneness with our authentic divine nature. This is the evolution of man's soul back to unity consciousness and the very purpose of man's extraordinary experience here on Gaia. Conversely, when viewed literally, the religious construct has this concept of falling from a spiritual existence into a physical manifestation codified as penitence for the consequences of the original sin resulting in the man being cast out of heaven in a fallen, sinful condition. Man is created in the image of *the one who is greater* for this very purpose, and man's sin is by design, represented by the ignorance of his true spiritual nature. Recall that God said that they would die if they ate of the tree. Well, Adam and Eve did not die but were instead expelled from the garden. What happened is that they made a choice, the first choice of their free will experience, and symbolically chose to die a spiritual death in order to have an experience of duality knowing both good and evil."

After a long pause, Zegula responds, "Dawa, that helps to explain what I was trying to say. I'm anxious to learn more about these current events." Dawa responds, "Yes, Zegula, that was indeed most helpful. It helps me to understand both mankind's' creative prowess and the teachings of the Apostle Paul. Paul addresses man's dual nature on several occasions, and it seems to be the cornerstone concept of the mysteries that he often refers to. Allow me to meditate on these thoughts for now, and let's get back to the business of your next journey. You're most definitely more prepared than I could have imagined. Thank you, Zegula." "You're most welcome, Dawa. It has been an interesting exercise merging your knowledge of observation with my knowledge of man's thoughts. Most helpful indeed", says Zegula adding, "but before we move on, you mentioned something that has given a reason to pause and reflect further. As I recall, God commanded Moses to make the brazen serpent which served a noble purpose. Jesus did make a specific reference to it, comparing the raising up of the brazen serpent to His own crucifixion. But didn't Moses have the brazen serpent destroyed because the Israelites began to make it an object of worship and committed the act of idolatry? I wonder if Jesus wasn't alluding to that risk as well as it pertains to man creating a religion that focused on worshipping Him versus His God and His Father exclusively? It certainly seems that the concept of idolatry is a slippery slope indeed and a challenge for most all religions. I'm anxious to learn more about this new religion of Christianity, but I'm most interested in gaining a better understanding of how man is made. That discussion will be a good time for me to share my thoughts on the progeny of Adam and Eve, Cain and Able, and later Abraham and Isaac, as they all point to the same dual natures of men, the lower-self first, the *natural man,* and the higher-self second the *spiritual man,* helping to explain the saying *those that are first will be last, and those that are last will be first.* But Dawa, you have me intrigued by your curiousness regarding the teachings on man's blindness, as I am not yet familiar with those teachings. Would you please elaborate on this concept before we move on?"

"Oh yeah, that's right, Zegula," offers Dawa. "The parables of Jesus regarding the blind men have always caught my attention, especially the references to Him coming out of Jericho as He headed to Jerusalem. But now I'm starting to see the bigger picture Zegula. To begin with, Jericho means *'the moon city',* and well, I suppose that explains some of my curiosity," as Dawa gives off a little chuckle. "For all the millennia leading up to your last Journey of Saffron, recall how man would worship the creation of the Ethereal Council members as a mystery and one of coexistence, with reverence even. Man could witness how I would light up the night sky and marvel at my beauty and mystery. Mankind, at this point, believed that I was generating my own source of illumination and incorporated that belief into a component of their worship of me even though I knew it to be an illusion as the source of my light is merely a reflection of Saffron's. But I must admit, it was a very intoxicating experience to have all of mankind worshipping *Me,* as I eagerly embraced the effects of this illusion. I realize that you haven't been around to witness man's science revolution, but to get to the point, this reverence has all but evaporated with the advance of this knowledge. Man has since redirected this reverence into the quest for more knowledge and into a variety of ideologies, rendering our relevance nothing more than science projects. The Council is no longer a mystery insofar as mankind is concerned, and the creation's nature has been rendered lifeless and an irrelevant part of their everyday lives. Man's spiritual evolution appears to have taken a similar path."

Dawa continues, "As the story of the Exodus from Egypt unfolds, the first stronghold that the Israelites had to overcome once they crossed over the Jordan river into the Promised Land was the fortified city of Jericho. In the sacred texts, Jericho signifies the intellect as an external or reflected state of consciousness. The moon is not illumed by its own means but instead reflects the rays of the sun even though, to the eye, this is not apparent. It's here where the relation of the moon to the sun is that of the intellect to the Spirit. The intellect believes that it is expressing the light of understanding, but the science of Being reveals that it shines by reflected light. Even as the moon is part of this creation's planetary system, the intellect has a legitimate place in man's consciousness. It is when the intellect becomes egotistical, thinking that it originates its own light, it forms the adverse consciousness, which is man's internal adversary, the devil, the serpent of old. The carnal mind in man will always be out of harmony with the divine. Jesus passed through Jericho on His way to Jerusalem, much like the Israelites did when entering the Promised Land. Jerusalem, as the holy city, is the spiritual heart center of man and represents the opposite of Jericho, the domain of serpent-controlled self-willed consciousness. Mankind must contend with a version of their own Jericho as they spiritually ascend into their new Jerusalem."

"In one story," continues Dawa, "the man was blind from birth, and the blind man asked to regain his sight in another. All of mankind is blind in their ignorance from birth, while others later claim from their intellect connected to the practice of religion that they *'See.' And Jesus said, 'For judgement, I came into this world, so that those who do not see may see, and that those who see may become blind' (John 9:39).* It's here where Jesus says to those claiming to see that they must become blind again in order to continue their spiritual ascension and enter the kingdom of heaven through the proper door; through the Shepherd's door versus climbing up the other way, saying; *'If you were blind, you would have no sin; but since you say, 'We see,' your sin remains,' (John 9:41).* Man must open his eyes and receive sight in order to traverse through the intellectual trap of the adverse mind. This is the essence of our Father God's grace and the liberation from the bondage of sin. Unfortunately, mankind has done much to fortify its intellectual stronghold in your absence Zegula and those having knowledge of God, or those that God knows, must acknowledge their blindness and then to endeavor to regain their sight so that they may find His door. I think that I'll pause there for now as we will delve deeper into this concept as we explore what the last book reveals about the kingdom of heaven within man. We need to focus on the task at hand and get you ready, Zegula, for your next Journey of Saffron."

THE JOURNEY OF SAFFRON

The Condition of Mankind

Zegula acknowledges Dawa's suggestion as Dawa quickly begins providing insight into Zegula's next journey. "Zegula, as you are obviously aware, man initiates creation here on Gaia through his thoughts. Those thoughts become manifested to create everything not natural on Mother Gaia, everything from things, institutions, images, and ideologies, everything not natural to Gaia. Man's desires are insatiable, and he's quite industrious. While every other life form on Gaia has a singular conscientiousness and only takes what it needs in the moment to survive, man's dual nature has no such constraints. Creations for convenience, comfort, pleasures, and all manner of indulgences are the footprints of mankind's lower nature. Since your last journey, man has managed to initiate an Industrial Revolution that has helped to supercharge population growth challenging Gaia's fundamental integrity. Maintaining an environment for 7.7 billion irresponsible creators has overwhelmed Gaia's design. Something must change. Next, man created the Information Revolution. Unlike the Industrial Revolution, which mostly had a negative impact on Gaia for the benefit of man, the Information Revolution has had little effect on Gaia but has had an unhealthy impact on man himself, of which he is mostly unaware. This revolution has effectively shrunk Gaia and electronically connected all of mankind. Think about the last time that you sojourned Zegula, man's lifestyle was still functioning in the village environment and encompassed the hunter/gatherer mindset with nothing like the technologies of today. The village was comprised of extended families, with all serving a specific purpose and having a role towards the collective support of the community giving man meaning in his work and relationships. That has disappeared so quickly that man's gene pool has not adequately evolved to accommodate these lifestyle shifts. Man is simply not prepared to live in this manner, a life devoid of true community and disconnected from family."

Dawa continues, "This void has spawned the promotion of, and competition between, countless ideologies, belief systems, and social structures which man easily attaches. The result is disassociation, an isolation reliant on an electronically connected humanity. The distractions are innumerable. Man has become overwhelmed with himself, because of himself, and humanity has fractured. Man is universally functioning from his *natural body* nature, believing himself to be separate from all our Father God's creation. This disassociation is reflected in many faith-based belief systems that render this world as insignificant; one to be saved from and transcended, looking to the afterlife for its purpose, rendering this experience to be a mere bridge to another existence. This leads to a disassociation of responsibility and accountability for Mother Gaia and other humans. The practice of these beliefs effectively embezzles away the value of this world in favor of what's next. The erroneous application of man-made doctrines and practices has largely squandered the gift of salvation that Jesus Christ intended to deliver by causing man to look outward for a God that *saves man* in the afterlife as compared to resurrecting the Christ within during man's present physical incarnation. The hope held out for the opening of the eyes of man's hearts is the essence of this Gaia experience."

Dawa plows on, "Then there is a version of this overall lack of inherent meaning, or nihilism, that manifests as a lack of higher values where even those values that held the highest worth have become to reflect no value at all, resulting in the overall destruction of values. This leads to a need to replace old values with new ones causing man to collapse into involvement in more secular causes and movements in order to find meaning. This turning towards ideologies for meaning leads to totalitarianism tendencies which result in a near-total giveaway of personal freedoms in order to align with others having similar nihilistic views of this life. This life-negating nihilism becomes addictive, as it's the path of least resistance and the domain of man's *natural body* nature. Zegula, much has changed. Our Father God has given the Council of Concurrence the authority to align our efforts for the first time to best serve man's need to reverse these trends; to help man awaken and become aware of his true nature. Zegula, you've returned with an unexpected Glow, having a profound positive effect on all of Mira. The Council believes that your energy can be the key to carry along on the Journey of Saffron and act as a sort of a virus to first effect the transition of the other drops, leading to an infiltration on all of mankind, serving to free the Christ energy within, helping to liberate them from the bondage of the flesh."

Zegula was astounded at the wisdom and ambition of Dawa. That God our Father would permit the Council to align their efforts towards these ends represented a seismic shift in accepted protocols. Things were critical, it seems. What was Zegula going to see on this next Journey of Saffron? Would his Glow have the desired influence? Zegula responds, "Wow, Dawa, I don't know what to say. I suppose that I simply must experience what man has created. So, it's time for me to go? What am I supposed to do differently? I've already learned about the law of least resistance and have no control over the path of my journey; what is expected of me?" Dawa responds, "The Council can help guide your path by coordinating with you. Now that you have the Glow, we can communicate with you along the Journey of Saffron and will be able to move you around. But we've determined that this next journey will have one objective, and you will not return until it has been achieved. If we are to discover how to help man on his journey, we need to first learn how to guide and direct the other drops so that they can find the Glow, for the drops have been impacted by the human condition and have become more fearful. This impedes awareness, while increasing resistance, leading the drops further away from the Glow. Your task is to take another drop along on this next journey and bring her to the Glow. We must see this happen, Zegula." Zegula reacts, "Her? Who is her Dawa? Don't I have a say in this matter?" Dawa replies, "Zegula, the Council has determined that sending a drop that has never experienced a human before on the Journey of Saffron under your tutelage would present us with the highest probability of success. We can then focus on how to transition the traumatized drops. We think that's going to be more problematic; it has been a long time since a drop has found the Glow, with none other than you managing to hold onto it, and Mira yearns for more of this energy. That virgin drop is Zarya, and you will meet her on the day of your departure. The Council will facilitate a coupling mechanism so that you and Zarya will always remain tethered during the journey. We can't have you worried about losing her along the way. This coupling will enable you to feel Zarya's thoughts as you travel and aid in her discovery of the Glow. Zarya will not be able to discern your thoughts, however, as Zarya's transformation will be up to her and dependent upon her level of desire to let go of the resistance."

Zegula Prepares a Strategy

Upon hearing this, Zegula quietly agreed, and Dawa faded away as the orange-red radiance of Saffron began to appear on the eastern horizon. He was feeling more than a tinge of frustration regarding Dawa's directive, as he was ready to go, right now; to head out for the nearest concentration of humans to begin his quest. But this changes things. Zarya does not have the resiliency that the Glow affords, and he will need to develop a more subtle thoughtful approach to avoid losing her in the chaos that's sure to come. Zegula determined that he would approach the process incrementally, broken down into three phases. The first part of the Journey of Saffron would be to simply experience Mother Gaia in the most natural way possible; to travel to a remote unadulterated area on Gaia. This would allow him to get acquainted with being tethered to Zarya and how she would react to the various stimulations without worrying about man's influence. Zegula would direct the journey to focus on the prime directives to nourish life on Gaia and cleanse Mother Gaia. This presumably low-stress journey would enable Zegula to respond to and calm Zarya's tendency to resist. The experience of separateness is always one of limitation and unease. It's so very easy for drops to lose their sense of connection; their sense of simply being, instead of outwardly focusing on their own expectations and on the feelings and beliefs emanating from the other drops.

The second phase would be to experience some of the machines and other tangible creations of man. Man had already proved to be quite the creator the last time Zegula journeyed; what could they have possibly come up with to top what they had already built over two thousand years ago? And how was man able to create the means to support so many people? Dawa says that this Industrial Revolution period represented the turning point for humanity. It also began man's unintended assault on Mother Gaia. We'll see what that's all about soon enough.

The third and final phase will be to venture into the large cities and experience how mankind lives in this relatively new urbanized ecosystem. Dawa says that man wasn't meant to live in this manner and that his gene pool evolution remains far behind these changes. To think that man can create at a pace that surpasses his own ability to accommodate is a hard concept to grasp. And Dawa says that man himself is mostly unaware that this has happened; that the residual fallout from the tangible creations has led to more complexions in man's intangible creations. What does that end up looking like? What is this Information Revolution situation anyway? When did man continue to create beyond his ability to keep up with the consequences of his creations? Surely man knows better right? Why can't they just press the pause button until humanity catches up; to catch their breath and coordinate alignment with each other? How far out ahead can they get without becoming completely overwhelmed, or has that already happened?

Zegula was in the middle of his strategy presentation to Mira and Azul when Zarya showed up with her two friends Gali and Iluka. Azul barks out, "Zarya, where have you been? You've missed some very important discussions. And who gave you permission to bring along your friends? This journey isn't for them." Zarya was clearly happy and giggling under her breath, answering, "I just got caught up catching some waves with Gali and Iluka, Azul. I mean, I don't know when I'll be back to get to do that again; it's the most fun thing to do. Some of these Journey's to Saffron can last a very long time you know," as she giggles again. "Yeah," Iluka chimes in, "it's a cool feeling when you turn into a drop at the top of the wave; when we separate from Mira; it feels like an eternity before we tumble back into the foaming turbulence. It's as if time stops, and it's like you're not even a drop anymore, looking around at all the other drops. So cool!" "I hear that it's because of the Krystal; that having the Krystal while being separate keeps it from being scary," adds Gali. "That feeling Iluka is the closest that we can get to having the experience of finding the Glow while you're here with me," responds Mira. "To experience the freedom of physical separation from me and the Krystal, while also remaining aware of your true nature is the essence of the Glow. It's a feeling that will come back to you the moment that you stop resisting and accepts 'what is,' lifting the veil on the Journey of Saffron. It will eventually happen for each drop on all of Gaia; we just don't know how many journeys it will take; it's different for every drop, but you can ride as many waves as you like," Mira says with a wink. As expected, Azul could not hold back his intensity, "Okay, enough of that silly chatter; we have to get back to Zegula's presentation." Zarya giggles again and says, "You know Azul, you should probably go wave riding yourself…you seem a bit uptight," as one of her friends barely holds back their snickering with a little snorting sound. Azul's lips tightened as he looked down to compose himself. After a deep breath Azul shakes his head, saying, "Well, Zarya, that sounds like a good idea. I could use a vacation and think that I'll do just that after you and Zegula depart. But for now, you're going to want to hear what Zegula has planned for you."

Zegula finished explaining his strategy to the team, asking for any questions. Dawa unexpectedly joins the conversation, catching Zarya and her friends off-guard. "Zegula, I must say that's a very well-put-together strategy. It does provide Zarya with a process that appears promising. My only caution is this. Even the Council is concerned for this journey, as not even the Council knows how the current levels of dark energy are going to affect you; *if it's even a little bit,* your ability to not give into your own resistance will be put to the test. You need to be prepared to adjust your plan without hesitation and remain fluid, *hhmmm,* no pun intended." Zarya giggles as she raises her hand to ask a question, "What happens if we become untethered? This coupling thing sounds sketchy to me." After Mira assured Zarya that it would work out fine, Zarya blurted out one last question, "What about Gali and lluka? Can we tether them to us too," she asks. Zegula responds curtly, "Zarya, that is not possible; it only works for two drops; besides, this trip doesn't need any other distractions. It's imperative to learn how best to lead drops to find the Glow; Mother Gaia is counting on us." lluka speaks up, "How about hooking me up with Gali? Why not? We can experiment that way to see if two going together can accelerate the experience. Come on, please?" An exasperated Zegula, shaking his head while glancing back and forth into the eyes of all who were there, was hesitant to respond. Even though he felt his own reluctance to agree to this proposition, he sensed a different vibe coming from the others. Azul took a quick look down and raised his head towards Zegula. Azul's expression said it all, with his one eyebrow raised, followed by a tiny upward wave with his hands; he gave a bit of a *why not* gesture. "Awe, come on Azul, don't make me do this," blurted Zegula, "this idea is absurd; how am I going to keep watch over those two newbies tethered together? They're either going to kill each other with their conflicting resistance or, well, *come on,* why are we considering this?" Nobody said anything. It was a convicting silence, and Zegula knew what had just happened. "All right then…let's do this," he says with a heavy sigh. "You guys are going to regret suggesting this…be careful what you ask for. Gali, are you sure that you're up for this? We have no idea how long this journey will take. I, for one, can't imagine the torture of being strapped to Iluka for a thousand years. That boy lives for the adventure," Zegula chuckles softly. Gali looks over at Iluka for a long minute while everyone else stares directly at Gali. "Gali," chimes Azul, "that's a pretty heavy burden buddy; think carefully about it. However, I will provide my opinion if you're interested." Gali pauses for a moment and replies, "I'm in. Admittedly I am apprehensive about it and, in all honesty, feeling a tinge of anxiety. But I've been friends with Iluka from the beginning and trust him. Do you hear that Iluka that I'm going to trust you with this? I only agree with this as I'm intrigued by the prospect of discovery, and we'll never know if we don't give it a go. That's the adventure Iluka; determining if two are better than one. That's the mission Iluka so let's don't get distracted, okay?" Iluka lets out a celebratory shout and says, "you bet, Gali, let's do this; love you buddy!"

Upon hearing this, the Council of Concurrence immediately convenes a meeting to facilitate the tethering's. Dawa begins, "We're here to send you on a very special Journey of Saffron, recognizing that it may take more than one journey to determine if this will work. There's so much that can disrupt this plan, as we've never attempted to accelerate the way to the Glow. Ancient wisdom has always suggested that attempting such a measure would only feed into the resistance, making the journey even more challenging. Having said that, we simply must trust that *the one who is greater* will guide us to a successful outcome. Our intentions are noble, and the situation is dire. You see, Zarya, Gali, and lluka, the Council believes that if we can learn how to capture the essence of Zegula's Glow and use it to infiltrate the other drops on the Journey of Saffron, then it's possible to use that energy to influence man. Man is electric, and so is the Glow. It's the most expedient way to transmute the loving energy of this creation directly into man. Perhaps this energy will help to restore mankind's connection to Mother Gaia, as well as to the purpose of their personal spiritual journeys. The Council does not want to engage man with the destructive tools available to Gaia to gain man's attention and instead prefers to trust that man will awaken to the need to love her back. That's the philosophy behind this experiment to use the energy from the Glow to help awaken mankind to their connection to the divine, which we believe will transmute into a loving obligation to care for Gaia in more responsible ways. We all know that we are one with *the one who is greater,* but mankind is completely consumed with itself and has lost its way." Mira respectfully raises her hand to make a comment and begins with acknowledgment from Dawa. "Remember that your basic training still applies. You will always end where you begin, no matter the amount of resistance you put forth. You will not perish even though you will experience that element of fear. Your travels are not a function of choices but the byproduct of your nature. Try to remember; *the essence of your journey is found in the journey itself.* That's what will lead you to the Glow."

Saffron commends Mira's message, "Mira, that is a great reminder and the ultimate reassurance. Your experience of duality is limited, and you will always end up where you began. It's time to use our collective essence to have a greater influence on mankind than what mankind is having on Gaia. Now I do want to take this one-of-a-kind opportunity to make an observation that may be helpful in managing your fear. This initiative must be successful and planting this seed may help you to remember. While you are here in Mira, you've come to know that my role is to provide Gaia with warmth and light, representing life and the unconditional love of our Father God; and of course, to illuminate Dawa," as she gives Dawa a loving wink, "as this represents my spiritual nature. But I too, have a dual nature as it relates to the Journey of Saffron. In the illusion of the journey, and because you no longer have the perceived protection of the

Krystal, as even that is part of the illusion, I become the antithesis of this loving nature and something for you to fear. You will come to recognize me as *Helia*, your primary nemesis on the journey and the source of your primary form of resistance. You will be tempted to blame all your setbacks on Helia, justifying your own resistance. Having something or someone to blame obscures your reality and responsibility as to how each drop is to conquer this fear. Overcoming the fear of Helia and recognizing my true love nature will be the cornerstone event of your finding the Glow. The key is to not fear the warmth when it's time for the breath of Kalani to pick you up. Remember to embrace the warmth as the love of Saffron; this will serve to help you let go of the fear of *Helia* and to see only me."

Determinism - It's All About the Start

After a brief ceremony to consummate the tethering's, the two teams prepared to depart. Saffron offers up a final thought, "I'll be working with Kalani to ensure that we begin your Journey of Saffron away from a large human population center and work to help keep all of you together. What we cannot predict is the impact that man's creations will have on your path, as some of these will defy the laws that have directed the drop's journeys since the beginning of time. It's also important that you realize the only way that we can track your movements is through Zegula's Glow. So Zegula, if you can't see one of us, then it's highly likely that we can't see you." With that being said, the breath of Kalani swept in and picked up Zegula with Zarya and then Gali with Iluka. They all rose into the warm ocean breeze, wrapped up in little bubbles because of the tether that attached them. Kalani was moving swiftly now and joined the crew with a mass of other drops that were circulating together at high speed. As the storm pressed forward towards landfall, the crew found themselves rising ever higher and closer to the center. The energy being released was intense, causing it to feel as if Kalani was angry and wanted to push us as far inland as possible. Oddly the feeling amongst the untainted gaseous drops was one of no resistance or fear but instead one of an anxious expectation. What awaits them when they turn back into drops and fall to Mother Gaia?

The storm ferociously slams into the shoreline, hurling the drops like mini projectiles against anything in its path. Buildings were being blown away while trees were being uprooted, with a massive volume of drops washing over Gaia. Zegula and crew still found themselves high in the clouds as the storm subsided further inland. Where was Kalani taking them? As the storm slowed, Zegula and crew found themselves circulating in a wide outer band as they were distanced from the storm. It was here where they were met with colder air and began turning back into drops. A massive gust of Kalani caught them as they began to fall towards Gaia. Zegula was catching glimpses of Saffron and blue skies as they hurtled toward the ground. The first thing they hit was a leaf, slowing them down enough to fall softly near the trunk of a majestic elderly oak tree. Zegula could see that they had fallen in a valley where the massive oak tree stood alone in the open field. It was clear that the ground desperately needed this rain, leaving Zegula to anticipate what was about to happen next.

As Zegula and Zarya were slowly sinking deeper into Gaia, they were suddenly sucked into a tiny sliver of the oak tree's root finding themselves being pulled into another much larger section up above them. What is going on thought Zarya. "Zegula," anxiously shouts Zarya, "what is happening? Are we being pulled, well, up? Is that supposed to happen? I mean, what about the laws? Going up doesn't jive with the law of gravity or the law of least resistance; how is this natural? It can't be right!" Zegula laughed under his breath and assured Zarya that it was as it should be, explaining that they were in a tree. Now that Zegula had the Glow, he could remember all the other times that he ventured through trees. In his opinion, it's one of the greatest feelings that the Journey of Saffron can provide as it's how Mira and the Journey of Saffron keep Kalani vibrant. Kalani would surely suffer without the trees, placing Mother Gaia in great peril, and without the drops, well, *there would be no trees*. On the other hand, there was quite a commotion going on just above. Just as Zegula had jokingly alluded to when the tethering experiment was discussed, Gali and lluka were engaged in a life-or-death tug-of-war tussle. *They were freaking out.* "Gali, would you just calm down…this has got to be the *'Way'* I mean, we're going back up, dude," screams lluka! Gali adamantly expresses his disagreement shouting back, "Come on man, going up like this is not natural…nope…don't wanna go up lluka, but I can't stop it from happening no matter how hard I try! And you certainly aren't helping matters Iluka. Quit tugging on me!" "Yeah, right, buddy," says Iluka with an antagonizing jerk on the tether.

Zegula was learning more about having the Glow and found it exceedingly helpful that the Glow facilitated the art of communicating with all the other drops as if they all had the Krystal without even having to speak. With this new perception, he was becoming aware of the fear and resistance coming from the other drops while also sensing that some of these drops had been on this particular journey for a very long time. Like Gali and Iluka some were nervously hopeful that going up would be the *'Way,'* while others were resisting with all that they had. The one consistent message coming from the drops moving into the roots was a maniacal obsession with finding the Krystal, believing that it would *save them.* Before he could answer Zarya's desperate plea, Zegula felt a tremor running through the roots and heard a mysterious voice coming from, well, *the tree?* How could that be? He's never talked to a tree before; not in a billion years; three billion years ever; never? "*Who* said that? W*hat* said that? W*here* did that come from?" with the sound of Zegula's voice causing the tremors to electrify!

"My name is *Quesnel,* a warrior oak in the service of protecting our mysterious Kalani. You're traveling through my shadow! My shadow has only ever known darkness, and yet your light energy has me vibrating with an ecstasy I've never experienced! *Who* or *what* are **YOU**?!?! You're not just a drop; you're not like the others! Where did you come from? Have you been sent by *the one who is greater,* the one that our Mother Gaia has *prophesized*?" bellows the voice of Quesnel. Zegula was startled and dazed by those questions. "My name is Zegula, and yes, I'm *just a drop* Quesnel on the Journey of Saffron with my new friends here. Well, we're actually on a mission of sorts as well. Sorry to have caused such a commotion." "A mission," questioned Quesnel, "what kind of mission, Zegula? Did our Mother Gaia send you? Could that be possible?" Zegula was about to answer that he was most certainly not a party to a prophecy when he was compelled to ponder those questions further. "Well, Zegula, cats got your tongue; speak up my friend," compels Quesnel. "Well, Quesnel, to be honest, I was sent on this mission by the Council of Concurrence; at the urging of, well, Mother Gaia, but she said nothing about a *prophecy*

Quesnel," stammers Zegula. Both Quesnel and Zegula became solemn and reflective, while Quesnel's shadow vibrated with joy.

"*the happening* Zegula…the prophecy of *the happening*! Have you not heard of *the happening*?" Quesnel questions skeptically. "The prophecy foretells of a time when Mother Gaia would be distressed by mankind and that the Council would send out a cry for help to *the one who is greater* to save her. And that *the one who is greater* would send out a most unlikely hero to begin the process of renewal; to begin the transition to the New Earth; the revival of Mother Gaia. This prophecy would somehow involve mankind and cause them to love her differently and to be more careful with their creative powers. Really Zegula, have you not heard of the prophecy of *the happening*? You are, after all, a most unlikely hero, are you not? You are but *just a drop* as you say?!?" Zegula's memory immediately snaps back to Dawa; to what Dawa had said about him. Zegula just thought at the time that Dawa was handing out excessive and quite inconsequential platitudes. *But* this was an overwhelming and surreal moment for him as he recalled that conversation. The *'one'* he thought? The vibrations were getting more intense, causing them to rapidly accelerate upwards through Quesnel's shadow as Zegula pondered that thought.

The new energy that Quesnel was absorbing, combined with the peace and wisdom of Zegula's Glow, was having a positive effect on the other drops. It seems that their resistance was fading, and they were all feeling expectant that this was, in fact, the path to the *'Way,'* the path to being saved by the Krystal. It was a longing for something unknown within the drops, perhaps a longing to be out of the Journey of Saffron with its dangers and detours and safely home where the mystery of the Krystal would be revealed. It didn't take long before the crew breached the surface and began climbing up the trunk of Quesnel. Although Zegula knew that the ultimate destination was to reach the leaves of Quesnel, the other drops were content to relax into this newfound energy. On the other hand, Quesnel was looking for an explanation and knew that time was short. Neither Quesnel nor Zegula could slow down the ascent, and Quesnel's excitement only exacerbated that problem. Curse those pesky natural laws of cause and effect.

Quesnel implored Zegula for more information. "Zegula," asks Quesnel, "is there anything that you can share with me to shed light on the purpose of your mission? Could this be the beginning of *the happening*? We don't have much time before you are absorbed into one of my leaves and not able to speak with me. I can't seem slow down my vibrations. It's been a most unlikely and fortuitous opportunity to experience your special energy. Thank you, Zegula!" "Quesnel," replies Zegula, "it's difficult for me to imagine that I'm part of *the happening's* prophecy, but I do have reason now to suspect that I am. You see, I had a very interesting conversation with Dawa preparing for this journey" "What was that!" interrupts Quesnel, "you've spoken with Dawa? That can't be possible for a mere drop. How does that even happen, Zegula? Have you spoken with any other members of the Council?" Zegula slowly shakes his head in disbelief at what is going down in this moment. "Yes, Quesnel I have, even Mother Gaia and Saffron. I suppose that having the Glow has caused me to forget how unusual that is, which is why I'm becoming suspicious that this very well may be the beginning of *the happening*. So yes, Quesnel, I am afraid that I may be the one prophesized. I've been charged with finding out how to help the drops find the Glow; to expedite that process so that we can collectively help mankind in their Journey of Gaia. The hope is that we can influence mankind from the inside-out as we are concerned that working on them from the outside-in will only make matters worse. Man is a special creature that way. Their fear rules them, and that approach would only cause more resistance," answers Zegula.

Quesnel solemnly responds, "Mankind, hmmm? You wouldn't know it now, but I've had plenty of experiences with man over my 250 years. There used to be many of us in this valley, but now I am the only one remaining. Initially, I thought my crookedness was a curse as I looked around at all the tall, straight, mighty oaks. They towered above me, reaching for the sky, as I spread out amongst their midst. Then one by one, they were cut down by man and hauled to the mill for processing. You see, a crooked tree doesn't fit into the mill Zegula. So now I'm thankful to be a crooked tree as it's afforded me a long life protecting Kalani. I've also hosted many a man; providing shade as they traveled through. I've even had lovers meet here under my branches. It's been a great life Zegula and made even more special with having met *the one*." Zegula replies, "Well, thank you, Quesnel, and yes, you are a lovely, crooked tree. Thank goodness you weren't cut down. But man is also having an impact on the drops Quesnel. Have you noticed a difference?" Quesnel answers, "Most certainly, Zegula. Even though the drops have always seemed preoccupied with where they were going and never focused on where they were in the present moment, they were not annoying. But that has changed over the last 100 years, Zegula. It's as if they now think that they can control, or should control, where they are going. I've learned to ignore their negative energy and let them through as quickly as possible. I don't even mind those times of drought anymore. I'd rather be thirsty than to feel their self-absorbed anxieties." Zegula nods in acknowledgment, adding, "Yes, I've already picked up on that anxiety. You see, Quesnel with the Glow that I have, I can pick up on the drop's memories, including the memories of the humans that they've experienced. It's been over two thousand years since I made the Journey of Saffron, so all of this is very new to me. Man is much the same way, either looking back at the past and carrying all that baggage along with them or looking ahead, obsessed with destination expectations. They are rarely focused on the present moment and have become addicted to their own anxiousness. Oh boy, here we go; good luck Quesnel, hope to see you again, buddy!" "Bye, my friend, my hero buddy, go get 'em' all right? You can do this! Hey, and give Dahlia my best. She's a most gregarious darlin' of a leaf! She's one of my most prolific little creators too", as Quesnel's voice fades. With that, Zegula and crew were whisked away into Dahlia, a vibrant oak leaf surrounded by acorns.

Zarya was flabbergasted by what she had just witnessed, but she didn't have a moment to approach Zegula about *the happening* and his involvement. If it were true, then she was also part of it, but what did that mean? Just then, Dahlia speaks up, "Whoa there, pardner' something just cranked my engine up ten notches. Don't know what you brought in here with you cowboy, but boy-oh-boy, it feels like a bucking bronco. Oh, okay, that's a sight never seen, two drops tied together like that. Kinda strange, you know. Those other two buckaroos over there look a mess, all tangled up and such, fighting like two bull bucks with their horns stuck together. Well, aren't you guys quite the posse? You're just in time, too; needed a little juice given how you jacked things up." Zarya was intrigued by such a sprite personality. "Hey there, Dahlia, my name is Zarya, and this is the great sage Zegula; we're on a mission," pipes Zarya while receiving a stern stare-down from Zegula. "Well, how's that little cowgirl? What kind of mission could you be up to; looking for a way to put a lid on that Glow, you think?" Dahlia giggles out. "Well, as a matter of fact, that Glow is the start of *the happening;* what do you think about that," brags Zarya. "Well, howdy yippee ki yay, what do you say? So, you're here to save Gaia? Mother sure needs some help. I'm just getting started and would sure be singing the cowboy blues if I don't get a chance to evolve further. You see, a leaf is the first of my incarnations. It's a very short trip; you know, just one season if I'm lucky. Squirrels, you know, come up here trying to get those acorns wreaking havoc around here. That's what I want to be next; an acorn so I can become a tree like Quesnel. It's been a hard ride with Kalani blowing us around. It's like riding a bucking bull, but I wouldn't change it for the world", says Dahlia. "Yes, the first ones are hard, Dahlia," says Zegula, "but I must warn you; they don't get any easier as the lessons keep getting more difficult. I recall one of my earlier experiences as a honeybee. I got a little angry and shot my stinger, and that was it; poof, back where I started; just like that", Zegula laughs. Zarya has no recollection of where she started and asked, "What's so hard about it?"

Dahlia looks over at Zegula with a grin, "Hmmm, I'm not real sure how to answer that one and don't want to be made the fool, you know. Not a good look for a cute cowgirl like me. How about it, ol' wise sage; time to rodeo up; you got this one?" Zegula considers the question, "Well, it's a big thought, and I don't think we have that much time, but I'll try. Our Father God is omnipotent, omniscient and omnipresent. There is no limitation on *the one who is greater.* So, what does he go and do? He creates limitations for Him to experience through His creations. It's an opportunity for consciousness to experience greater awareness through manifesting in the physical plane. We are a part of our Father; well, our Father is in us; making all the Gaia creation a part of Him; experiencing limitation. It's quite difficult for us to be separated from Him; you see, He must make us forget that, or else it's pointless, and agreeing to be so limited when we came from being limitless is a difficult thing to do. It starts with you, Dahlia, with the crescendo being man's submersion into a world of duality. That's what we are all hoping to experience, becoming sons of our Father God; and it's not going so well for man currently, which is why *the happening* is important. See, kind of a difficult concept to digest. Speaking of digesting, Dahlia, I think it's time for you to create." "Yep," replies Dahlia, "seems so. I have this invisible gas thingy over here and need to create that gas thingy over there, and I need you guys to get into the mix! It's the way us leaves keep the mysterious Kalani healthy; get on over here; time to giddy up and roam the range pardners." And just like that, Zegula and his crew were caught up with the breath of Kalani on their way towards another adventure.

Only Kalani knew where the drops were headed as they were caught up in a cloud that seemed to be standing still. Gali and lluka were holding onto Zegula and Zarya in anticipation of what was next while Zarya was assaulting Zegula with a series of rapid-fire questions. Being turned into a mist was a surreal experience, and even though it's happened thousands of times for each drop, the veil of forgetfulness caused each Journey of Saffron to feel as if it was the first. Zegula was most certainly the main attraction, with all the other drops not sure what to think of him. Although he was fully aware of his primary directive on this journey, he couldn't focus on Zarya's distress, as he was distracted by the bombardment of thoughts coming from the surrounding drops; struggling to process this disparate array of information. But while he may have been the primary curiosity, Zegula was preoccupied; being enamored with Kalani and the mystery surrounding her complete independence; for not even the Council could command her and instead would beseech her cooperation when needed. Zegula was intrigued by her seemingly unlimited implicit authority to move about the face of Gaia without concern for boundaries or any apparent restraint related to the natural laws. How was the precision of the Council impacted by the indiscriminate nature of Kalani's behavior? Perhaps Kalani really was the breath of our Father God; invisibly moving about Gaia with absolute intention versus this perceived randomness. Zegula could feel that if he could just quiet his mind, he could embrace the peacefulness of Kalani's movements and capture the essence of the meticulous care she displayed as she secretly came and went. But the noise; so much noise coming from all around him. How can the thoughts from these other drops create so much noise questioned Zegula. And then; in an instance; his peace was abruptly violated as if it were never there at all.

"Zegula; Zegula; *hey, Zegula*! Why aren't you answering me? You're supposed to be focused on *me* right now?" screams out Zarya. Before Zegula could gather himself, lluka jumped in, "Hey, where are we headed Zegula?

I mean, we're barely moving, and Zarya's been tugging on your tether like she's never been in a cloud before. Zarya is there something wrong? Do you know something that we don't? You can't make this all about *you,* you know. I mean Gali, and I want the Glow too; where are we headed, Zegula!" Zegula snapped to and snapped back, "lluka shut the…be quiet for a second. I think, what the heck, I don't know; only Kalani knows, and she doesn't reveal such things, so relax lluka. And as for *you,* Zarya, this journey has just begun, and I'm trying to digest more information than I ever imagined. My Glow is more than enough for me to manage right now; give me a moment, please." With that, Kalani came to life and cranked up her pace. The cloud magically grew and rose, swirling and gyrating as if Kalani had suddenly become angered. As Gali began admonishing lluka for his precocious behavior, the energy in the cloud became electric. Without warning, Kalani sent a massive lightning bolt traveling sideways throughout the clouds. The thunder that followed was deafening, sending a vibration out for miles. The next bolt of electricity struck a tree on the ground ending its Gaia journey and incinerating it where it once stood proudly. This time the thunder was fierce and well *personal.* Kalani was pissed off about something, and she was clearly sending a message to the insolent drops that she carried along. One after the other, the strikes came without interruption, destroying anything that Kalani's savage energy touched. The might of the creation was on full display, with Kalani acting out her frustration with a sleeping Gaia. Mankind has no answer for this kind of energy, and it was being made clear that only the love of *the one who is greater* was protecting humanity from her wrath.

The storm persisted until it settled directly above Quesnel, sitting alone in the valley below. And then it happened; in rapid succession three bolts ripped through Quesnel, turning him into a smoldering pile of charred oak ashes. Zarya screamed out as if Zegula had the answer, "Noooooooooo, not Quesnel and Dahlia; why, why Zegula?". Then out of the darkness and turmoil, they all heard a voice that pierced through the chaos, *"the happening* is a mystery that unfolds as *the one who is greater* reveals; it's not to be announced as something that you've determined! Your purpose is to simply BE Zegula! Anticipating and speculating on what is to come is a construct of man and only serves to heighten anticipation of what may be. It's in this speculation that expectations are formed, leading to fear, robbing you of the gift given by *the one who is greater*, which is the moment that you are in. It's there that you will find what you seek. Fear will take you from the *'Way'* Zegula, and any effort towards anticipating the prophecy alters its very trajectory. BE in your journey Zegula and trust the process, as you are where you are supposed to be, or you would be somewhere else!" Nobody has ever heard the voice of Kalani or could it have been a declaration from *the one who is greater*, as it was certainly His power on display. And with that, the storm subsided as unexpectedly as it had begun. Zegula was visibly shaken, while the dramatic incident seemed to have dulled his Glow. Gali and Iluka stopped their precocious tug-of-war games as they searched for an understanding of what just took place. What kind of story were they involved in? What was going to happen next? How could they possibly know for the intensity of this experience has already surpassed anything they'd ever experienced prior. Zegula was silent as they rose higher and higher into the sky. Then they heard the voice once again saying, "Hear this," replies Kalani, "my friend Quesnel's journey is not complete. Quesnel will get his wish and become like that of a drop, but not of this world. As for Dahlia, her destiny is her wish; she will rise again with the essence of my power displayed as a majestic oak like none other before; right where Quesnel once stood proudly. It's all part of the plan of *the one who is greater*; trust the process our dear and faithful warriors."

Zegula's Urban Experience

With that profound pronouncement, Kalani raced on westward to the great Spire of the fourth Jewel. It was summertime, so Zegula knew that they wouldn't be caught up on a frozen snowcap, but he didn't know if they would fall on the windward or leeward side of the Spire. Zarya was already nervous as they had been traveling for over a week, and the looming Spire looked troubling to her. "Zegula," asks Zarya, "what is that rising to the sky in front of us? It looks like we're going to fly right into a wall or something." Zegula answers, "Zarya, that's one of the great Spires of Gaia; the greatest of the fourth Jewel." "Well, Zegula," responds Zarya, "that doesn't help me much as I don't know what either one of those is. What's a Jewel Zegula?" "Well, Zarya, a Jewel is where most drops go for the

Journey of Saffron. There are seven major Jewels on Mother Gaia, and this one is the fourth largest. Dawa tells me that it's become the most important Jewel of them all," answers Zegula. Zarya replies with another question, "Zegula, why is it the most important? Why aren't they all the same, Zegula? I mean, doesn't Mother Gaia think of them all as the same, just as important as any other?" Zegula responds, "Well, yes Zarya, I suppose that Mother Gaia does feel that way, but it seems that mankind has altered the character of each Jewel in unique ways; each Jewel is different Zarya because of mankind's influence. It seems that this fourth Jewel was set apart to serve a special purpose. The last time I ventured through this fourth Jewel, I didn't experience or even see a single human. You see, Zarya, this is a very recent settlement for humans in mass and only made possible by mankind's Industrial Revolution that Dawa speaks of. Much of what's on this westward side is mostly desert and unsuitable for man to settle; there's not enough water for them to build a community around. Dawa wanted me to experience this part of the fourth Jewel first so that I could see first-hand what's happened as man has put great stress on Mother Gaia and themselves." "You would think," begins Zarya, "that mankind would have learned from the experiences with the other Jewels how to live here without harming Mother Gaia. Zegula do humans learn from their own history? I mean, do they ever evaluate what they've done right and what they've done wrong before doing the next thing? I mean, surely they're capable of that, aren't they Zegula?" "Zarya, that's a great question and one of the things that I hope we can answer, but for now, I just don't know. It seems that they really don't if we're compelled to ask such a question at all. Zarya I'm sure that they must start out with good intentions; then over time, it seems that they repeat the same pattern of self-destruction over and over and over. Based on the memory feedback that I'm picking up from the many drops that have recent human experiences they haven't seemed to learn from history and appear determined to repeat the same mistakes. This has led to the overwhelming sense of apathy and futility emanating from the drops; a deep lack of faith that mankind can reverse this precipitous decline into depravity. Dawa has carefully observed the maturation of this fourth Jewel with great curiosity as it determined to set itself apart as a country favored by *the one who is greater,* at least that's what the founders believed they were doing. They were committed to governing themselves differently than any other human communities that went before it. Even though it's not the largest, this fourth Jewel quickly became the heart center for all of Gaia and, for a time, was the most influential of them all. Dawa informs me that in a very short 250 years, this influence has waned significantly and that at any moment, it could be rendered too compromised to be a positive impact on others. Zarya, how can anything build and then deteriorate that fast? Most of the decline has happened since the beginning of the Information Revolution; just a short 30-50 years or so. It seems that now the largest and the oldest of them all, the first Jewel, the one identified as the Red Dragon, is once again threatening to become the most influential but not in a positive sense."

Zarya was about to ask another question when Zegula interrupted her, "Zarya there will be more time to explore the activities of man especially as it relates to what's happened here with the fourth Jewel. The redemption of the seven Jewels is the purpose of *the happening,* as the Council cannot influence man's spiritual ascension into becoming sons of God until we get Mother Gaia healthier and more awake and, the creation needs sons of God to be able to usher in the New Earth. All of this becomes meaningless if we can't save her. For now, I need to focus on how to help you find the Glow and keep mine; let's direct our thoughts on those things. Gali and lluka quit fighting and stay close. *Where is Kalani taking us,*" whispers a concerned Zegula? "Zegula," Zarya snaps back, "how can I find something when I have no idea what I'm looking for, hmmm? I mean, what am I supposed to be thinking about? Really, everything is moving so fast, and I can't help but be sad for Quesnel and Dahlia. Was that supposed to happen? How does that help us to find the Glow Zegula? Hmmm? What should we be expecting exactly? I know I'm missing something, and I've heard some of the other drops that have been muttering about the Krystal for a long time. Is that what finding the Glow is all about, the secret of the Krystal?" Before Zegula could come up with an answer, a blast of warm air pushed them up high over the Spire, falling as drops once again on the western side of the Great Continental Divide.

Zegula reached out and grabbed the tether connecting Gali and lluka, assuring they would all stay together. They quickly cascaded along the rocky slope towards the smallish clear blue mountain lake below, picking up sediments as they moved along. Zegula thought how pleasant it was to sense the cool air under the shade of the mountain as he eagerly anticipated carrying the much-needed minerals to the lands beyond. This all felt familiar and natural as the drops appeared to be solemnly relaxing into the beauty of the journey. The peace of the journey was suddenly broken as they moved further into La Poudre Pass Lake, located in the Rocky Spire. Zegula knew that from here, they would be moving into the Colorado watershed, one of the 24 Deacons, and on towards the Gulf of California, where they would once again reunite with the Krystal of Mira. Dawa informed Zegula that this had become a very important Deacon due to the migrations of man out to this desert-like southwestern region of the fourth Jewel. Zegula was picking up on the increasing thoughts and distress of the surrounding drops as they all contemplated the journey ahead. Many were wondering if they would make it all the way down to the Gulf of California or if they would be sucked up and diverted for the purposes of man's creations as before? Others just wanted to stay in the peaceful waters of La Poudre Pass Lake, looking for any way possible to get out of the water's flow. Zegula could sense that this journey had become a burden for many as he sensed skepticism and resentment amongst the drops, as if even allowing themselves to imagine they could make it back to Mira had become a futile proposition. And then the fright of the haunting presence of Helia above was all-consuming, for his scorching rays meant certain death.

"Hey fellows…look over there at that crew!" shouted out a drop as it pointed over to Zegula. "Have you ever seen a drop lit up like that? And check out how they're tied together; that's not right." "Hey, you over there, you'd better stay away from us if you know what's best for you," yelled out another. With that Iluka lashed back as Gali tried to restrain him, "Hey buddy, back off; we're here to help Mother Gaia, so chill out!" "Help Gaia?" questions the drop, "Why help Gaia when she's not helping us…eh? We're trying to get back to the Krystal, and she keeps taking us in the wrong direction. Mira is over there," as drop points towards the west, "but that takes us to where Helia goes to hide so we just need to stay here where it's safer. I don't trust Gaia," as it struggles to resist the current. Another drop disagrees, saying, "Nope, Mira is that away," as the drop points to the south, "I was told by a very smart drop that it's that direction, and he has a big following, so he must be right!" And then another joins the fray,

"No, no, no, it's that way," pointing to the top of the Rocky Spire and the Great Continental Divide, "we should've been dropped down on the other side as that's where Mira is, and I hear that Helia isn't on that side!" Then all the drops begin to argue amongst themselves, making claims that only they know the *'Way'* to the Krystal. Meanwhile, they are all being carried along with the current no matter how frantically they resist. Zarya looks at Zegula, "Zegula, what are we going to do? They're afraid of your Glow Zegula. Why would they be afraid?" "Yeah, Zegula, where are we headed?" questions a fearful Gali.

A frustrated Zegula found himself lost in thought, wishing that Saffron and Kalani would sweep in and carry him far away from this madness. Zegula was struggling to keep his attention on helping Zarya find the Glow, knowing that she had begun to question if that's what she even wanted anymore. He was starting to sense that the power of his Glow was fading as the negative energy around him increased. Dawa had prepped Zegula for this part of the Journey of Saffron, informing him that this desert Deacon served as the lifeblood for over 40 million humans. This represented over 50% of the population that was influenced by the Rocky Spire and represented a population growth of more than 40 times over the last 220 years for this region alone. This rapid population growth and accompanying industrialization was overwhelming Gaia's ability to sustain mankind's expansion as well as the environment overall. Dawa explained that mankind had built 15 dams on the main stem of the Colorado watershed and hundreds more on the surrounding tributaries in order to capture and use this water in support of man's purposes. Zegula was anxious to make it to the bottom of the lake, so they could start the rapid descent towards the cities below. He was ready to experience this new breed of urban-oriented humanity, temporarily letting go of the idea of finding Zarya's Glow, for that would have to wait until he could find his own bearings.

The crew finally made it to the mouth of the river and began to turbulently descend the southwestern side of the Rocky Spire. As the river would wind, the drops would be yelling that they were going in the wrong direction, with others claiming it was the right direction. The resistance was futile and pointless, as the river would suddenly make a turn serving to repeat the cycle all over again. After tumbling down the mountain for a couple of days, the exhausted crew suddenly found themselves in one of the many manmade reservoirs located along the route. Zarya blurts out, "Zegula; I need off this tether right now. Your Glow is getting a lot of attention, and it's not the good kind. I'm not sure if I even want to do this Glow thing anymore. I just want to get back to the Krystal. Can you do that, Zegula? Release me now?" Just as Zarya finished asking her question, the crew was being sucked into a large round opening just under the surface of the reservoir, and there was nothing that they could do to stop it. Just like that, they were moving briskly in a completely dark cylinder. The drops were all freaking out, with some becoming most animated. "Awe, no, not this again; I'll never get back to the Krystal. I don't want to see another human…ever!" shouted out one in disbelief. "Yeah, me neither. I'm tired of carrying their shit all over the place!" said another. "And I just escaped from one of their machines that I was stuck in for years. It totally sucked! I was all mixed up with chemicals being heated up over and over, in total darkness no less. I nearly gave up on finding the Krystal, and now this!" said another. "Hey Zegula," yells out lluka, "what's up buddy, this isn't the law of gravity at work…you ever been in something like this, Zegula?" Zegula replies, "No, lluka, this is a first for me. I'm not sure what this is or where we are going." A drop responds, "Well buddy, I'll tell you where you're going; you're going to *hell* is where you're going; where millions and millions of those jacked up humans live. Once you get into one of those massive human anthills, you can't get out. I'm telling you, it's *fucking hell!* Hey, what's up with that Glow thing anyway?"

Zegula remained silent as his crew sent question after questioning his way. Zegula could feel his energy fading just as Dawa had feared. He knew now that he couldn't help the others find the Glow under these circumstances and was more than willing to untether from Zarya. Zegula knew that it would have to wait until they returned to Mira and that he would petition the Council just as soon as he could emerge in a place where he could be seen. For now, he would have to find a way to hold onto his Glow and persevere through this trial. Zarya began to tug on the tether out of fear and anger. Why did she agree to this, she thought? What was going to happen next? Well, that was a question that was about to be answered. The crew was being pulled up and down and sideways as they sped along, and after several days of this, they abruptly stopped. After a moment or two, they were shot into a small tray located in a very cold space. Before they knew it, they were frozen and locked in place. While Zegula was thankful for the peace and quiet that comes with being frozen in place, he was also perplexed by this most unnatural situation. He had quickly learned the pointlessness in planning this Journey of Saffron, as the law of least resistance and gravity clearly no longer serve as the fundamental determinants. Man's creations have changed all that; now, he's experiencing yet another of man's inventions by being artificially frozen in a little tray. Where was he, and how long would he be here? Once again, it didn't take long to get an answer as the ice cube that he was frozen in was dropped into a cocktail glass and immersed into a crystal brown liquid. Although this was an entirely new experience for all of them, he began to sense this might be the moment they've been waiting for.

After a minute or two, a few more ice cubes were dropped into the glass, and another cascade of warm crystal brown liquid enveloped them. And then it happened; they were released into the powerful mixture and quickly swallowed. As the drops traveled downward, they gradually began to pick up on the uncomfortable energy pattern emanating from this middle-aged man. It was as if they were all holding their breath, waiting to see what would happen next as they were absorbed into the man's bloodstream. Almost immediately, they began to feel the infusion of the Krystal pushing out the remnants of the crystal brown liquid resulting in a dramatic sensory overload. All at once, the drops could silently communicate with the other drops circulating around in the man's body while simultaneously discerning this man's thoughts. He was distraught and beaten, sitting alone at the bar as he stared stoically into the barrage of images coming from one of the dozens of screens hanging on the walls surrounding him. The man would stare down into his cocktail glass, softly shaking his head, and with his irrational thoughts raging out of control, would periodically glance at his cell phone expectantly; occasionally scrolling at even more random images just begging to be distracted. Not only was he sitting alone, but he felt all alone and hopeless even amidst this barrage of visual stimulation. His mind was stuck processing the same questions over and over in an endless do-loop. *What the fuck just happened? How could I possibly have seen this coming? Why did I let this shit happen? I thought he was my fucking friend, a Christian friend, no less! How do I deal with this evil bastard, and how can I stop this fucker? But I'm so fucking god damned tired. I'm broke; what are my fucking options. I don't want to do this anymore. Just put a bullet in your brain, you stupid fuck. Can it even be fixed? We were so fucking close! What a lying sack of shit, and he does so while inserting the name of God into every conversation. What a fucking fool I've been. Think you stupid son of a bitch! Think, damn it, think!* He looks up and, under his breath, quietly says to the bartender, *"I'll have another,"* as he brushes his finger across the cocktail glass. He solemnly rests his head in his hands as he glances back into his phone; then the internal rant begins anew.

The constant barrage of lightning and thunder racing up the man's spine blew right through his heart center and into the throne in heaven. The twenty-four elders responded by pushing out powerful electrical charges, with this frenetic energy being mercilessly dispersed throughout his body. The combination of this energy and the alcohol were blowing cells apart, thankfully serving to numb his desperate mind. The circulating drops became universally disoriented while the display helplessly paralyzed Zarya and her friends. They all could sense that the man wanted to die, that he wanted it to end, that he was tired of the pain. But there was much more going on amidst the noise. There was another war raging in his thoughts. The unexpected failure triggered feelings of shame and humiliation, and the voice in his mind was angrily taunting him. It was obvious that the man's identity rested on his ability to plow through such adversity, but now he was truly stymied. Not only did he admonish himself for this level of incompetence, but he also knew that others couldn't love him as the failure he'd become. This internal anger burned in his psyche as self-hate and self-persecution, with the voice in his mind using it against him. *How could you let this happen again, you stupid fuck? I trusted you to make this happen, and you didn't listen to me. Why do you continue to trust these people? When will you learn that you keep attracting these kinds of people into your life? Just because they claim to be godly doesn't mean they aren't playing you! Wake up, you stupid fuck! It's the same fucking pattern as the time before and the time before that! I can stop that shit if you'd just let me be in control! But no, you want to figure it out. You're hopeless! Yeah, and now you're seeing the pattern play out yet again with this woman of yours! What were you thinking in the first place! Ha, that's it; you weren't thinking were you buddy; nope; you just needed to plug that hole didn't you; the stupid fuck that you are! Yep, she's going to hurt you bad, buddy, and you fucking deserve it! You've already been crushed financially because of it. Yeah, that's going to be a juicy and embarrassing story, you stupid fuck! Yeah, go ahead and kill yourself; it's better than feeling that shame and humiliation yet again! How much of this shit can you take anyway? It's your damn fault, and you know that I'm not going out before you! You're an idiot! You're on your own now, buddy, nobody, wants to be around you; you toxic piece of shit!*

Zarya was about to say something when Zegula preemptively shut her down, "Not now, Zarya," said Zegula, "I don't have the answers right now. This man is overwhelmed by his thoughts, and something in his mind is angry about his repeating patterns. Man's persona is inherently fearful and cannot handle the shame and humiliation that comes with failure. But there's something in the psyche of man that will endeavor to keep him suffering in order to stay in control. I sense that *the one who is greater* is at work somehow, but the man remains unaware of the laws of the inner man. His coping mechanism of drinking away the pain appears to be driven by an inner war between two natures. *The one who is greater* wants to lead him into other means to deal with the battle within, but he's just not yet aware of awareness. That's the purpose of suffering Zarya; to wake man up to knowing his divine nature; it's a fine line. A part of man wants him distracted and thinking that waking up is a continuance of his natural tendencies while adding spiritual thoughts to the process. It's an internal deception of sorts. That process ends up taking man deeper into his slumber."

Zarya speaks anyways, "Zegula, do you really think that he wants to kill himself like that? I mean, humans are why we are here in the first place, after all, right? How can living produce such thoughts, Zegula?" "Zarya," Zegula begins, "the world they're living in is moving very fast and full of an endless array of choices. Free choice has consequences Zarya and some of those are hard lessons to swallow. Knowing that he betrayed himself brings pain, which is what he's trying to reconcile. Something in his conditioning has set him up to blindly trust the people that are attracted to him, and some of those people are attracted to him simply for that reason. He's susceptible to being manipulated, and he's just now realizing that. He feels that not only has he let himself down, but worse than that, he believes that he's disappointed those he loves the most and believes that they cannot love him back as the failure he believes himself to be. He's learned love to be a feeling that is conditional. In his early conditioning and programming, there's something in him that intensely fears being humiliated; what humans fear is ultimately what they manifest. It's how they learn Zarya, that their thoughts also create; always without fail; it's how they're made Zarya. I'm working with Dawa to figure out how man's psyche functions, as it's paramount for the success of *the happening*."

The man stands up and tells the bartender that he will be right back. With that, Zegula and the crew find that they are being flushed down the toilet and into a winding dark pipe that is connected with other pipes filled with drops carrying human refuse. This journey was most disgusting and unlike any the crew has experienced. The pipe became larger and larger, with more drops merging into the semi-liquid flow filled with all manners of human waste. The flow eventually grew to become like that of a small underground river dumping into a series of filters and treatments. It wasn't long before they were forced through a very fine membrane and into a treatment vat being flushed with disinfectant chemicals. The drops were then funneled into yet another pipe and pushed back out into the artificial water cycle for yet another urban adventure. It's been so long since the drops have seen the rays of Saffron or the light of Dawa. The maze of underground pipes is daunting and disorienting for the drops. The natural laws of their original nature no longer apply with these types of experiences helping to explain the defeated condition of the returning drops. How long can a drop get caught up in this manufactured experience wonders Zegula, as he contemplates his fading Glow.

The drops managed to travel through several more cycles before encountering another human. The first was being dropped through a showerhead leading right back down into the spaghetti bowl of underground rivers. It was here where Gali and Iluka were swept out of sight and not to be found. The next trip took Zegula and Zarya through a manic dishwasher and flushed right back into the endless flow of refuse. The next experience found them being poured into a boiling pot of drops used to cook some vegetables, and then you guessed it; right back they went into the dungeons below. All the while, Zegula's anxiety increased as he felt his Glow disappearing. Zarya was numb and was no longer asking questions. They both gave up hope on finding Zarya's Glow, given that Zegula wasn't even able to hold onto his own. Dawa searched and searched for any sign of Zegula's Glow, not even knowing what city he ultimately ended up in.

The next journey promised to break this tiresome cycle after they were squirted into a plastic water bottle and placed on a delivery truck. At this point, all they wanted was to see the light of day and get their bearings.

A young lady taking a hike in the desert landscape was carrying the bottle they were sealed up in. Helia shown brightly and hot as the young lady walked briskly through the canyon, pausing briefly to take a drink. Zegula and Zarya quickly sensed the absorption of the Krystal as her body readily accepted the much-needed hydration. The energy was much different this time as her thoughts were totally focused on the phone in her hand. She was an attractive woman and had made several posts as she hiked along. The images from the phone bombarded her mind as she scrolled endlessly through one account after another. Her mind was clearly enjoying the nature that surrounded her, but it was not at peace. Her thoughts revolved around her sense of self-worth as she looked for likes and comments coming from her posts. Although she was with a couple of friends, they were distracted as well, doing the same thing with only the occasional superficial interaction. *How many likes did I get? I thought that I'd get more likes. Why didn't he like it? Should I post a TikTok instead? I'm going to stop liking hers if she doesn't start liking mine. Is that a good pose? I should've posted a different pic from the other side; that's my bad side. I'd have more followers if I had bigger boobs or was taller like her. How can she have 100,000 followers, and I only have 1,000? I am prettier than her, right? I wished that I could travel like she does. What else do I need to do to be able to make a living as an influencer? Should I do my lips and have veneers on my teeth? She has such nice teeth. Those boobs are way too big, but I guess guys like that.* And at the same time, the critical voice in her mind is going: *You're just too short to look like that, so just give it up. You're too fat to get many likes; pictures just make you look even fatter. Your friends are way cooler than you. You need to show more skin like they do chicken! You need to get rid of that deadbeat boyfriend if you want to be an influencer. He doesn't let you post the risky stuff; you know. Just tell your parents to go to hell and do what you want. You should just block them anyway; that's what your friends do, you know. You don't wear enough make-up. Your nose is too big, and you need some Botox, so your face doesn't move when you smile. Those influencers don't have wrinkles when they smile, you know.* And just like that, Zegula and Zarya were whisked away by Kalani as the perspiration evaporated off her face.

THE PSYCHE OF MAN

the Thinker and the Wanter, 'IT' and the Sonship

Zegula waits anxiously for Dawa to rise into the night sky. It's perfect timing, as Dawa will be full tonight and singularly focused on the conversation. This would be the first time that a drop came back from the Journey of Saffron with the ability to remember all that had happened, and it was almost more than Zegula could absorb. Zegula was certain that Dawa was going to be both intrigued and concerned based on what he was about to reveal. Dawa was about to receive a full download of man's thoughts and a deeper knowledge of how man is made. Our Father God has certainly created the most unusually marvelous Being in man, mused Zegula. Dawa greeted Zegula eagerly, "Zegula, my friend, it's so nice to see you've made it back from your journey. Fortunately, it was a shorter sojourn of just seven full moons, but sadly I see that the others did not find the Glow. The Council awaits your assessment of the potential success of *the happening*. Mira; Azul; it's great to see you here too. Based on my observations, there's much for us to contemplate." "Thank you, Dawa," both Mira and Azul said at the same time. "We've all been waiting to hear as well, especially since *the happening* is no longer a secret," says Mira. "Well, Zegula, what do you have for us? What have you learned about man," questions Dawa? Zegula shakes his head ever the most slightly, knowing that Dawa has no idea the difficulty of that question and the complexity of the answer.

"Zegula begins, "It's great to be back with each of you too. The journey was much more intense than I expected," adding, "and Dawa, you couldn't have been more right about my original plan. Planning in phases lasted only a day, and from then on, it was distraction and reaction. The energy is overwhelming, and I found myself resisting having the energy crushed out of me at times. Under those circumstances, I don't see how the drops can find the Glow, but I do think that I'm missing something, and hoping that you can help. But first, let's take on the question of the present condition of mankind, as man's energy is nothing less than frenetic. How our Mother Gaia has her level of temperance is nothing short of divine. We must figure this out because what I can say for certain is that the change must come from the inside out of man; *the happening* is the only way; we must figure this out. Man will not respond to pressure or influences from the outside-in, as their nature wasn't designed that way; those influences just set off *triggers,* giving them something to *react* to. I mean, we know that their nature is to create continuously, right? And the nature of creating begins with thoughts, right? So, these reactions invariably cause them to create something else. It's in their reaction to stimuli that they create. Awe how am I going to say this?" says an exasperated Zegula.

The others patiently remain silent, knowing that Zegula needs a moment to think about it. Zegula puts his hand over his mouth, looks around, and raises his other hand, imploring the others to wait for a second longer and then begins anew. "Imagine with me, okay; man is in constant motion; constantly evolving; evolving as a response or as a reaction to his environment. Now imagine that his environment is ever-changing and morphing at a pace equivalent to his creations, meaning that mankind is constantly responding and reacting to his own creations. It's circular. I mean, imagine this dynamic sort of spinning upwards, okay? Now imagine over seven billion creators reacting and responding to each other's creations which is really nothing more than thoughts becoming manifest; creating new stimuli to react or respond to. This constant motion is frenetic. It's frenetic if it's not intentional, meaning a creation with an intentional outcome. BUT this isn't really true either, as what is intended for one man may simply become something to react/respond to for another. So, let's just stop that thought right there; stimuli will generate a thought, which manifests a creation, which generates yet another set of stimuli spiraling up; never ceasing."

Zegula continues, "When drops first encountered humans, these stimuli were mostly centered around the need to meet their basic daily survival needs. The corresponding creations resulted in ways for their families and village or community to work together to meet these needs more expediently and conveniently, with every man having a role and accountability to the others. Well, those thoughts come from a very specific place in the mind of man. For simplicities sake, I'll call it the desire mind, or better yet, '*the Wanter*' mind, which is the seat of emotional energy. In this more primitive capacity, the desires of *the Wanter* remain limited and not subject to much corruption, generating thoughts revolving around simply meeting the basic physical needs of *the lower self.* However, *the Wanter* is motivated by the fear of not being able to secure what it needs to survive or to thrive and is constantly subconsciously comparing itself to others. Now we need to consider that the motivations or the associated thoughts related to surviving are quite different than those related to thriving, with both having the capacity to become destructive. The types of creations arising from *the Wanter* are more concrete and tangible, growing more complex as man's creative capacities expanded the process of spiraling up, remember? As man progressed through the millenniums, there came a need for more organization and the creation of belief systems. Now, these types of needs require a more collaborative approach and come from the intellectual mind. I'll call this guy '*the Thinker*' or the self-willed intellect of the lower self...*although this guy is often times delusional pretending that it is the higher self.* Think of *the Thinker* as the guy that acts as man's conscious and, when awake, takes dominion over the thoughts streaming out of *the Wanter,* but when unconscious or asleep, acquiesces this control to some other place; remember this idea conceptually as it becomes the cornerstone of the *natural man* persona. Comparatively speaking, the thoughts arising from *the Thinker* are more intellectual in nature, resulting in more intangible creations and more difficult to comprehend. But they are creations, nonetheless. Since *the Thinker* is also motivated out of fear of being wrong and bringing humiliation and shame, the desires here tend to lead to the need for control; to control the outcomes of these intangible creations as *the Thinker* will do anything to avoid feelings of humiliation or shame. *The Thinker* can become most harmful due to this need for control. All right let's leave this here for now but realize that there are several layers to consider with each persona in order to more fully understand both *the Wanter* and *the Thinker*. One other thing before we move on, I need to add that these two can often operate independently of each other, believing that they are really separate from everything else. That will be clearer in a moment. Together I will refer to them as components of the lower self, or the *natural man*."

Zegula continued, "All right, consider that *the one who is greater* created man in His image in so far as Spirit having a physical experience. So that's the third dynamic at play within the inner man, that the *natural man* is not aware he is a divine creation and is one with all things. Man's journey begins in this nature, and mankind doesn't realize it due to his mostly unconscious *Thinker*. It's here where we must pause and acknowledge the elephant in the room and ask the question, what was our Father God looking to accomplish with this design? What is His desired outcome? Understanding that I've learned the secret of the Krystal and how it may lead me to the next iteration, what is it that man must experience for our Father God's expectations of the entirety of this creation to be met? God created this experience for a purpose; what is it? Obviously, we are forced to speculate what this might be, but with speculation, our thoughts have the freedom to think of these mysteries without boundaries. So now I'll give you my thoughts on this matter, but first, are there any questions before I move on?"

Dawa chimes in, "Yes, Zegula, I have a question. You have given us two interactive natures that influence man's behavior alluding to the thought that there may be more. Are there more than these two?" Zegula responds, "Dawa, the short answer is yes. What I'm doing here is compressing several influencers, as you put it, into both *the Thinker* and *the Wanter* in order to develop a structural understanding of man. On top of that, the *natural man* is very much a product of his specific environmental conditioning and programming. Man is most susceptible to being molded by his experiences, particularly from early childhood, and the matrix of possible outcomes is practicably incalculable. And then there's his divine nature that he is not yet awakened to and how that subliminal internal conflict plays out. Then there's the ultimate wild card; what active role may our Father God be playing in any given moment in the lives of all of mankind, if any? I mean, these are things that we can't see, and it's a challenge to discern the true source of man's thoughts when intermixed in this complex environment. For purposes of this conversation, I'd like to focus on coming up with a foundation with which to make these assumptions, to allow ourselves to speculate a bit to form a foundation to help draw some temporal conclusions until we learn more, you see. Determine a starting point so we can make decisions regarding *the happening*. We need to find a solution and that requires us to develop a decision tree filling in the gaps with agreeable assumptions. Is everybody on board with that?" Zegula prepares to continue, with everyone nodding in agreement.

Zegula moves along, "All right then, let's begin with considering that *the one who is greater* wanted to experience the only thing that He lacks, which is for Spirit to experience limitation. To this end, our Father God created man and his dual nature in order to experience this limitation. Our first assumption is to temporally conclude that there was something important for Spirit to experience from this world of duality through man. Based on what I learned from the Buddha and from Jesus Christ was that this experience was to progress through two stages; first, the *natural man,* or a persona dominated by the characteristics of the lower self, and second the *spiritual man,* or a persona dominated by the characteristics of the higher self. This transition appears very difficult for man to make as it must navigate through *the Thinker* and *the Wanter* first and yet a third entity that we will get too next. But first, what might Spirit be seeking from the *natural man* persona? This presents a bit of an enigmatic conundrum of sorts as the Buddha concluded that the desires originating from *the Wanter* led to suffering and that man's life was only suffering. Why would Spirit seek such an experience when it's already perfect? You see, Dawa, it's here that we remain stuck unless we make another assumption. What I will add is that the *natural man* believes that this is all about *'IT'* and can't see beyond itself. Remember what I said a minute ago about a situation arising when *the Thinker* is mostly unconscious and not in control of *the Wanter* and how that was a component of the *natural man* persona? Well, *'IT'* becomes the part of man's psyche that fills that void, becoming the pseudo arbiter of man's consciousness. Think of this guy as being *the serpent* in the mind of man who is managing the energy and thoughts of *the Wanter.* It's this dynamic operating between *'IT,' the Wanter,* and man's myriad of conditioning and programming experiences that serve to create the ego-self, and it's this ego-self that creates the false-self projection that is presented to others as who they are. Now we won't get into this any deeper here, as it will make more sense in a little while but remember that this is all occurring subconsciously in man. But I will leave this thought here for now; first, let's look at *the Thinker* as Adam, man's conscious that starts out unconscious or asleep; second, let's look at *the Wanter* as Eve, man's subconscious that was initially beguiled by the serpent due to Adam's neglect so to speak; next look at *'IT'* as the serpent mind which assumed the authority of Adam while Adam was unaware of what Eve was up to; and hence we have what makes up *the natural man* persona."

Zegula continues, "So, my next assumption is that even though *'IT'* plays a major role in this experience, which we will dig into deeper, *'IT'* is not what this Gaia experience is about, as that decision pathway ends abruptly right there. So that would mean that Spirit must have this experience of suffering in order to progress to the ultimate objective. And through my observations from the thoughts of mankind, is that man is stuck in the *natural man* persona. In some manner or form, *'IT'* has created a world that has mankind stuck. It was my hope that Jesus Christ had delivered the solution to free mankind from the grip of *'IT'* but unfortunately, that has not happened. It's actually much worse. Why is that? What's happened to the message of Jesus Christ? That's what we need to explore, as that's the secret to releasing the Christ energy that Jesus signifies and modeled. Before we dive in deeper here, I will add that there is also the next objective for Spirit, which can only be achieved once the transition has reached the collective tipping point for the salvation of mankind. You see, I'm beginning to understand the correlation between the objectives of the prophecy of *the happening;* when the Glow reaches the tipping point aiding to facilitate the mass salvation of mankind. It's all connected, Dawa. It's all connected to the hope of *the happening;* the rebirth of our Mother Gaia."

The others were mesmerized by these revelations while gazing at Dawa in anticipation of his response. Dawa replies, "Zegula, I find this to be disturbing, to say the least. First, we haven't yet found the answer to helping the drops find the Glow, and you came close to losing yours during the last Journey of Saffron. We know that all drops finding the Glow have eventually lost it, and we don't know why. It appears that the efforts of *the*

Thinker and *the…*," Dawa's attention fades off at that comment. "Zegula," asks Dawa, "do you think that *'IT'* is purposefully working against our Father's wishes here to subvert His will? Is that even possible? He did create them after all?" Zegula shrugs his shoulders ever slightly and responds, "Dawa…I think that making that assumption is reasonable under these circumstances. I do believe that to be true. But it's most certainly strange, as I also don't believe that it's intentional; I don't think mankind knows what they are doing; *the Thinker* and *the Wanter* are totally submersed in reaction mode, or under the dominion of *'IT'* seemly as if that is how they're made. What I feel is that mankind's pace of creating; a collective reaction to an overwhelming stimulus; is a shared subconscious response to the threat *'IT'* perceives. *'IT'* fears its very existence and has fiercely created firewalls and such to subvert any attempt by Spirit to reveal itself in man. The *natural man* is aggressively slaying the *spiritual man*. In Biblical terms, it is the *spirit of Cain* killing the *spirit of Abel* over and over and over, yet again. As the pace of this form of protective creating spirals upwards the influence of the Christ energy is spiraling downward. Mankind has lost its connection to the Christ and does not even comprehend it. The *natural man* is holding on with desperation and invariably robbing mankind of the peace and joy promised by the Gaia experience. *'IT'* would prefer to inflict this pain, even on itself, rather than giving up its power. *'IT's* fear of losing control is that great."

"All right, Zegula, I have some questions about the reference to the *spirit of Cain* and the *spirit of Able,* but first, how was *'IT'* able to neutralize the message of Jesus Christ? Wasn't He sent to liberate mankind from this design," asks Dawa. "Well, Dawa, now we're getting to the root of the problem. The easy answer is yes, certainly, Jesus as the son of man, was sent by our Father to show man how to release the Christ energy within them, and that's what His life was about to show man the *'Way'* to salvation; to becoming sons of God just as He is. And to that end, Jesus came onto the scene as the only begotten son of God, the first among many brethren to follow, and in His being *the first* son of God meant that He was initially **the only** son of God; at least here on Gaia that is. Now Dawa, I'm intentionally emphasizing that point as its key to understanding what happened next. I'll need to make several points here for this to make sense, so hold off asking questions until I've finished."

Zegula continues, "First, remember that our Father God gave man free will. It's the nexus of the world of duality; for man to exercise his free will towards the revealing of his own divine nature; to recognize that as his true nature. The gift that the Christ energy offers requires man to seize it for himself; to claim it to a spirit of adoption as sons of God, and only then can the energy of the Helper engage as promised. The Helper is in a sort of standby mode until man has consciously released it; man must give the Helper the authority to act, and to do so, man must believe in his heart that he is worthy; but *'IT'* can't believe from the heart and instead convinces man that loving from his intellect is the same thing. To act upon *what* you may be asking; to subdue and eradicate the influence of *'IT'* and reconcile an awakened Adam; the higher self or the conscious Self; back into unity consciousness with a submissive Eve; back into one nature with the divine; into unity consciousness; a new consciousness. I think that I'll refer to that part of the inner man as *the Sonship* and that new consciousness as the *Christ consciousness*. Well, then, you may be asking what needs to happen before man decides to take this action. That's a question that I believe requires another assumption Dawa. Perhaps it's when the Spirit in man has been satisfied with the physical experience. What might that be, you ask? Well, if life is suffering as the Buddha concluded, and certainly our Father God doesn't suffer in His existence *without limitation* but does experience suffering in a world of limitation here on Gaia. The *Sonship* within man apparently passively participates in the plight of the reaping and sowing arising from the consequences of the decisions and creations made by the *natural man;* perhaps it's when Spirit has sufficiently suffered and determines that it's *time for the sleeper to wake up* and move onto the experience of what comes next; for what awaits those who have become sons of God; those souls who have ascended into this new Christ consciousness?" Dawa chimes in, "Well, the sacred texts address this situation directly, and it certainly seems to suggest that it's by design and an expected component necessary to fulfill mankind's Gaia experience. Keep in mind that references to Gentiles are synonymous with one being in the *natural man* persona or otherwise consumed with the lusts of the world; *'For the time already past is sufficient for you to have carried out the desires of the Gentiles, having pursued a course of sensuality, lusts, drunkenness, carousing, drinking parties and abominable idolatries, (1 Peter*

4:3)." Zegula responds, "Yes, it must be by design and the word 'sufficient' used there is relevant for one to come to know both good and evil as a perfected Spiritual Being must require man to endure a multiplicity of both good and evil experiences in order to *know* both. I know...I know these are big thoughts, but we are compelled to draw some inferences to be able to continue this contemplation."

Without a pause, Zegula keeps going, "Second, notwithstanding the obvious challenge above; that *'IT'* is going to vehemently resist the *Sonship's* efforts from *'waking up'* the unconscious *Thinker,* as *'IT'* will be fearing for *'IT's* very existence, we'll first revisit the concept of original sin as it will help to better understand the first point. Man's fallen nature is referred to as original sin in their practice of faith. Now man's fallen nature, or man being banished from the Garden of Eden, was man falling out of unity consciousness and into consciousness fragmentation and into duality, here on the physical plane. Man fell into ignorance as to mankind's true spiritual nature. It's here where we must make another assumption. Let's assume that Spirit, or the soul of man, agreed to this Gaia experience. Otherwise, we would have to view the Gaia experience as some sort of penitence for the participating Spirits or souls, and that's a much larger fear-based assumption to make, requiring one to become a scriptural samurai in order to force fit the concept with the sacred texts. I mean, why would our Father God design this extraordinary experience with such a glorious prize if it's a byproduct of a rebellious and fallen nature? Here's where I'm going with this second thought; we know that Jesus, the son of man, was without sin, right? We also know that Jesus was *perfect,* and he told His followers to be *perfect* as our Father God in heaven is *perfect*; implying that so is He; meaning there's no way for mankind to be *perfect* unless Jesus was as well, right? Now we've also learned that Jesus *learned obedience through that which he suffered.* We also learned that Jesus rejected the notion that He was *good* whenever mankind would make that assertion about Him, right? Jesus's response was that the only one that was good was our Father God in heaven, right? So, here's the next assumption; Jesus knew that any discussion regarding man's morality was a trick of the *natural man;* a trap made for the benefit of promoting the *natural man*; does that make sense? Jesus also knew that Christ is *perfection,* just as our Father God in heaven is, right? So, our assumption will be to deduce that a reference for mankind to be *perfect* is not about issues of morality because that would be impossible if even Jesus refused such a notion; that He was good. So, the assumption is that *perfection* referred to here is representative of man *coming into* or *waking up* into his true nature; his *perfected* Spiritual nature like Jesus *the first* son of God and *a* son of God when he inevitably has His first fellow *brethren* son of God, which would be in essence *the second* son of God, joining him. So, this reference is that our Father God only sees our Christ perfection once man has transitioned from a son of man into a son of God; when man has awakened; when the eyes of man's heart is enlightened; when his *natural man* persona has been crucified and resurrected into reconciliation with his true Christ nature. It's at this juncture mankind receives his *salvation; it's when our Father God sees man as perfected, which would appear to be the primary objective of man's Gaia experience.* All right then, you'll need to have that perspective to understand what happens next."

The Apostle Paul & the Religion Mind

"So Dawa," Zegula continues, "back to your question of how did *'IT'* hijack the Jesus message? It may already be self-evident if you're paying," Dawa abruptly interrupts with, "All right, Zegula, let me try to answer this one; I think I see it." "You bet, Dawa; I was hoping that you would put the pieces together," acknowledges Zegula. Dawa begins, "I've been an eager observer of the sacred texts and man's created institutions, with religion being one of the most difficult for me to understand. It has such a noble purpose, yet it appears that across Gaia that it has been more divisive than unifying. It's constantly self-destructing and contradicting itself through judging and comparing the various faiths and inter-denominations. They're all trying to justify their foundational belief system but can only do so by denigrating others. But it's really quite brilliant what *'IT'* has pulled off here. I mean, Zegula, you cannot un-see it once you see it, right? Seeing it this way also helps to understand what the Apostle Paul's ministry focused on as well. Hmmm," pondered Dawa, "I think I may be seeing the connection to *the happening* Zegula. Do you see it too?" "Well, Dawa," ponders Zegula, "not really, not fully yet, I'm still shaken up with almost losing my Glow on the last journey, and I still don't know what caused it, so no, I don't see what you see, Dawa. I'm just trying to walk my thoughts forward the best I can, hoping to see some connection."

Dawa continues, "Very well, hopefully, this will help. It's clear that man creates indiscriminately; without intention; that mankind created everything that is not natural on Gaia. We also agree that *'IT'* is fearful… that *'IT'* is fearful and uses fear to self-perpetuate its existence. *'IT'* will do anything to avoid detection and keep man from *'seeing'* the true Christ message, for *'IT'* cannot help itself. The institution of religion was clearly a frustration for Jesus and later, for Paul. In fact, Paul warns that man has not received a spirit of slavery; leading to fear again, subjugating man to the desires of the lower self and continued subjection or control of *'IT,'* but that you have received a spirit of adoption as sons of God. Paul tells us that the mind set on the flesh … *'IT'* … is death, *meaning to remain in the natural body nature*, but that the mind set on the Spirit is life and peace, because the mind set on the flesh is hostile toward God; for *'IT'* does not subject itself to the law of God, for *'IT'* is not even able to do so, and those who are in the flesh cannot please God. Paul goes on to say that those who have received salvation are not in the flesh but in the Spirit *if indeed* the Spirit of God dwells in you. I'm beginning to sense that the *'if indeed'* in that statement is perhaps the most significant *'if'* in all of humanity, for *'if'* any man does not have the Spirit of Christ, then that man does not belong to Him, and *'if'* men are living according to the flesh, that *'IT'* must die. Paul was directing this warning to those that were practicing their religion, believing that they had become spiritualized and had already achieved salvation. The sacred text also refers to those in this religious mindset as *'the blasphemy by those who say they are Jews and are not but are of the synagogue of Satan.'* The references to Jews here are symbolic and have nothing to do with the individual's ethnicity. This usage targets those who believe they are spiritualized, as evidenced by their religiosity and practices, while remaining blind, naked, and unaware that they remain in the *natural man* persona. Jesus understood the potential depths of this deception, referring to those in this condition as attempting to enter the kingdom of heaven through the wide gate by climbing up to the throne some other way. To remain blind yet proclaim that *'You See'* is the most precarious place to be as it's those that must become blind again in order to enter by the narrow gate. It's those that Jesus Christ lamented on the cross by saying, *'Father, forgive them, for they know not what they are doing'."*

Dawa elaborates further, "Zegula, this thought takes me back to the concepts introduced regarding blindness and nakedness. I know that I said that we would revisit those ideas when we circle back to the meaning of the last book, but I need to work through this right here. Bear with me, Zegula, I'm simply thinking out loud. Oh boy now I'm distracted with an errant connection I haven't considered before. Recall that the Apostle Paul was one of these zealot practitioners of the Jewish faith and had sat on the Sanhedrin Council back in his day. He was one of those that could be put in the category of believing that he could *See*, right? But what happened when he experienced his miraculous conversion while in the road to Damascus? He was struck blind. This symbolizes this concept whereby Paul had to become blind again before he could proceed towards finding the narrow gate; the door of the shepherd Jesus speaks about. Then after three days the scales fell from Paul's eyes allowing him to see. This event parallels the meaning of the resurrection of Jesus three days after His crucifixion. I'm still trying to understand the meaning of the scales falling from his eyes. Alright, back to the first book, when Adam and Eve were *naked and not ashamed,* which was their condition before they ate of the fruit from the tree of knowledge of good and evil. This signifies that they were still in unity consciousness with our Father God and in the garden. Upon deciding to know good and evil, they agreed to participate in the world of duality only made possible by a physical incarnation on Gaia. It's at this point that they ate of the fruit of the tree of the knowledge of good and evil, initiating the fall from unity consciousness and into a physical incarnation. Becoming *ashamed* of their nakedness signified that they were aware of their newly modified consciousness, which now incorporated the serpent persona of the ego-self. The recognition of this awareness is signified by Adam and Eve clothing themselves with the fig leaves. This concept is expanded upon in the last book when the fifth Spirit is opened, but we'll leave the expansion of that thought for later. The next thing that happened to Adam and Eve was they were clothed by God in *skins* and expelled from the garden. It's at this moment that Adam and Eve became unaware of their nakedness and began their Gaia journey in the *natural body earthy* condition and without shame, *the first of the ways of God."*

Dawa continues, "The *skins* here signify the covering of the ego-self, which is symbolically corroborated by the tent of goat hair that covers the tabernacle carried by the Israelites throughout the Exodus. Paul fully develops this connection in his writings, with this concept also reappearing in the last book, so I don't want to distract us from trying to connect those dots just yet; we'll deal with it then. For now, I want to remain focused on determining how the symbolism of nakedness correlates to the symbolism of blindness, as these references serve as the explanation of the immense significance of that *'if.'* So, to be naked and not aware, meaning that one is not clothed and unaware that they should be, is where every human incarnation begins. Taken one step further, to be unaware of your nakedness and proclaim that you are not naked is to man's shame and condemnation, meaning that salvation from this condition is not possible. What this is saying is to signify the very real risk of being deceived by the serpent persona; man's self-willed intellect; his ego-self. It's here where man, in his spiritual pursuits, is led to believe that he has become spiritualized while remaining in his serpent persona, the *natural man.* That's the meaning, or the serious warning, found in the Apostle Paul's ominous *'if.'* This warning is magnified in the last book with the following: *'Behold, I am coming like a thief. Blessed is the one who stays awake and keeps his clothes so that he will not walk about naked and men will not see his shame'* *(Rev 16:15).* This warning occurs during the Battle of Armageddon, man's personal war of the inner Self signifying the need to first become aware of your serpent persona in order to win the battle. It's easy to be deceived by *'IT'* into believing that your salvation is secured, for it is how the devil defends his earthly domain. This is also signifying the relevance of the references to garments of white when he who overcomes has conquered his *natural body* signified by casting the Red Dragon out of heaven. More on that later. Alright, let's take a deeper look at the symbolism behind the concept of blindness."

Dawa begins the explanation of the symbolism behind blindness, "Alright, let's go. There are two natures of blind men in the parables of Jesus. One was blind since birth, and the other asked to regain his sight as Jesus was leaving Jericho on His way to Jerusalem. Being born blind means the same thing as being naked and unaware. Since all of humanity is born naked and unaware, let's begin with the blind man blind from birth. To start with, this is a test presented to Jesus by the Pharisees, the religious leaders of the times. The Pharisees, being focused on doctrines, asked Jesus: *'Rabbi, who sinned, this man or his parents, that he would be born blind? Jesus answered, "It was neither that this man sinned, nor his parents; but it was so that the works of God might be displayed in him"'* (John 9:2-3). What are the works of God that are symbolically being referred to here? It's the Adam and Eve story of the Spirit agreeing to incarnate and the making of their first free will choice. This man was born into the *natural body* persona and did not know it was the first of God's ways, yet he was symbolically displaying the works of God. This is how mankind's Gaia experience begins; being dead to your true spiritual nature; involution of the soul; with salvation being a return to unity consciousness; evolution of the soul; taking us *From Genesis to Revelation*. As we will see in the last book, this moment occurs at the opening of the fifth Spirit before the throne, which is where the inner man's dual natures see each other for the first time, initiating the internal Battle of Armageddon. Therefore, Jesus answers this man in a most peculiar and controversial manner when asked who the son of man is, *'Jesus said to him, "**Both** of **You** have seen Him, and he is the one who is talking to you,"* (John 9:37). It's here where the *Sonship* fully recognizes its divine nature and where 'IT' realizes that it's the internal false prophet as merely an illusion to overcome and that its time is short. They both see the truth as this is when the Spirit of Truth is released into the battle as suggested by Paul's words: *"The Holy Spirit is signifying this, that the way into the holy place has not yet been disclosed while the outer tabernacle is still standing,'* (Heb 9:8). The outer tabernacle made of goat hair signifies the Spirit within remaining under cover of the ego-self serpent persona. It's not until the ego-self is acknowledged can the veil be torn away, and the truth revealed. *"Therefore, brethren, since we have the confidence to enter the holy place by the blood of Jesus, by a new and living way which He inaugurated for us through the veil, that is, His flesh,'* (Heb 10:20) and *'This hope we have as an anchor of the soul, a hope both sure and steadfast and one which enters within the veil, where Jesus has entered as a forerunner for us...,'* (Heb 6:19,20)."

"Now Zegula," continues Dawa, "it may appear that I'm grinding on this concept somewhat unnecessarily, but there is a reason for this attention. What I see is that this experience must happen during man's incarnation and not after his physical death; the second death referenced in the prophecy. Man is dead to his spiritual nature because the serpent controls the intellectual domain of the mind of man. It's the ego-self that must die and then be resurrected, or reconciled, into the true Spirit of the *Sonship* set to occur during the present incarnation. However, that is not the construct of man's religious practices. We'll explore the consequences of man failing to accomplish this objective when we look deeper into the last book. But for now, let's look at how the interaction with the Pharisees played out in this parable, for it appears to me that Jesus is pointing out the root of the problem regarding humanity's practice of religion and its pursuit of spirituality. Jesus tells us why he came into the world in a very concise manner, saying; *'For judgement I came into this world, so that those who do not see may see, and that those who see may become blind,'* and then the Pharisees responded, *'We are not blind, are we?,'* with Jesus saying, *'If you were blind, you would have no sin; but since you say, "We see," your sin remains,'(John 9:39-41)*. It's here where man, to his shame, is naked without his clothes on. In this condition, man is blind to his nakedness and de facto declares that he is not naked and that he can see. Man does not see his own shame in this scenario. Furthermore, it's the extrapolation of man's self-willed intellect deceiving him into believing that he has become spiritualized that gives rise to such a delusion and symbolized by those that climb up to the throne in heaven by the other way, meaning the wide gate. This condition correlates to the concept of being spiritually lukewarm presented in the last book and when your sin is attributed unto you. We'll discuss that next but first, let's look at the other blind man.

"Alright, I need to get through this quickly, so here goes," begins Dawa, "what does it signify to first be born blind as all men are; then secondly, to be able to see, or more accurately, in this symbolic representation, to claim that you have sight as the Pharisees do in this story; and, then thirdly, to then desire to become blind again so that man can then see? At this juncture, if the Pharisees above would have acknowledged that they have been deceived by their intellect into believing that they have sight, they would be placed into the same position as Bartimaeus, the man who asked Jesus to restore his sight. As I just noted this happened to Paul but unknowingly." Zegula interrupts, "Dawa, another key symbolism in the parable regarding Bartimaeus is that this encounter occurred as Jesus was coming out of Jericho, the city that symbolizes the fortified self-willed intellect and on towards Jerusalem, symbolizing the heart center in man. The self-willed intellect and the serpent persona create this diversion, and where the devil is symbolically sitting on the throne in heaven. Jesus symbolically went into and out of his own experience of overcoming the intellectual will and is signified further by His third temptation in the desert. The first temptation related to the earthly man. The second temptation related to the holy city of Jerusalem, the heart center in man. And the third related to the heavenly man whereby the intellect deceives man into believing that he has become spiritualized and assumes the throne by the other way." "I agree, Zegula," says Dawa, "what I'm seeing Zegula, is that much of the institutionalized practice of religion is stuck in the same condition as these Pharisees leading to misplaced doctrines. We will also see the cumulative effect of missing the scripture's symbolic meaning, which by default leads to a reliance on the intellect and misapplied pearls of wisdom; losing the benefit of intuitive wisdom; but I suppose that's what *'IT'* is all about isn't it Zegula? *'IT'* is a tactical genius."

Zegula replies, "Yes, Dawa, but it is so nuanced as man truly believes that the illusion is real. I mean, it seems as if viewing these lessons primarily through the literal lens oddly reinforces this illusion. Awe, I don't know what I'm trying to say; just allow me to attempt to summarize the stories about being blind and wanting to see because the concepts of sin and salvation, and forgiveness are all connected through these symbolisms, and I'm honestly a bit confused, as it's not matching up with how man believes." "Very well, Zegula," adds Dawa, "and then I'll give you some additional thoughts on sin. That may help with some of your confusion." "Okay, Dawa," begins Zegula, "Jesus said something here that caught my attention, well two things, actually. The first is He said that if you are blind, then there is no sin. And then he said if you say that you see, then you must become blind. I'm assuming here, but it sure sounds like he is saying if man comes to recognize that he cannot see; seeing the error of his ways; then man is restored to the same place as the one born blind; without sin. Right, Dawa?" "Hmmmm, well, yes, that appears to be what is implied; continue," replies Dawa. "Alright," says Zegula, "that's the first scenario. Now, if man is blind and every man begins in that condition, yet says that he can see, then his sin remains. It's here where I'm assuming that when man says that he can see that it's referring to him believing he is seeing the true nature of his spiritual condition, while in actuality, he has been deceived, and he remains naked and without his clothes on; in his shame; in his *natural body* persona still. Do you agree with that, Dawa?" "Hmmmm, yes, I'm following Zegula, the trigger event causing man to say that he can see; the moment that man becomes known by God, or vice versa, when man comes to know God; it's the purpose of the law of Moses Zegula and what I was going to get into next." "Okay, Dawa," continues Zegula, "that sounds great but stay with me here. This is scenario number two, when man's sin remains. Next, we have the blind man from birth receiving sight. It's here where Jesus says that 'Both of You' have seen me, signifying that the man has awakened into his true divine nature, the *spiritual body* attaining salvation. Are you following me, Dawa?" "Yes, Zegula, please continue," says Dawa. "Alright," as Zegula moves along, "This third scenario kind of contains two situations as I see it. The first is that he is no longer blind, and the eyes of his heart have become enlightened. The other part of this scenario goes back to the first. If man remains blind from birth, then sin isn't attributable to him; I think this is what is meant by God's grace, and I'll explain why in a moment."

Zegula plows on, "The second part of the first scenario is kind of tricky, but first, we must make a critical assumption; that this man has determined that he desires to become blind again in order to pursue the proper door into heaven; to the holy place within; to alter the way he is pursuing his spiritual ascension; no longer being deceived. Let's call this scenario #1 Part Two. So, in scenario number one, man is without sin and is not known by God or does not know of God, so there is no sin, God's grace. Now, this isn't suggesting that this man hasn't done anything bad or evil it's just that it's not attributable as sin unto him and merely representative of the program; to know good and evil. I think that it's this man that scripture describes as being cold. The man in scenario number three is in the clear, having attained salvation, and is hot as compared to cold. Then there's scenario number two, whereby the sin remains. I believe that it's this man that scripture refers to as being lukewarm and at the greatest spiritual risk of being spit out of the mouth of the Lord. Our Father God said that it would be better to be cold than in this position. Now back to scenario #1, Part Two. This man has become blind again in order to pursue his faith. Dawa, it's here where I believe that the grace of God applies for the second time. In one, there is no sin, but man does not attain salvation either. What does this mean when the scripture says that salvation will happen to all men in the blink of an eye; all will be changed? There's more to this question, and we'll leave it there for now as I want to get into the other half of this thought. In Part Two of the first scenario, the nature of the *scriptures* suggests that God comes to know man's heart and shows mercy and grace to those that are aware of their dual nature; their innate divine nature and the serpent persona, '*IT*,' and, on the right path at the time of their earthly physical death. But it is a mystery for certain. Alright, I went through that to address the following concepts."

Zegula continues, "Recall from an earlier discussion how Jesus quoted Isaiah saying that He came to '*proclaim to the captive's liberty and to those who are bound the opening of the prison*' meaning that He was here to show the '*Way*' to salvation. The Hebrew word used here for *liberty* is the root word that was translated into Greek to mean *forgiveness* in the Gospels. Dawa, I must say that proclaiming liberty to the captives is not the same as being anointed with the power of forgiveness. But that's not my point. The above scenarios are presented by Jesus to be a form of guidepost or preset parameters governing this Gaia experience for man. If there is no sin for the blind or for the awakened, then there is no application for actions of active forgiveness in these scenarios. The path to liberation is preset, and the application of forgiveness is passive; it either applies or it doesn't, and this is why Jesus says, '*You are forgiven*' or, '*You have been forgiven.*' Jesus doesn't ever say that '*I forgive you,*' and the one time that Jesus pursued an active act of forgiveness outside of the preset parameters is when He appealed to Father God that He forgive those that crucified Him and those that say *they see but are blind;* the only ones where the sin remains. Jesus makes an impassioned appeal directly to the Father to do so. Why would Jesus be compelled to make that plea when the recipients of the requested forgiveness were the same people that were putting him to death? If there ever were a time for Jesus to exercise such authority, it would've been at this moment, and He didn't. Then we get back to this concept of sin when it's not necessarily applied to every man the same. What is the usage of sin here, Dawa, if it's not universally attributed to man's moral behavior exclusively?

Dawa answers, "Those are interesting observations, Zegula, and a very good question. It seems that dismissing the essence of the symbolism in these concepts has led to more support for the Jesus narrative that was set in motion during the 3rd and 4th centuries. And having to understand sin within the context of your observations surely crowds the concept that there is a sentient third-party Satan *out there* that we are battling against. Let me give this a try, Zegula; you've caught me off guard, however. Paul spends a great deal of effort defending the importance of the law of Moses while at the same time explaining that man will move beyond those practices once the law is *written on their hearts*. Through this transition, man learns to live from his heart; symbolizing unconditional love or God's love nature; and away from living from man's self-willed intellect; symbolizing conditional love; which is the *natural man's* love nature. Paul further elaborates by holding up the law as always relevant, as it was the law that revealed sin to man. It was the intention of the law to assist in making man aware of their *natural body* nature. What is sin? If we allow that debate to be about morality, which Jesus says that even He is not good, then the conversation remains a construct of *'IT'* and played by *'IT's* rules. However, Paul was teaching that sin represents the fallen nature of man; from spiritual unity consciousness into a physical incarnation or consciousness fragmentation; with the law beginning the process of revealing man's ignorance of his true nature, the Christ within. *'IT'* was fearful of man understanding this process of going *within* to witness his thoughts, for that's where *'IT'* can be observed, in the practice of meditation or prayer. So, what did *'IT'* do as a defensive measure? What *'IT'* did was quite disingenuous but very effective, nonetheless. We need to remember that our Father God tells us that *'IT'* is the *most subtle and craftiest beasts of them all* and *'IT' is hostile toward God*. Mankind has not sincerely thought this concept through and must heed these warnings beyond a fear-based construct. Incorporating fear into the dynamic is playing this very serious game by *'IT's* rules."

Dawa is rolling along, "Now Paul is making it clear that the practice of doctrine is a construct of the *natural body* and why the law reveals sin; why it reveals man's ignorance. *However, this requires man to become aware of awareness and learn the art of observation in order to see it.* In *'IT's'* desperation, *'IT'* made the relevance of doctrine to be a primary focus of the practice of religion and even went so far as to distort some of these doctrines to prevent man from understanding the law of God in the inner man that Paul eagerly agreed with. How was this accomplished, you ask? If you don't want man to agree with the law of God in the inner man, as Paul concluded was good, then the goal becomes to implement methodologies to divert attention away from that inner place to something *outside of man.* That starts with Jesus' message and what He represents, which then opens the door for the need for a form of Satan to enter the picture."

Dawa continues enthusiastically, "Now I can see how understanding man from this perspective is critical for knowing how to approach our misunderstanding of the secret of the Krystal and the prophecy of *the happening;* we missed it Zegula; what the Krystal represents in our own story!" Zegula chimes in, "Hmmm, please continue, Dawa; you're still ahead of me here." Dawa nods and continues, "The *natural man* in its practice of religion has taken the position that Jesus Christ, was really Jesus Christ, our Father God incarnate, and not the son of man showing man the *'Way'* to becoming sons of God themselves. Well, it's subtler than that as religion still holds up that the process they've created results in their salvation, which is the event that awakens man into his true divine nature because they've pitched it differently; to a process of *being saved* instead of *awakening.* By looking to Jesus as 'God,' it puts man in a position to conclude that he really isn't worthy at all and can't be like Jesus, and to think otherwise would be a sin, the worst of all moral sins…in and of itself. This leads to man concluding that he really has little to do with his own salvation and that man is in a hopeless fallen *moral* condition. This requires the positioning of Jesus as a savior in the absolute sense versus as a brother. The impact of this shift led to perhaps the most profound and limiting doctrinal practice of them all; how to approach our Father God. Recall that the Buddha practiced the art of meditation, as did Jesus. Jesus was critical of the way the religious leaders of his day would behave, praying *outwardly* in public, bringing attention to themselves, and suggesting that they would be better off going into a closet; in a dark place alone. Today's religious practices largely dismiss the art of meditation as a *New Age* practice and not suitable for teaching to those it is to steward. Once again, *'IT'* has maintained control of the process of making appeals to our Father God on behalf of man, sending the focus outward and away from the inner man. The Roman church has even gone so far as to have another man intervene on behalf of others to approach *the one who is greater* regarding the confession of man's sins. Furthermore, this practice offers little to no opportunity for man's *divine nature* to commune directly with our Father God, severely hindering the ability of our Father God to speak to man or for man to hear Him. *'IT'* just makes too much noise flooding the mind of man with indiscriminate error thoughts. There is little to no emphasis on how to guide man into a practice of stillness and into one of observance of thoughts within most modern religions. The sacred texts refer to this: *'For we are His children. Being children of God, we ought not to think that the Divine Nature is like gold or silver or stone, an image formed by man's art and thought (Acts 17:26,27)."*

Dawa continues, "Now *'IT'* didn't stop there, even though that alteration alone would probably be a sufficient distraction. As we've acknowledged already, *'IT'* also created an evil third party 'Being' *out there,* accusing this invisible third party of being the source of evil that man must contend with. Not only does this serve to take focus completely off the *natural man* and *the evil in man's heart, the Thinker* and *the Wanter under the dominion of 'IT,'* it thoroughly negates the reality and the purpose of this creations duality experience by misdirecting the law of reaping and sowing; karma; abdicating man from taking ownership of the circumstances leading to his own suffering and away from his own ascension. *'IT'* can now remain in control of the mind of man and play this out indefinitely. How? *'IT'* acts as man's moral authority pretending to be his higher self; 'IT'* pretending to be man's spiritual conscious arbiter; *'IT'* pretending to be *righteous; 'IT'* pretending to be the awakened *Thinker* in order to maintain the deception. Taking this a step further, *the Thinker* and *the Wanter,* being coerced by *'IT,'* learn how to play off the other using fear and guilt as means to punish immoral behavior. This effectively serves to maintain control of man's mind while effectively diverting attention away from the inner man."

Zegula steps in, "I just had a thought, Dawa, on the duality experience that may be helpful. Do you mind?" "Certainly not, Zegula go ahead, but I do have a story I'd like to get into when you're finished as I see where the sacred texts actually give us two additional names for both *the Thinker* and *the Wanter* and may help to explain the mystery of the scales that fell from Paul's eyes upon receiving back his sight," replies Dawa. "Understand; I think I'm beginning to see where you are going with this, and I look forward to hearing your thoughts on the Glow and *the happening*. The concept of duality is a bit of a paradox. You see, man believes that this physical experience is real, I mean, it is real for him, but it is not his true nature, so it's more like an illusion that is going to end at some point. The sacred texts tell us that all of humanity inhabits a temporary earthly dwelling, or body tabernacle, and should see themselves to be aliens and sojourners while in this physical manifestation with the objective of seeing the day the morning star rises in their hearts. (1 Peter 1:13,14,17,19; 2:11). Now we've speculated on what that looks like in a few ways, but I think that I can be even more specific. Like you, Dawa, it's starting to come together for me as well. Duality is the experience of opposites and the choices arising from man's reaction to those opposing forces. It's the only way for man to have an experience of exercising free will. What's present in every choice that man makes is an *expectation,* that is the key behind the duality experience. Think about good and bad; causes and effects for a moment. Deep down, man is consumed with only himself as man in this *natural man* condition is really nothing more than *'IT,'* with *'IT'* being all about self-preservation. *'IT'* is always making choices with an expectation attached to them. When an expectation is not met, *'IT'* will obsess about what went wrong and where to place the blame, focusing more on evaluating the cause and less on the effect. *'IT'* has a very difficult time letting go of an unmet expectation, as it becomes a reflection of its own failure or deficiency. *'IT'* will not accept this outcome, which leads to the next expectation. Unlike before, where the choice preceded the unmet expectation, here we have the next expectation providing the impetus for the next choice, a choice made subject to and in reaction to the emotions related to prior unmet expectations. *'IT'* is mostly unaware that this has happened. Okay, stay with me here. As man becomes aware of awareness and begins to observe his thoughts, the focus of an unmet expectation will begin to migrate more towards an analysis of the outcome and not the cause, becoming more conscious of the present moment. What has happened is past, and recognition that *'what is'* the present moment is man's reality. In this state of increased awareness, man will begin to let go of attachment to expectations accepting that opposites exist by the grace of the other, and gradually learns not to be triggered into reacting to unmet expectations. This is the process of moving away from making choices from the intellectual mind full of expectations towards the heart without expectations, or unhealthy attachment to expectations. The gap between opposites begins to shrink the more that man lives in the present moment, from the heart, moving him beyond duality and back into non-duality. Choices are made from a place of wisdom and more intuitively as compared to making choices from the intellect and subconsciously. This is synonymous with going from consciousness fragmentation back into unity consciousness, completing the process of transitioning from the *natural man* into the *spiritual man,* and why man's diligent practice of meditation is so critical. It's from there that man can learn to control impulses leading him to go from reacting to triggers, as if on autopilot, to responding with intention. Hope that helps; I mean, it helps me to think along those lines as it relates to what we can do to influence the situation on Gaia," says Zegula.

"One last thought Dawa…I've learned that our Father God is quite active in the affairs of man and will move to discipline man when He determines. Discipline from the Father comes in the form of consequences related to poor choices and error thoughts and can be confused with the natural consequences arising from the duality experience. Looking back at your analysis of blindness and nakedness, our Father God will be most active in disciplining those who sincerely desire to evolve but are blind, believing that they can see or are naked, but remain unashamed. There's an applicable story in the sacred texts that demonstrates this quite clearly, certainly as it applies to the religious doctrines you've discussed," finishes Zegula.

The Battle Within: The Story of David & Goliath

Dawa picks back up with his thoughts, "Thanks, Zegula, that is helpful to understanding the interplay between matters of the psyche in the *natural man.* I think the story that you refer to is about Job, and yes, I agree that it's appropriate and does connect with the story I'm about to speak on as well. The battle within the inner man is esoterically depicted by the story of David and Goliath as an unfoldment of spirituality. *'IT'* serves to direct the affairs of the ego-self construct between *the Wanter* and *the Thinker* that you've described from the discernment of men's thoughts.

From my knowledge of the ego-self gained from eastern philosophies, these can be broken down into five basic qualities. The first being form, matter and body. The second is feelings or emotions. The third is cognition, memory and thoughts. The fourth is volition; free will and/or desire. The fifth is consciousness; self-awareness or the 'I' identity. These five components collectively make up man's ego-self and give man the unique and individualistic experience of physical existence. Humanities destiny is to be ruled by this ego-self insofar as man ultimately realizes that an ego-driven existence is really an illusion. For this illusion is nothing more than an amalgamation of man's thoughts that have given rise to the internal belief system that this projected persona is real, as is the illusion of the world that *'IT'* has created. By inference, then, the concept of duality is also an illusion, as you have suggested, Zegula, as experiencing opposites such as good and bad are merely necessary and relative to support the experiences required for man to learn the source of his suffering; his unrestrained lower nature."

Dawa moves along, "In the story, Goliath is in a standoff with King Saul, with Goliath signifying the fear-initiating state of the ego as evidenced by his imposing size, his weighted spear, and impenetrable armor. The Goliath in man uses fear to control by taunting King Saul with its intimidating fierceness and by a projection of its own lack of fear. These are some of the same characteristics associated with Leviathan described in the story of Job that we'll explore a bit later. King Saul, on the other hand, signifies the personal will or sense consciousness, the docile ineffective consciousness in its *natural man* nature. David symbolizes divine love, with his name meaning the *well-beloved of the Lord*. David uses a stone to slay Goliath with the stone symbolizing the Spirit of Truth, the indwelling Christ at work. The conflict between King Saul and David represents the war in the inner man between the head and the heart for control; symbolized by King Saul as the self-willed intellect and David as divine love. In this scenario *the Thinker* and *the Wanter* are in a stand-off serving to perpetuate the existence of *'IT.'* Here, in this story, it depicts that the personal will functioning in sense consciousness would destroy or sacrifice its own soul before giving up its control; signified by the death of Jonathan, Saul's own son and the numerous attempts by King Saul to kill David. Everything in man that does not recognize and acknowledge its source in our Father God must finally die to things spiritual, such was the eventual death of King Saul and Jonathan in this allegory."

Dawa moves along, "Back to Goliath, the giant Goliath, it says it was six cubits tall; has six pieces of armor; and weighed 600 shekels. This gives us 666, the number of the unregenerate man. It's also interesting to consider that man is made of carbon, and the molecule of carbon is comprised of 6 electrons, 6 protons, and 6 neutrons; once again; 666; the number of man. This number represents the ego-self or the beast inside of man, and we see it in other places within the sacred texts. As we have determined, this beast is often referred to as Satan, which textually really means *the adversary* within. In Revelations, John has a dream in which this beast appears and is cast out of heaven. Religious practices, through means of a literal translation, have reconditioned this beast to be the third-party tormentor that *'IT'* needs to divert attention away from its own destructive nature. However, this dream, like most all within the Bible, is intended to be understood *spiritually,* which Paul tells us the *natural man* cannot comprehend. This was a dream of the war Armageddon that takes place in the inner man with the beast being cast out of its pretentious control of the higher self, out of heaven. In Revelation, this beast is sitting on the throne but not by his own power and is correlated to Rome. Rome signifies the self-willed intellect pretending to be spiritualized. This is the war that Paul refers to as being waged in his members and the enmity between man's dual natures that Jesus came to show us how to reconcile."

Dawa continues, "It certainly appears than man created Satan in his own image as what better way for *'IT'* to hide. Satan represents the state of mind in man that believes in its own sufficiency independent of its creative source, the state of mind formed by man's personal ideas of his power and completeness and sufficiency apart from God. Satan is the deceiving phase of mind in man that has fixed ideas in opposition to the truth; he is the adversary, the one who opposes; the hater; the accuser that makes man believe that his *fallen nature into moral 'sin'* completely bankrupts him, requiring man's need to *be saved,* as compared to man's fall into 'sin' in respects to his ignorance regarding his own true Spiritual divine nature. It is virtually impossible for man to recover his true nature upon adopting the mindset that a third-party Satan is real, dismissing the beast within. Now the Satan of the Torah, as represented in the Book of Job, is quite different from the version depicted in the New Testament. In Job, God tells us He was the one responsible for the adversity brought upon Job and that He essentially sanctioned Satan as His minister of wrath and dispenser of discipline. Sometimes it is difficult to discern between the discipline brought on by our Father and the consequences of outcomes related to 'IT' and 'IT' will do everything in its power to divert this blame outward diverting attention away from 'IT,'" says Dawa.

Dawa elaborates further, "The story has it that David gathers five smooth stones and enters the battlefield with Goliath. David slings a stone of truth into the forehead of Goliath, with the forehead signifying this false center of consciousness. Goliath is slayed, and David goes on to slay the other four giants of the ego-self, as represented by the remaining four stones. So why do I believe that this story is relevant to *the happening*? What have we learned by looking at man's religious doctrine, the beast, Satan, and the stories? Belief systems are a construct of the imagination of 'IT' and are ingrained into man from the day they are born into this physical experience. These belief systems don't stop at religion, and many of the other institutionalized belief systems are pursued with the same religious fervor from the same influencers. It's the nature of the *natural man;* to deceive mankind and to be hostile to our Father God in order to preserve 'IT's false-self persona. So Zegula, are you ready to pick this up?"

"Absolutely, Dawa, I see where you're going, and it's as if my eyes were just opened. Can you see my Glow growing? Dawa, even though our creation is mostly subjected to natural laws, we still have a belief system to contend with ourselves; we just didn't see it. Having said that, we come from the same Christ energy as man and have forgotten that. We consider ourselves to be complete and whole while we are in Mira and have the Krystal to connect us. Our belief system has been to learn to let go of resistance while on the Journey of Saffron, which is the 'Way' to the Glow. However, the secret of the Krystal was learning that our essence, our power, was not in the Krystal after all and that we could better serve Mother Gaia while on the Journey of Saffron without it. So, there were drops that learned the lesson along the 'Way' and later lost it. We've never figured out why until just now. What we've missed is the same thing man is missing; awareness of our divine source, the Christ within each drop; that the power of the divine is in us whether we are on the Journey of Saffron or in Mira with the Krystal. Our belief system has spoken of the special power of the Krystal, and that's what we've been holding onto or have become attached to. It's most certainly special when it comes to helping Mira restore those drops returning from the Journey of Saffron, but it is not the source of our power, our essence. That's the secret, Dawa. We need to teach the drops to be still and not to resist while also becoming aware that they have been empowered by the Christ within, too; it's then that they will find the Glow and cease being afraid; cease resisting allowing the Christ energy to flow freely through Gaia" Zegula answers enthusiastically."

THE CONDITIONED
COLLECTIVE

Enlightenment & the 2nd coming of Christ & the Antichrist

"Zegula," Dawa begins, "this discussion has been a great reminder for us all. *For since the creation of the world, our Father God's invisible attributes, His eternal power, and divine nature have been clearly seen, being understood through what has been made, so that all creation and man are without excuse because that which is known about God is evident within them; for God made it evident to them (Rom 1:20).* This brings us back to the process of salvation for man and another doctrine that has become a stumbling block for man's ascension into enlightenment. Understanding the nature of this misplaced doctrine may help to better equip the drops to see how the nuances of this kind of ideology contributes to the advent of other types of destructive man-created belief systems."

Dawa continues, *"I pray that the eyes of your heart may be enlightened (Eph 1:18)"* comes from a letter that Paul writes to the church in Ephesus. The word 'enlightened,' as used in the Bible, is synonymous with the word *'salvation,'* amongst others, such as *'established,' 'awakened,' 'incorruptible,'* and *'resurrection.'* These words signify the milestone event of when *'IT'* loses its dominion and Eve is reconciled back with a redeemed Adam, Eve's first love, just as Jesus Christ, serving as mankind's example, put to death the enmity between these two warring natures signified by His crucifixion and resurrection. It's here where man's false persona will be supplanted with the authentic Self. When is this milestone event supposed to take place? It's when Christ will appear a second time for *salvation* as it is written in the sacred texts, *"so Christ also, having been offered once to bear the sins of many, will appear a second time for salvation without reference to sin, to those who eagerly await for Him" (Heb 9:28).* Does this process; the second coming of Christ; unfold continuously, while man is alive in this physical manifestation, or is to occur in one single magnanimous event with religion referring to this as *the rapture;* manifesting at some uncertain point on the horizon, determined to occur even after man's physical death? To help answer these questions, we will explore the controversial doctrine of *the antichrist,* for man's misunderstanding of this concept is clearly the brilliant work of *'IT.'* Once again, we will see how *'IT'* will seek to have man looking outward for the resolution of spiritual matters versus exploring the law of God in the inner man as the *'Way'* to salvation, to the enlightenment of the heart. It's here where man's religious doctrine teaches that the antichrist is a single literal individual that has yet to be revealed, with this individual leading a one-world government that is hostile towards our Father God. It's here where these major religions believe that a future golden age will be ushered in with the second coming of Christ but only after enduring a period of merciless persecution and horrific bloodshed."

Dawa continues, "So what does the term antichrist refer to? The sacred texts state this, *'…and every spirit that confesses not that Jesus Christ **is come** in the flesh is not of God; this is the spirit of the antichrist, of which you have heard it is coming, and now it is already in the world'* (1 John 4:3) and *'Children it is the last hour; and just as you heard that the antichrist is coming, even now **many** antichrists have appeared; from this, we know that it is the last hour'* (1 John 2:18). We can see here that the antichrist is not an individual neither is there an *end time* at some point in the future where such a unique person will be revealed. John makes it clear that there are many antichrists and that even 2000 years ago, it was already the last hour. So, what is the core issue here, and what could *'IT'* be up to? This is how I'm seeing it. The antichrist refers to a mindset in man, or a man-made belief system, that denies that the salvation of our Father God *comes to mankind while man is alive in the flesh.* Let me put it another way. Notice how the sacred text uses the present and imperfect tense when it states that *Jesus Christ 'is' come in the flesh.'* This denotes a continuous action. It did not say when Jesus Christ came or that He *has come* in the flesh which many translations erroneously reflect. In other words, Jesus Christ coming in the flesh *is a continuous event happening in the flesh* and this seemingly innocuous mistranslation distorts the intended meaning of the antichrist but does serve to support the narrative of mainstream religions. It's clear that this transition from the *natural body* into the *spiritual body* is set to manifest in man, during the present incarnation, right here on Gaia. The man who denies this has the spirit of the antichrist, the serpent persona. So, the antichrist is anyone living in the past, present, or future that denies that there is a spiritual resurrection that takes place in man's fleshly body. The resurrection, or enlightenment, or the second coming of Christ, *does not happen after man's death;* for the opportunity for salvation, or for *being saved*, is passed. But once again, redirecting man's attention in this manner serves as an effective doctrine, a construct of *'IT'* keeping man looking outward to a future event of being saved and away from looking inward at the law of the inner man for salvation." Zegula elaborates, "Dawa this brings to mind another similar mistranslation found in the Lord's prayer cited by Jesus demonstrating the lack of understanding regarding the underlying symbolism. Jesus was pointing to the inner man in this prayer with, *'your kingdom come, your will be done, in earth as it is in heaven,' (Matt 6:10),* when the most common translation has it saying, *'upon the earth,'* instead. This has man looking outside of himself for the meaning behind this prayer." "Yes, Zegula, that directs mankind's attention to the events happening on the physical earth while Jesus was directing the intent of the prayer towards the spiritualization of the inner man."

Dawa continues, "The *Beast* of the Bible; *666* being the mark of the *Beast,* is the active works of *'IT,'* the spirit of the *antichrist*. The sacred scriptures report that there are currently many in the world, with the gate being wide for those with the antichrist spirit. The reference being made to the *world* here represents the sum of all of *'IT's'* creations here on Mother Gaia and the way these creations distract man *away* from the journey within. *Enlightenment* is the same as the *second coming of Christ* for it's the authority of the Christ that initiates the enlightenment experience. It all connects, and it's here where we can conclude that the Bible is a sacred spiritual text for all of humanity to learn from and not intended to serve as the foundational text for the practice of man-made religious doctrines.

As we will see in a moment, this *push-pull* effect that *'IT'* deploys by the delivery of offsetting *fear and love* dynamics solely designed to manipulate and control the mind of human's is quite effective and serves as the model for many other coercive belief structures. This methodology creates a form of trauma bond between man and the item that man is attached to, be it a belief system or another individual. We will explore that next and correlate that analysis to the religiously promoted fear of *the one world government and Armageddon* I referred to earlier," Dawa concludes while looking at Zegula expectantly.

"Dawa," responds Zegula, "once again, that is consistent with the thoughts that I picked up from Jesus Christ. He taught that the kingdom of heaven was within and admonished the religious leaders of His time for shutting off the kingdom of heaven for those following them. He goes on to say that not only do the religious leaders prevent those following them from entering the kingdom of heaven, but neither will the leaders themselves enter in, frustratingly referring to them as hypocrites. He also refers to this dynamic as the *blind leading the blind* and we can now understand the significance of what it means to be blind. The practice of religion remains a construct of the *natural man; of 'IT,'* and *it's the responsibility of the human seeking to become enlightened to circumvent the myriad of misdirection's coming from 'IT.'* Recall that Jesus Christ provided a stern warning about how disruptive his message was and that letting go of a restrictive belief system is most certainly uncomfortable for any man. Man becomes most attached to the comfort and validation that accompanies shared beliefs and surely fears being ostracized by his peers should he question those beliefs. We must think about these matters further, but for now, I'm anxious to explore matters related to trauma bonds more thoroughly, as I believe that there is a distinct pattern here. Perhaps those thoughts will help to discern how to address man's belief system attachments."

Ideological Warfare & the Religion of Totalitarianism

"Now Zegula, as you've already alluded towards…the religion mind is not limited to just faith-based institutions," Dawa begins, "it's simply how man is made. The Apostle Paul teaches that the *natural man* is first, and the *spiritual man* is second. This is shown repeatedly in the sacred texts. The firstborn of Adam and Eve was Cain, with Able the second. Cain represents the *natural man*, or lower self, persona, while Able represents the *spiritual man*, or higher self, persona. The same applies to Abraham's progeny, with Ishmael being first and Isaac being the second, along with Isaac's progeny, with Esau being first and Jacob being second. Their stories reflect how the *natural man* persona eventually acquiesces to the *spiritual man* persona, usually through self-destructive compulsive actions. But because the *natural man* is first, all belief systems are always the constructs of *'IT.'* It's like the natural laws that the creation must adhere to, so must mankind recognize and navigate through the natural laws related to how he is made, for Spirit's experience of duality demands it."

Dawa continues, "The religion mind Zegula, along with the other coercive belief systems that *'IT'* has evolved into, reflect ideologies that man has become attached to. Now please understand that I don't use that term, religion mind, with any derogatory intent but rather as an indication of the nature of the underlying commitment to such ideals. The *natural man's* persona is remarkably susceptible to conditioning and programming by his worldly environment and is inherently driven to attachment by the fundamental love nature of *'IT.'* Once again, it's how man is made and this construct, or characteristic, is necessary for the experience of duality. It is as our Father God intended. I've diligently observed the manifestations of man's intangible creations and can see these conflicting ideologies' outward impacts. But once again, I'm most curious as to what influencers drive man to have such thoughts. That I cannot see Zegula, and it appears that even mankind remains largely unaware of these dynamics. I do know that Jesus Christ had much to say on this matter, and I would ask you to elaborate on his warnings in this regard, for I believe it will help to explain what I've observed."

"Very well Dawa, I think I understand what you're seeking," begins Zegula. "Notwithstanding the number of men and women that I've journeyed through, recall that I can now discern the memories of the other drops and what they've encountered as well. There is a very distinct pattern that originates from relational trauma experienced by mankind in general. Out of these relational traumas flow a variety of adaptive relationship strategies that enables man to accommodate his perceived lack. It's the cumulative effect of these traumas and offsetting relationship strategies that serves as the foundation for man's conditioning and programming. This process of adapting to traumas, or even to unmet expectations and the like, leads to a continuous process of conditioning based on the success, or lack thereof, of the adaptive relationship strategies that man chooses to deploy in order to address this sense of lack. This process continues until man becomes aware of what he is doing to himself and decides to address it. This marks the beginning of the enlightenment process leading to man's salvation; when he has unwound much of this conditioning and returns to his authentic Self, his true nature; the *spiritual man* persona. Now before I move on, I need to make an important distinction that we will circle back to later. At the juncture when man begins to sense that a course correction is warranted, *'IT'* is already working to anticipate how the man wants to feel. Suppose man continues down the path determined by the *Wanter*. In that case, it's very likely that the man will go even further down into the persona that *'IT'* desires and further away from the authentic self. The process will make the man *feel as if* he is making progress, while the opposite is his reality. *'IT'* will not allow man to go inside if man remains unaware of the wisdom regarding the Christ and the Helper."

Zegula continues, "Now, Dawa, I'm going to focus on a particular relationship dynamic as it's the one that seems to have permeated the structures of these competing ideologies. Once again, it is a very ingenious construct of *'IT'* to have a multiplicity of competing ideologies with which to act upon the others; essentially serving to validate all of them as one attempts to destroy the efficacy of the other. Said differently, so far as *'IT'* keeps the warring parties *reacting defensively* to the criticisms of the other, then the intended impact of the ideology's purpose continues to be promoted. The winner of these ideologies, or the one that is right, becomes irrelevant, for the objective is to simply promote fear; the fear of being wrong; the fear of humiliation; the fear of lack; the fear of safety; and on it goes. This fear leads to the opportunity to control, and with control comes power; this is the agenda of *'IT'* and of all the intangible creations of *'IT.'* From here, man can commit all kinds of acts of evil with justification; with righteous indignation even. This is the condition of mankind Dawa."

Zegula moves along without pause' "In regard to personal interactions, this can best be summarized by the nature of the narcissist and the codependent relationship, for it's the same dynamic at play in the competing global ideologies working today. The," Dawa interrupts, "Zegula hold up for a second; I have a question." "Sure, Dawa; what is it?" "Zegula, once again, I don't know the thoughts of man, but I do think that I understand what you mean when you refer to a man's conditioning and programming. It's how they're made, and I get it. But I don't understand the extent of man's knowledge regarding their own conditioning and programming. It's one thing for man to be unaware of his true divine nature, as that is how he is made; the *natural body* is first; but is man also unaware of how his conditioning and programming affect his thoughts and his decisions? Can man behave in a manipulative manner and yet be unaware that he is being disingenuous?" asks Dawa. Zegula responds with bemusement, "Dawa, now that is a very astute question indeed. It's puzzling to witness man's thoughts in these matters. You see … I mean … it kind of depends Dawa. Now, much of this behavior is the byproduct of *the Wanter,* for you see, *the Wanter* is the source of all matters related to *surviving* and *thriving. The Wanter* desires things and remains contented so long as it gets those things. It's not uncommon for man to remain in this mode of operation for most of his life, which largely depends on how much pleasure he seeks; and gets; and how much entertainment he craves; and gets; keeping himself sufficiently distracted from having to rationalize that behavior. It's why Jesus Christ proclaimed that it's harder for a rich man to inherit the kingdom of heaven than it is for a camel to go through an eye of a needle. Why would a man *seek* to be aware if he gets everything he desires? So, if this is man's condition, then yes, Dawa, that man will remain quite unaware that he is behaving in a manipulative manner as its most convenient. It's not until man must be accountable for his disingenuous behavior will the need arise for *the Thinker* to become involved. It's here that man will be jolted from being unaware by necessity with *the Thinker* taking charge but can quickly fall back into his stupor provided *the Thinker* does a proper job of covering for *the Wanter;* they are very good at covering for each other, for you see, *'IT'* will avoid the feelings of shame and humiliation at all costs; even if it requires unjustified shame and humiliation misdirected towards another; for it's here where the fear of shame and humiliation, being averted, has been replaced with control and power over another; an elixir and source of immense energy for the celebratory *'IT'.*"

Zegula gets back on point, "Now the narcissist uses all kinds of tactics to prey on the naivety of the unsuspecting codependent much like those that control the narrative of these man-made ideologies. These tactics include gaslighting, projection, triangulation, scapegoating, victim playing and others. And I will add here that it's much easier for those in power to coerce followers of a belief system ideology into codependent tendencies than it is for a narcissist to maintain control of a codependent individual experiencing an intimate relationship, for it is here where confirmation bias tends to kick in, aligning one's beliefs with the thinking of the group. These tactics create cognitive dissonance within the mind of man, causing them to seek alignment within their own thoughts in manners that they would not otherwise engage, serving to soften the inherent and intentional contradictions. It's here where the push-pull effect of the oscillating and offsetting fear/love dynamic is most effective. Now Dawa there is much to contemplate regarding cognitive dissonance, and I will leave that for the discussions when we evaluate our strategies for *the happening*. I'll leave it there for now and hand it back over to you."

"Well, Zegula, that was certainly a helpful introduction but woefully incomplete. I have many questions still, but I will respect your position and express my concerns nevertheless," responds Dawa. "Dawa," responds Zegula, "yes, your right; it was incomplete but stay with me here, please? These are the men that Jesus Christ warned us about; *the ones that come to man in sheep's clothing but inwardly are ravenous wolves (Matt 7:15)*; those that use our Father God's name towards the justification of their own vanity; to the disguise of their own vanity induced manipulative behaviors. I need some time to gather my thoughts on the matter." "Fair enough," replies Dawa, "it was helpful in explaining what I've observed regarding these ideologies. So, thank you, and I look forward to hearing more from you on this matter, Zegula. This push-pull effect of the fear/love dynamic is clearly at the center of these ideologies. It does create a sort of trauma bond for those following the doctrines. Allow me to test my assumptions by thinking out loud here. The Apostle Paul clearly tells us that the *natural man* cannot comprehend the mysteries of the sacred texts and that relying on literal interpretations leads to death. Paul goes so far as to tell us that the story involving the progeny of Abraham was an allegory *(Gal 4:24)* and that the meaning of the husband-and-wife metaphor was a great mystery, whereas we see it as yet another reflection as to how man is made. I say that to reference once again the religious doctrine that the last book has been interpreted literally to suggest the antichrist was an individual who would set up a one-world government that would usher in a period of great tribulation for mankind. This supposition introduces much fear and trepidation amongst the followers of this faith. It's a great distraction nonetheless, and it's here where the offsetting prospect of *being saved* by a loving Father God sets in motion the cognitive dissonance that you refer to Zegula."

Dawa continues, "When approached literally the Father God of the Torah appears to be an unpredictable and irrational God, an angry God even. And that *the one who is greater* even created a being that has been allowed to torment man, basically nullifying the concept of reaping and sowing; concepts we've already acknowledged. Furthermore, we've already recognized that every creation that's not natural on Mother Gaia is the work of the creative nature of mankind; that man's thoughts are the genesis of creation here on Gaia. It's undeniable. So, when the major religious institutions preach on the fear of what has been revealed '*literally*' in the Book of Revelation…releasing the collective thoughts of those agreeing to these inevitable outcomes into creation; because that's where thoughts go; I've concluded that the religious institutions themselves; this ideology; has in and of *itself* created the advent of the one-world government ideology. This incessant fear has manifested to bring into being the very doctrine which is to be feared. *'IT'* is using these conflicting ideologies to manifest the very thing that *'IT'* needs to perpetuate *'IT's* Self. The religions call it Satan, but we know it to be humanities collective *'IT!'* It's so subtle and crafty as to be practically indiscernible."

Dawa powers on, "Zegula it appears that there exists a sort of tug-of-war between the ideologies of religion and those of the State; meaning the nature of the governments that mankind chooses to be subject to; man, governing mankind. Mankind intrinsically appears to be willing to subject itself to the concept of complying with the wishes; or designs; of a creator Being. However, when those practices begin to incorporate unnatural doctrines of belief that contribute to this cognitive dissonance discomfort, then the door gets slung wide open for the introduction of other indoctrinations. Humans are drawn to affiliate, and when the natural affiliations are withdrawn by the designs of their environment, then they seek solace from their fears elsewhere. I'm observing this shift occurring with emerging political structures possessing all the earmarks of a religious movement. The totalitarianism ideology shares many characteristics with organized religions even insofar as they both share the promise of a future golden age for those aligning with those respective ideologies. This fascist ideology seeks to control the innermost thoughts of its followers and, like religion, does not promise happiness to those who do not convert. Not only is their aim to change political and social institutions but does so with the intent to remodel the nature of man and society."

Dawa continues, "These politically motivated institutions pursue the totalitarian religious transformation using various methodologies, each contributing to and enhancing the effects of the cognitive dissonance emanating from each. It's a powerful fear/love concoction made possible using the electronic media tools provided by the Information Revolution. When the State can create continual crises and then unilaterally determines the resolution, assuring that only *it* has the resources and means to deliver said resolution, it creates a Stockholm Syndrome effect on the overall population. Thus, the abuser becomes the perceived safe haven; a person or entity that man can turn to for comfort, mercy, or relief from the perceived threat. Two others commonly used proselytizing methods are demagogy and pedagogy, with the former being the spreading of State propaganda throughout the social construct and the latter being the ideological indoctrination of the youth through compulsory schooling."

Dawa continues, "This alternation of fear and love triggers free-floating anxiety and confusion related to the associated cognitive dissonance and serves to create this trauma bond between the citizen and the State, a bond that lies at the basis of all cults. Persistent delivery of this alternation within an isolating environment such as *'TT'* has created results in a dissociated, loyal and deployable follower who can now be instructed to act in the interests of the leader rather than in his or her own survival interests. Such processes of brainwashing rest on the creation of stress or threat with no avenue of escape other than compliance, whether voluntarily or by coercion, to the apparent safe haven of the totalitarian regime or group. Totalitarianism is a fanatical religion that can never achieve what it promises. The more power the State is granted, the more corrupt those in charge become, for *'IT'* cannot help itself. Corruption is *'IT's* destiny for *'IT'* is hostile to *the one who is greater,* and *'IT'* cannot please our Father God," says Dawa.

Dawa addresses Zegula, "Zegula, much has been said about love, even how it may be used as a manipulative tool to cause this cognitive dissonance, but I haven't heard your thoughts on how love is reflected in the thoughts of man. How does the duality experience affect man's perception of love? I'm beginning to sense that love has many colors in the construct of *'IT.'*" "Dawa," responds Zegula, "yes, that's an accurate observation. It's all very nuanced, and even man is confused and misled by these feelings of love, for they are sourced from various motivations. These motivations can originate from fear; the need for safety; the need for acceptance; the need from perceived lack; the need for companionship; or they can originate from the want to satisfy desires for pleasure and intimacy; or can even arise from the need to support a belief system out of duty or loyalty. It's all interconnected and often end up revealing contradictions within the thoughts of man."

Three Love Natures: the Thinker; the Wanter; the Sonship

"Now Dawa," begins Zegula, "love from mankind's perspective of duality is a difficult subject for the creation to grasp. The creation is not burdened by free choice or the forces of the will like man is, so I'll simply introduce these concepts to you, and we'll explore these thoughts more thoroughly once *the happening* has been fully established. I will compress this discussion of love as a contrast between the three primary sources, or participants, that man finds *within* his being. I believe that the most obvious and most primitive of these would be love originating from *the Wanter*, the unregenerate heart center. Man's desire nature can motivate in a variety of ways, with most of the motivations afflicted by a myriad of expectations guided by man's feelings. It's here that I will offer up that *the Wanter* loves from the seat of expectation, with many of these compromised by mutual expectations emanating from the targeted recipient or, said in a nicer way, the benefactor. Passion comes to mind when *the Wanter* is the pursuer. Considering our next level-up source of love, *the Thinker*. I'm suggesting that this love comes from the intellect. Love is a decision process, a choice, and pursued out of duty and, once again, with expectation attached. Together *the Wanter* and *the Thinker* are reflected as *'IT,'* the *natural man* persona, with *'IT'* driving the entire love experience until this nature has been reconciled into one with man's divine nature. This is simply how man is made. *'IT'* loves conditionally as, by definition any source of love that includes attachments and/or expectations is rooted in fear, no matter how subtle, and is conditional loving. For man to say that he loves anything unconditionally from this nature is either self-deception or due to a lack of understanding of what that means. The third source of love is from the heart of man. The regenerate heart loves unconditionally and without expectation. This love emanates from the Christ consciousness nature and is the primary goal of man's incarnation. God's desire is for His children to evolve, through experiences of suffering on this physical plane; through duality or consciousness fragmentation; into a ***knowing*** of His love nature; that would be creations hope for man; that man returns to unity consciousness."

Zegula continues, "Upon the initiation of love by *'IT,'* whether by desire or intellect, love tends to hold its course for some period whereby the subjects are committed to meeting the expectations of the other. It's quite possible for this type of commitment to be maintained over an entire lifetime, evidenced by many long-lasting relationships. However, it's not uncommon for love out of passion to morph into love out of duty or loyalty without even realizing it. That's the nature of commitment. Absent this steadfast commitment to meeting expectations, this love begins to be challenged by *unmet expectations*. One unmet expectation tends to naturally bleed into the next while being met with offsetting energies and exacerbated by the other partner. Many of man's expectations are the product of how the individual first experienced or learned love, which for most of mankind is an unknown quality as it happened before they were cognitively mature. When one combines this unknown quality with an unmet expectation, the process becomes more complex and tends to start spiraling in a downward motion, feeding into even more unmet expectations. It's here where many a therapist makes a living."

Zegula continues, "On the other hand, love from the heart and without expectation is much harder for man to find. I mean, how does *'IT'* love without expectations? Is it safe? Well, in asking that question, it becomes clear that expectations originate from some underlying fear, with fear recognized as the overriding emotion of *'IT.'* Love from the heart loves without fear, making the question of *is it safe* mute, for unconditional love *just is.* When love is sourced from the heart, this energy is not burdened by expectations, or fear, or judgment, which tends to beget a reciprocal greater love response from the other party. This elevated love energy then triggers a corresponding release of love energy from the receiving party, resulting in a love that spirals upward seemingly without limits. I'll leave it right there for now, and like I said, we will explore love more deeply when we begin approaching man as a function of *the happening.*"

Zegula pauses and has one last thought about love, "Dawa, I'm going to attempt to correlate this love dynamic to the totalitarianism mindset that you've described, as I think that I can demonstrate a relationship. *'IT'* is inherently fearful forgetting that as a Spirit Being there is nothing to fear. However, *'IT'* knows that Spirit is asleep in man and will do whatever *'IT'* can do to keep it that way. As long as man exists subconsciously from *the Wanter* persona, Spirit will not awaken. *The Wanter* is most fearful regarding the matters of surviving and thriving, as it's here where a man's pride resides most prominently. Much of *'IT's* determinism is based on judging and comparing one man's condition against another's. The more that *'IT'* can do to level the playing field by normalizing the outcomes of surviving and thriving permits *the Wanter* to be less fearful, and *'IT'* can relax. This is why man rarely rejoices in the success of others, even if they are friends, for the pride of *the Wanter* considers this a poor reflection upon them. Creating an environment whereby individuation is muted, and outcomes equalized will systemically diffuse this kind of energy. But such a scenario has a cost and requires a place for this dissipated fear energy to go."

"Back to totalitarianism for a moment," continues Zegula. "This trauma bond phenomenon that gets created through cognitive dissonance involves the idea that man becomes attached to his fear, with this fear being validated if he can align with others that share the same fears, the same ideologies. But if in the process of adhering to an ideology man can become less fearful, it always comes at the expense of personal freedoms. How do you suppose this give and take; this exchange; is reconciled in the mind of man; by *the Thinker*? *The Thinker* wants to placate *the Wanter* and quiet the mind of *'IT'* for fear that persistent drumming of anxiety may wake up the *Sonship*. *'IT'* is working manipulatively to have man accept this bargain. So, *the Thinker* turns this reduction of fear energy into a form of love energy directing it to the source of the relief, the ideology responsible for the reduction of fear, while recognizing that it's also the source of the crisis events leading to the causes of the fear that's being mitigated. This is one of the panaceas of ways that man deceives himself and unsuspectingly grants permission to be controlled by those in power and may help to explain the fanaticism behind these ideologies. Before we forget Dawa, I'd like to elaborate on the story of Job as it's another example of how *'IT'* deceives man. It may be helpful in recognizing how *'IT'* assumes the presumptuous position of the higher self and then how *'IT'* responds when *the one who is greater* takes disciplinary action to redirect man's attention. I also believe that a portion of the story reflects directly on the creation of the ideologies that we're witnessing throughout mankind. It's that concept that I will focus on at this point."

Job: the Battle Within & Beasts of the Psyche

Zegula plows along, "Now, Dawa, I'll only be providing a brief summary here, and we can go in deeper when the timing is right. We need to complete the preparation for the next Journey of Saffron, and I need to meet up with Azul and Mira. Much like the story of David and Goliath, which is about the battle within, the story of Job is a story of the Self ascending through suffering. In brief, the story begins with Job representing the Self, attempting to become spiritual through the *natural man* nature. The Lord initially acknowledges the righteousness of Job, which Job has overtly expressed himself, but also realizes that Job is unaware that he is functioning from this *natural body* nature and has been deceived by *'IT.'* Job is blind but says that he sees. He is naked without his clothes and unashamed. Job signifies the pharisaical mind. At this point, the Lord is meeting with the sons of God, presumably discussing Job's plight; a man truly seeking the *spiritual body* transition that Paul reveals. Job has a good heart so to speak; fertile and ready for the trials to come. It's here that Satan shows up and appears to be curious about this conversation regarding Job's misdirected religiosity. I can only imagine that the Lord, understanding this immense desire coming from Job, determines to show Job mercy and grant him closure and completeness regarding his wishes to be a *spiritual man* and not an *earthly man*. But Dawa, compassion from the Lord can be a harsh experience, for *'IT'* does not relent easily, and the Spirit does not negotiate with *'IT,'* for it is a zero-sum game at this point."

Zegula continues, "Satan was given permission to extract the Lord's discipline in the hopes that Job's condition would be revealed to him, helping to facilitate this transition. It's here that I will suggest that Job existed in *the Wanter* persona as he had been extremely blessed with having everything that he desired materially, with *the Thinker* subliminally acting as Job's higher self. Job was being unknowingly deceived while also handsomely enriched by *'IT.'* So, the story goes that Satan delivered the Lord's discipline as the Lord had sanctioned, and what did Job do? The *'IT'* in Job's persona doubled down and refused to acknowledge any deficiency…a predictable move of self-preservation by *'IT,'* for *'IT'* had no choice. Unfortunately, but thankfully nevertheless, the Lord doesn't stop once this process begins and allows Satan to deliver another round of discipline. Now Dawa, this really does confuse Job as he truly believes that he is righteous and that God has rewarded him because of his righteousness, making him deserving of the bounties that he has collected. Job believed that he had earned his salvation and deserved his *special* treatment. It's here where Job had several of his friends appear in hopes that they could help Job reconcile what had happened. Now Dawa, these so-called *friends* signify components of man's psyche and the beginning of the internal dialogue, or rationalization, that takes place when this war is raging within the inner man. These friends represent the three components of the lower self; the mental body; the astral body; and the physical body; all of which work together to facilitate man's physical incarnation."

Zegula quickens his pace, "Dawa, Job could not accept the assertions that these three friends were making and continued to assert his own righteousness, defending his integrity at all costs. It's here when the fourth party shows up out of nowhere. This party proclaimed to be without guilt and would deliver only that which was the truth. I believe that this friend represents the Helper within; the Holy Spirit; for after he spoke, Job did not respond, and the Lord took over. The Lord then proceeded to thoroughly admonish Job resulting in Job ultimately recognizing his offense and acknowledging that his *eye* now sees what he had only previously heard with his ears. Job is a changed man; there was a purpose in his suffering, for it brought Job to his salvation. Even the Lord acknowledges that it was *the Lord that brought these adversities on Job (Job 42:11)*, with no further mention of Satan. The Lord also admonishes the three friends and says nothing of the fourth party's discourse, which by default would suggest that the Lord agreed with the claims made by Elihu. Throughout this process, the sacred text demonstrates the turmoil that *'IT'* is going through, fearing *'IT's* annihilation, the humiliation, and shame expressed by Job, the battle within."

Zegula plows on, "During the Lord's admonishment, he makes mention of two beasts which is what I want to focus on next. One is the Behemoth, and one is Leviathan. It's here that I will suggest that the Behemoth correlates with *the Thinker* and that Leviathan correlates with *the Wanter;* let me explain. Let's begin with Leviathan, one of the Lord's most powerful and misunderstood creations. The Lord describes Leviathan as a creature of terrible strength and fury and one that cannot be bridled by the *natural man, 'the sword that reaches him cannot avail, nor the spear, the dart or the javelin. He regards iron as straw and bronze as rotten wood. The arrow cannot make him flee; slingstones are turned into stubble for him. Clubs are regarded as stubble; he laughs at the rattling of the javelin' (Job 41:26-29)*. Leviathan is a mythical symbol that stands for a powerful force within man's astral natures: man's desires and emotions. This is why Leviathan is also a serpent of the sea. The sea is symbolic of the desires and passions of the astral body, which is responsible for man's emotions and the birthplace of man's pride. The sea is also symbolic of the flow of error thoughts emanating from the subconscious mind. The astral body is the great primordial sea from which the serpent's lower desire-minded ego-self arises. *'Leviathan looks on everything that is high; Leviathan is king over all of the sons of pride' (Job 41:33-34)*. The purpose of the Lord's discourse here is to speak to Job about the desires and passions of the lower mind amid his own ascension. The lower emotional desires are very much like the description of Leviathan as they refuse to be bridled, controlled, and used for positive influence unless they are purified and properly come under the control of the higher mind as *'Leviathans heart is as hard as stone' (Job*

41:24). Keep in mind Dawa that Leviathan is not inherently bad just as the serpent with Eve is not inherently bad. However, it is the charge of man to subdue and utilize this immense reservoir of raw emotional energy in spiritually positive manners in order to ascend into the higher self."

Dawa interjects, "Zegula, I have a question before you continue. You say that the serpent, or *'IT,'* isn't necessarily meant to be bad, but it sure seems to be the undesirable adversary the sacred texts speak of. How do you reconcile that statement?" A reflective Zegula answers, "Dawa, it's a difficult concept to grasp, but I'll try to briefly elaborate as we will get deeper into this thought as we affect *the happening* and deal with man directly. When a child is born, the authentic Self is what you see, but the child is virtually helpless for the first years of its life. It's during this timeline, the first seven or eight years or so, that a child learns to interact with this world. Every child, without exception, experiences some forms of trauma as they learn how to be loved and heard. It's here that the ego-self begins its development. The child must learn to protect itself from these trauma's rendering the ego-self as a very necessary component of the child's psyche. The ego-self subconsciously steers the child through these experiences by creating coping and defense mechanisms. Every time this happens, a child is driven further and further away from their authentic Self and an awareness of their divine nature. Addressing this trauma effectively wraps up the wound of an immature psyche behind these mechanisms and guards it against detection for as long as necessary. At this juncture, the ego-self is in protection mode and will defend that wound at all costs. These coping mechanisms are very difficult to detect while the child remains in the environment in which the wound occurred but tend to manifest more negatively when they mature. It's here where a child-wound coping mechanism will create a solution for an adult issue using the same immature psyche that has been wrapped up behind layers of defenses. Without awareness, these solutions can quickly become self-destructive patterns of behavior. This nature of the activity of the ego-self is what *'IT'* has been conditioned to do, and *'IT'* believes that *'IT'* is acting in the best interests of the adult host. It's this outdated ego-self that becomes more readily susceptible to the wild beasts of the *natural man* persona, hence the advent of the adversary. And Dawa, *'IT'* is an adversary insofar as man struggles to awaken into his salvation as, *'IT'* truly believes that *'IT'* is needed presently and largely in the same construct as *'IT'* was needed in the beginning. *'IT'* will vigorously resist, fearing that any other outcome is annihilation versus thoughtful integration." "Thanks, Zegula. You're right; we're not ready to expand upon that thought at this time," replies Dawa.

Zegula continues, "Very well, Dawa, the Behemoth is the target of this discussion as it relates directly to man's affinity towards a reliance on belief systems and the ideologies of institutionalized religion and political affiliation's that appear to be the root of the challenges facing our ultimate success of *the happening*. The Behemoths of mankind originate from the *natural man's* intellectual mind and the mental body. The Behemoth represents man's consciousness in an unconscious state, which the serpent mind or sense consciousness has hijacked. It's here where man operates in autopilot mode with the Behemoth having control of the subconsciousness power to create. *'The Behemoth is the first in the ways of God...and all of the beasts of the field play there,' (Job 40: 19 & 20)*, referencing the *natural man* who is first, and the *beasts* of the lower self are here with the Behemoth. *'The Behemoth's strength is in his loins and his power in the muscles of his belly,' (Job 40:16)*, referring to the location of the lower chakras. Dawa, the Behemoth, *the Thinker in subservience to 'IT,'* is the source of mankind's Behemoth's; man's global ideologies that are hostile to our Father God and representative of all the *natural man's* worldly intangible creations. The Behemoth represents the spirit of the antichrist and is the purveyor of the destructive machinations of mankind's nature. It's religious, economic, cultural, or political ideologies that are hostile to the revealing of the sons of God. The Behemoth's nature is to reproduce; the Behemoth's power is in its virility; the Behemoth is a tyrant; the Behemoth is full of pride. The beasts of the Behemoth can become violent when attacked and uses fear and intimidation to maintain their control. The *natural man* is helpless against the power of the Behemoth, *for its where all the beasts of the field play*. Herein lies the depth and necessity of the Apostle Paul's message of the Christ within and the purpose of the mission of Jesus Christ, for Christ is the only sword that can slay the Behemoth and Leviathan, much like we've learned that Christ is also the secret of the Krystal."

After a brief pause, Dawa chimes in, "Zegula, this is an unusual interpretation of the Book of Job and quite a departure from the literal approach preferred by those practicing religion. Religion holds Job up to be a righteous man and undeserving of the suffering he endured. In the story, Job is revered for his patience and steadfast faith, with religion teaching that Job should be emulated. In missing the symbolism hidden in the text, many religions even attempt to position Behemoth and Leviathan as actual creatures suggesting that the Lord is merely being boastful in front of Job. However, this certainly looks like another misdirection play by *'IT'* whereby *'IT'* ends up being honored while leaving man in his fleshly condition, leaving man unknowingly at the door of his salvation rather than leading him through it. I can clearly see how the pursuits of spirituality and the practices of religion bring mankind to the same door of salvation and how both paths are compromised by the deception of *'IT.'* It's at this point that Cain kills Abel yet again, robbing every man that fails to pass through that door of his spiritual birthright, that of becoming a son of God. It's very difficult not to have sympathy on mankind Zegula, as it's clear there is a sincere desire to honor *the one who is greate*r. It's just that they have lost their way due to their ignorance and conditioning; compounded by a corrupted belief system. They have become so intertwined with their own creations so as to be perpetually lost in the illusion. *'IT,'* through its thorough deception of mankind, has created a sort of collective subconscious negative energy that would appear to be the work of a third-party Satan, but we now know that *'IT'* doesn't need that. Instead, it is *'IT'* that created the concept of Satan for the very purpose of distraction and self-preservation. *'IT'* is a most subtle and crafty beast for sure."

Dawa continues, "Recall that I mentioned earlier that there were two other names for Adam, *the Thinker,* and Eve, *the Wanter*? Well, as usual, it seems Zegula, you're one step ahead of me here as I believe as you do that the Behemoth represents the unconscious consciousness in man under the dominion of *'IT,'* while Leviathan represents the subconscious in man that is also under the dominion of *'IT.'* It's a bit more complex as I also believe that the sacred texts show us that the Behemoth is acting in a subservient manner to Leviathan while in the *natural body* nature, as the Behemoth is unconscious of its designed intent to have dominion over the Leviathan. It's here where the unbridled latent energy of Leviathan overwhelms the sleeping, unsuspecting Behemoth. Both the Behemoth and the Leviathan are referred to in the Book of Enoch as being two powerful monsters; a female monster, whose name is Leviathan, dwelling in the depths of the sea; and a male monster whose name is Behemoth, dwelling in the dry desert. It says that they were separated on the same day, just as Adam and Eve were in the Garden of Eden and will one day be distributed for food to those that overcome. Zegula, you may already know where I am going with this, specifically regarding the other names for these two beasts, but I will leave that for a discussion after you return from the upcoming Journey of Saffron. For now, we need to focus on the finalization of that strategy so that we can ensure that we have the formula for guiding the drops to the Glow and the mystery of the Krystal. I do believe that we have found the proper combination to unlock that secret. The continued discussion on these two beasts will be more relevant once we begin the pursuit of *the happening* and the quest for the redemption of mankind."

The Secret of the Krystal

Dawa begins, "Zegula, I've asked Azul and Mira to join us as we wrap up our postmortem analysis of the first Journey of Saffron and prepare for the next one. I have to say it's encouraging to see how your Glow had fully revived to even surpass what we witnessed when you first returned to us." Mira chimes in enthusiastically, "That's right, Dawa, and I'll add that the seven seas of Mira have responded to Zegula's energy. It seems to have permeated even the most remote regions of my spirit." "Zegula," adds Azul, "although I don't fully understand what has happened, I will say that the drops preparing for their next journeys are in much better spirits. There's a hope that I have not felt for many a millennium. Unfortunately, not much has changed for those returning other than their rehabilitation is less traumatic." Zegula replies, "This is all very good news, and yes, I am feeling much better. Dawa saw it happen. The moment we realized that the secret to the Krystal was all about the Christ energy flowing through all things and letting go of the idea that the Krystal held the secret, my Glow responded immediately" "Zegula," inquires Azul, "do you have some ideas on how to incorporate this into a strategy for *the happening*? I mean, what is the secret to this power?" Zegula responds, "Azul, it's certainly a mystery, but I do have some thoughts to share. I believe that this revelation may be easier to deploy into a meaningful strategy than we could have ever imagined."

Zegula continues, "Dawa and I have learned a great deal about the condition of mankind and how he is made. Humanities struggle with the world of duality, which is, by inference, the essence of free choice; it requires that mankind realizes a spirit of adoption, a belief, and trust from the heart, that he is divine and that his spiritual power comes from the Christ within. Mankind is dead spiritually and, because of their dual nature, must rely on Christ to help fight this battle. It truly is a struggle for them to rise above the influences of the world they've created. But it's different for the other elements of the creation as it simply *is what it is* for us. Drops represent the first time a component of creation is asked to go through a learning process of sorts while every other component waits patiently to fulfill their roles and continue evolving. Drops are asked to let go of a belief system to learn the law of least resistance, for as we've learned, resistance is futile. Because our consciousness is singular, this process of letting go doesn't manifest as an internal struggle but simply one of revelation into awareness that we are one in Christ. Although man does have a belief system that relies on a declaratory process, I'm afraid that it's only a deception played out within the self-willed intellect of the *natural man*. So here it is, Azul. Here's what we need to do, using me as the example, the idealized drop, the first to have the Glow, to reveal this revelation to all those making the Journey of Saffron. It's crucial that the selected drops truly believe this revelation, and then I'm certain that Kalani and Saffron will do the rest! That's what I feel is my purpose of being Azul!"

Dawa replies, "Zegula, you truly are the chosen one; the One to show us the *'Way'* to *the happening*. How magnificent is *the one who is greater* to choose a single drop for such a glorious purpose!" Mira asks, "Zegula, can you telepathically send that message out to the seven seas and specifically to the twenty-four generals?" Zegula answers, "I can, and I will just as soon as we all agree that this is the right strategy." Dawa replies, "Zegula, we all trust you in this matter, and I promise to call a Concurrence to request full cooperation from the Council. Saffron can align her energy with yours, and Kalani can use her breath to encourage the drops on the journey to never stop believing in the revelation. We now know the secret of the Krystal and the power of Christ. Let *the happening* begin, Zegula!" And with that pronouncement, Kalani swept in without notice to carry Zegula towards the first Jewel of Gaia initiating *the happening*.

THE BOOK OF REVELATION

Dual Nature of the Sacred Texts: Exoteric & Esoteric

Dawa begins, "Now that the Council is witnessing the proliferation of the Glow, setting the stage for the redemption of the seven Jewels, I'd like to discuss the Council's progression of knowledge and how it might be used to address the condition of mankind in general. Zegula, your insight into the thoughts of man has been invaluable in enhancing my understanding of man-made belief systems, specifically religious institutions, and how man chooses to apply sacred texts towards those practices. Since we have previously determined that the only systemic way to approach developing a solution to improving humanities stewardship of this creation was to work on man from the inside out, it has become paramount for us to understand the kingdom of heaven within so that we may learn how to assist mankind in becoming aware of the purpose of this Gaia journey. From what I have gathered, there is a great deal of confusion and disconnect of what this may be, with many competing belief systems adding to the conflagration of ideals. This in general, has resulted in an overall increasing sense of apathy towards religious participation, which has been largely offset by an increased alignment with more politically oriented ideologies. I've concluded that the primary contributor to this disconnect is man's lack of understanding as to how he is made. There is no better indication of this lack of knowledge than how man interprets and practices his own sacred spiritual texts. I'll ask the Council to oblige me as I attempt to reveal the depth of this concern as I unpack the meaning of the final and perhaps most misunderstood book of the Bible. This is conceptually critically important, as this analysis will become the cornerstone philosophy behind the next phase of the creations efforts towards assisting *the one who is greater* in the revealing of the sons of God."

"I've come to understand that the scriptures themselves have a dual meaning and dual purpose," begins Dawa. "As Zegula and myself have already alluded to mankind is generally preoccupied with the exoteric or literal meaning of the sacred texts. The Apostle Paul aggressively posited that the *natural man* could not understand matters that are spiritual and that seeing only the meaning of the letter is death. To be clear here, Paul is not referring to death in the literal sense but death spiritually speaking. With that said, mankind's practice of religion is largely a study of historical events with an attempt to extrapolate the exoteric meaning into the conduct of their current behaviors. When looking in arrears, it's clear that many of the events were a manifestation of the prevalent beliefs and attitudes held by those in the various stories. And as we have noted, it's also clear that matters related to prophecy, taken literally, have largely become or are becoming manifest throughout humanity in general. Once again, we have acknowledged that anything man, and in this case mankind, focuses its collective thoughts on will absolutely manifest in some form like that imagined. Man's creative prowess is concrete and conclusive. This is happening in respect to the Book of Revelations, but here's the catch; the religious man believes that these prophecies are the predestined handiwork of *the one who is greater* and of Satan; and that these prophecies will materialize irrespective of man's attempt to proactively intervene. Once again, to say this differently is that *man believes that these events are happening to him*. However, due to mankind's inherent ignorance of its own nature, the Ethereal Council is witnessing quite the opposite occurring. The Council sees mankind's reality materializing as a byproduct of man's collective thoughts serving to actively will the evolution of the events currently unfolding. Remember, man creates everything not natural on Gaia, *everything*, even the fulfillment of prophecy, for *the one who is greater* knows this truth and wants it to be revealed to man, but man is simply missing it. Once again, to say it differently, mankind is hopelessly reacting to its own creating energies *expecting* a cataclysmic outcome that's out of man's control versus thoughtfully responding to a set of stimuli that mankind can most definitely alter towards the fulfillment of its highest purpose. But that isn't what '*IT*' wants. *The one who is greater* constructed the experience in this manner to help man see his creative power and hopefully reconcile the unfoldment of these events with an objective discernment of man's corresponding belief system components, asking; Is this belief rational? Do I truly understand why I adopted this belief? Why would a creator God honor these beliefs? What good outcome can be expected from these beliefs? Why won't man challenge his own beliefs, you ask? It's because of man's attachments, which always originate from a place of *fear*, no matter how subtle it may be."

"The other half," continues Dawa, "of this dual nature of the sacred texts relates to man individually…to how he is made. The esoteric or metaphysical thread begins in Genesis and ends in Revelation, with every story in between connecting through the embedded symbolisms. The Adam and Eve story touches every human being, beginning with Spirit agreeing to a physical incarnation. Next, every man must experience the world of duality by exploring his Cain and Able natures, with Cain, the *natural man,* being the first in the ways of God. It now makes sense to me to recall something that Cain said to God: *'Behold, You have driven me this day from the face of the ground, and from Your face, I will be hidden, and I will be a vagrant and wanderer in the earth, and whoever finds me will kill me,'* (Gen 4:14) meaning that the *natural body* persona, the *earthy* natured man, will eventually acquiesce to the *spiritual body* persona, Abel, the *heavenly* natured man. At some point, every man must experience coming out of Egypt, *moving beyond the spirit of slavery letting go of his ego-self persona*, and crossing the Wilderness into the Promised Land, *Christ's consciousness, or the new Jerusalem.* Every man must eventually kill his own Canaanites, *error thoughts,* and rebuild the body temple and the wall around his own Jerusalem, *the heart center,* and the seat of the subconscious. In the wilderness, every man must battle his own Goliath's by systemically slaying components of his ego nature, and like Job, must confront and slay the wild beasts of the inner man, the Beast of the Earth, the Beast of the Sea and the Red Dragon in his own battle of *Armageddon.* Upon emerging from this battle victorious, having experienced the dissolution of the false image that was his ego-self, man will see the illusion of what he thought his reality to be, leading to his own appropriate period of adjustment, *his thousand years of the Dark Night of the Soul.* And then this resurrected *spiritual man* will see the throne in heaven and be revealed as a son of God before the Ancient of Days, for this, without exception, is the fate of every man. Much like the drops and the Journey of Saffron, man must take this journey of the soul no matter how many lifetimes it requires, for once the process begins, it must continue till the end. Now let's begin with an overview of perhaps the most misunderstood book of the Bible, *Revelation*, for I believe that it holds the secret for the rebirth of Mother Gaia."

The Natural Body is of the Earth

"Man is truly fearfully and wonderfully made," begins Dawa, "and while Genesis demonstrates man's involution into consciousness fragmentation, Revelation demonstrates man's evolution back into unity consciousness. As the sacred texts say: *So also is the resurrection of the dead. It is sown a perishable body; it is raised an imperishable body; it is sown in dishonor; it is raised in glory; it is sown in weakness; it is raised in power; it is sown a natural body; it is raised a spiritual body. If there is a natural body, there is also a spiritual body. So also, it is written, "The first MAN, Adam, BECAME A LIVING SOUL." The last Adam became a life-giving spirit. However, the spiritual is not first, but the natural; then the spiritual. The first man is from the earth, earthy; the second man is from heaven. As it is earthy, so also are those who are earthy; and as the heavenly, so also are those who are heavenly. Just as we have borne the image of the earthy, we will also bear the image of the heavenly (1 Cor 15: 42-49).* The prophecy of this spiritual transition begins with a declaration that these are the things that must soon take place, signifying that the salvation of the soul has been made ready. It's now up to each man to make the decision to take this step. Then there are the messages to the seven churches. Esoterically the seven churches represent the seven spiritual centers of the human body and are also referred to as the seven Spirits that sit before the Throne of God. This concept correlates to the eastern religion's process of enlightenment related to kundalini energy rising through the seven spiritual centers called chakras. I will also explore the meaning of the two Beasts, the Red Dragon and the false prophet, as they correspond to the meanings of *'IT,' the*

Thinker, the Wanter, Behemoth, and *Leviathan.* In doing so, we will explore the meaning of the vision of the four beasts rising from the sea found in the Book of Daniel, as well as the vision of the Ram and the Goat that follows, as they are precursors to the Beast of the Sea, which is Leviathan, and the Beast of the Earth, which is the Behemoth, *the first of the ways of God.* The beasts of Daniel are tied directly to the four natures of the lower chakras, with these four lower chakras correlating to the letters for the first four churches, serving to help explain the prophecy found in Revelation. These first three Spirits are symbolized collectively as *the earth*, with the last three symbolized collectively as *the heavens*. The one in the center, the fourth Spirit, is different from the others and is what the battle of Armageddon is all about. And then there's the most important symbolism found in the prophecy; who is the *Lamb* in this allegory, who is the *only one worthy* to open the book containing the seven seals that *initiates* the opening of the seven Spirits sitting before the throne in heaven?"

Dawa continues, "As a recap, the story of man begins with Spirit preparing for a physical experience and the advent of Adam made in the image of God, both male and female. The next necessary step for man to have a physical experience of duality is to form Eve out of Adam, as that separation was essential for the laws of opposites to be possible. As we will see in the prophecy, there are two natures to Eve represented by two women who, in turn, independently represent the two Jerusalem's: Babylon and the new Jerusalem. The first is the one characterized as being in slavery to Babylon under the dominion of Rome, the self-willed intellect, and her name is Hagar, Babylon the Great. The image of Babylon the Great riding on the back of the Red Dragon signifies the unregenerate heart center under the authority of the self-willed intellect. The second is characterized as the woman giving birth to the children of promise symbolized by the birth of the male child, or the Christ within; her name is Sarah, the mother of all who holds to the testimony of Jesus, for Jesus is the spirit of prophecy. It's here when those holding to the testimony of Jesus become her children according to the promise, the second covenant that God made with the Israelites. Peter refers to this situation; *'She who is in Babylon, chosen together with you, sends you greetings, (1 Peter 5:13).* Sarah sits expectantly, waiting in Babylon, the unregenerate heart center, in hopes of giving birth to the to the promise in the hearts of men. To put a finer point on this reference, John makes mention of Sarah and her children in his epistle; *'The elder to the elect lady and her children whom I love in truth and not only I but also all of those having known the truth, (2 John 1:1).* This verse makes a peculiar reference to a lady that possesses servants or slaves or a mistress. Hagar was Sarah's mistress and is also in Babylon as, *'Babylon the great, the mother of harlots and of all the abominations of the earth (Rev 17:5).* The symbolism here comes from Hagar's progeny Ishmael, who is the first of Abraham's progeny and the precursor to the seven nations of Canaan; the source of all the abominations in the earth as signified by the three spiritual centers of the lower self.

Dawa continues, "The serpent represents the life force energy being manifest and necessary for the experience of Spirit coming to participate in a physical life, which suggests that the serpent shouldn't be summarily dismissed as a bad development; it's as God intended. It's at this point that an action was demanded to jump-start the involution of man, an event, so to speak, to set the story in motion. The serpent, being aware of the more vulnerable nature of Eve, the malleable subconscious mind, beguiled Eve in order to initiate this extraordinary journey of humanity. Now the only way for Spirit to have a legitimate experience physically manifested is for man to be unaware of his true spiritual nature; to be *asleep* to the reality of his divinity. Hence the meaning of the *natural man* as being first, with the objective of the journey being for man to travail through experiences of duality until man *awakens* from his ignorance and experiences his rebirth back into the *spiritual man* persona. It's here where we can acknowledge the key concept of the *natural man* persona; it's here, in the beginning, we find that Eve has left her first love, Adam, in favor of the authority provided by the serpent persona. Secondly, and confounding this opening dilemma, we find that both Adam and Eve are unaware and ignorant of their true spiritual natures, not remembering from where they have fallen. This opening dynamic leaves Adam the most vulnerable and ineffectual as he represents consciousness in an unconscious state subject to the errant leadership of the serpent, as Eve has unknowingly aligned with the devil. The subconscious Eve is being led by the Satan persona or sense consciousness, and it's the serpent's objective to keep Eve's first love, Adam, in his ignorant stupor. This is the *natural man* condition and is reflected in the imagery of Daniel's two visions."

Dawa races on, "The key to understanding the visions..." Saffron abruptly interrupts, "Dawa...I trust that you have a point to make, but I must say that I'm not following why you must take us into the minutia of what the sacred text's imagery can contribute to this discussion. We trust you Dawa, just please get to the point; Gaia still sleeps, and this kind of talk tires me." Zegula looks at Dawa and then does a double take back at Saffron. Zegula sheepishly raises his hand towards Saffron, seeking permission to speak with Saffron quickly responding, "yes...yes...Zegula go ahead, and before you do just know that it would not be possible for the Council to have gained this knowledge without your courage, so please consider yourself to be a pseudo-member of the Council heretofore and feel free to speak your mind; go ahead, let's get to it Zegula, Gaia still relentlessly turns while she sleeps, and I only have so many hours in the day." Zegula glances over at Dawa as he slightly stutters, "I...I...well, thanks...I mean...uh...okay...Dawa?" Dawa acknowledges Zegula with a bit of a grin, "Zegula, I feel the same way as Saffron and am anxious to hear your thoughts." Zegula gathers himself; "Alright, I was just going to comment that the situation with mankind is very nuanced Saffron. It always is such. I think that I know where you're going with this thought, Dawa. I just wanted Saffron to know that I think the Council benefits from such a cerebral approach as the situation with man morphs continuously. Well, the Council must gain an intimate understanding of the plight of man individually, while I'm thinking our approach to *the happening* will be best served to anticipate where the collective human consciousness is leading. Dawa is perplexed Saffron; by man's nature; I mean, there's a vast reservoir of knowledge contained in the sacred texts that unlocks the mysteries behind this Gaia experience, yet man, well, certain men, certain privileged men have chosen to misdirect humanity away from this knowledge for some other purpose. The strategy of the Council as it relates to *the happening* must recognize the subtleties of the serpent mind, or else it could totally backfire. As I see it, we have one shot at this. The moment the serpent becomes aware that we are on a mission to salvage mankind; *'IT'* will begin to shut every avenue down; every pathway; sabotaging every effort. Our strategy must be stealth-like and carefully targeted and why I think much of this knowledge is hidden in the symbolism and away from *'IT'*. Think of this; think of man being in a simulation that he's totally unaware of. Every participant is constantly thinking and producing thoughts; these thoughts spontaneously alter the simulation and affect the next move continuously. Now man may be oblivious to these nuances, but the serpent *lives for this*. This canvas that man calls the world is the masterpiece of the adversary, the devil. This connected collective human consciousness, was given free rein to construct the game and make the rules, and the adversary is a most skilled observer. We have one shot, and then we will be exposed," concludes Zegula. Saffron responds, "Zegula, I'm much too far away to see such machinations; it's clear that my love and energy are ineffectual when such a power is in control. But as you've said before, man is doing this to himself. It's no surprise that *the one who is greater* has become frustrated and went so far as to send *His Son* to show the *'Way'*. While *the one who is greater* knows how this experience ultimately ends, I'm beginning to see the seriousness of this effort and why our Father God is proactively involved with every life. It explains the exultation that I see when a single individual *overcomes* and why it's such a special designation to be accepted as a son of God. I must admit I've been remiss, somehow extrapolating my existence with that of man. But I was put in a place and limited by very strict and absolute protocols. That's really an easy mandate, as I see it now. Perhaps its why man tends to migrate towards similar dynamics; to put him*self* in a compromised position to agree to be somewhere whereby the parameters being pressed upon him allow him to accept a limitation on his expectations, providing an excuse for the failed realization of his *Sonship* potential. No matter how disillusioned, man has no such escape route, and much to our creator's disappointment, he continues to relentlessly compromise his opportunity for exultation at great expense and effort to create an alternative one. Well, there you go, Dawa and Zegula. I am certainly not envious of the challenge set before you and have suddenly become thankful that the expectations of my involvement are predetermined," with Saffron adding, "and to think that we came into this looking at you, Zegula, as but a *drop…oh my…oh my…*how we have so carelessly miscalculated the creativity of *the one who is greater*. Please continue, Dawa, and trust that I'll not miss a single detail."

Dawa picks back up, "Very well; thanks, Zegula for your input; as Saffron suggested, I too am beginning to second guess the envy for the drops that I held earlier. The Journey of Saffron is much more challenging than I had imagined. Okay, back to the key to understanding the visions of Daniel. We've had several conversations that have alternated the use of phrases that are largely synonymous. We've correlated the story of Cain and Able as a representation of the lower and higher selves, which points to the same meaning as the *natural man* and the *spiritual man*; as the *natural body* and the *spiritual body*; as the *earthy body* and the *heavenly body*; as the *corruptible* and the *incorruptible*; all language from the sacred texts referencing the same concept. The symbolisms found in the description of the visions of the beasts found in Daniel are also reflected throughout the Book of Revelation and, when viewed together, provides a clear demarcation between the one which is first and the one which is second. In my observations of this connection, I've also become intrigued by the interesting and quite unexpected hidden similarities between components of eastern religious practices and the Bible used by the western religions. The reason I suggest that it's hidden is that what I am about to reveal is not recognized as valid doctrine by those western religions, and I'm struggling to discern why that is, so I do believe that understanding why this might be will in some way have a determining effect on the success of our strategy about *the happening*. For now, I will attempt to simply overview the situation and expect that we must get into more of the finer points related to man's journey of the soul as the Council directs the redemption of the seven Jewels of Gaia, as there does appear to be an uncanny similarity there as well."

The Prophecy Construct

Dawa begins, "The prophecy of the Book of Revelation begins by telling us that this is 'The Revelation of Jesus Christ' given to Jesus Christ by God. Jesus Christ then determines that He will communicate the prophecy to His bond-servant John through His angel. This suggest that much of the prophecy is delivered to the reader of the prophecy in third person. Now Zegula, it's clear that you will have gained an experiential understanding of this prophecy through the amalgamation of the thoughts of mankind you have encountered either directly or through the memories of the other drops. I'm going to make a preliminary assumption here that those thoughts were primarily centered around finding the meaning of the prophecy as a reflection of what the resulting physical outcropping of these events would look like; on how these events would manifest *on* the earth and in the actual physical lives of humanity. Recognizing that we've come to understand the exoteric approach to reflect a literal interpretation and the esoteric as looking for the hidden meaning of the texts as revealed by the underlying symbolism and the allegorical meaning of the stories therein, this prophecy requires that even the literal interpretation find the meaning of the symbolism as that's how the prophecy is presented in its entirety. Recognizing this truth as a fundamental limitation on how to approach the prophecy's meaning, the predisposition of the mind that is accustomed to approaching the Bible's meaning literally has led to religious doctrines relying on predictions of what these prophecies physically create. The mind of the *natural man* seems to always gravitate towards this level of understanding, as it's consistent with the inherent practice of looking outwards for the meaning of events in the context that they are outcomes happening to mankind in contrast to outcomes emanating from within the collective mind of man. I'm thinking that the approach taken by the *natural man* persona correlates with the nature of the law of Moses as the first covenant of God and pertains to the manifestation of mankind's creative thoughts *on* the earth and geared towards the preservation of the soul of man. This approach is also reflected by the meaning of; *The first Man, Adam, BECAME A LIVING SOUL.*"

"In contrast," continues Dawa, "the esoteric approach to the interpretation of this prophecy requires us to discern these prothesized events from the context that they are happening within the psyche of the inner man. It's clearly a celestial natured prophecy as the letters are written to angels and not to the physical leaders of the churches so designated; the significance of which cannot be summarily dismissed. Taken exoterically, the celestial geography being referenced would be the totality of the physical creation as represented by the Ethereal Council, while also considering the invisible workings of the entirety of the cosmic hosts; the spiritual realm; working on behalf of mankind, and conversely, serving to work towards the detriment of mankind. Taken esoterically, the celestial geography being referenced in Revelation becomes the body tabernacle of the individual human. When considering the manifested outcomes exoterically many of these predicted future events will have little impact on the lives of those making these determinations, and instead have only served to establish doctrines based on the resulting fear-based outcomes. On the other hand, the esoteric meaning will have an immediate and meaningful impact on the spiritual ascension process that's being described. Why is that important? It's because the prophecy begins with telling the reader that the things being prothesized *'must soon take place,' (Rev 1:1)* and *'Blessed is he who reads and those who hear the words of the prophecy and heed the things which are written in it; for the time is near,' (Rev 1:3).* Furthermore, the exoteric approach is intended to be digested by mankind in mass as that is how the outcomes are manifest, while the esoteric approach to the prophecy is directed at humanity as individuals. The Revelation of Jesus Christ is directed at each human individually as the journey so designated by the prophecy is taken alone and must soon take place. I'm thinking that the approach taken by the *spiritual man* persona correlates with the concept of the Messiah as the second covenant of God and pertains to the manifestation of man's thoughts *in* the earth and geared towards the spiritualization of the soul; signifying the process of salvation. This approach is also reflected by the meaning of; *The last Adam, became a life-giving spirit."*

Dawa continues, "The Revelation prophecy is a very difficult text to dissect and understand. There are many characters to consider and many events to explore. It's very easy to get lost as there are more references to the Old Testament contained in the Book of Revelation than any other book of the Bible, with every single reference requiring a comprehension of the underlying symbolic meaning for the prophecy to be revealed. Considering that backdrop as our reality, I've determined that the one who reads the prophecy must have a basis of understanding of the characters involved in order to extrapolate the meaning behind the unfolding events and so should we. Since this is the Revelation of Jesus Christ, it stands to reason that Jesus is the most important character for us to understand; and we can't understand Jesus, as the son of man, unless we can also grasp the concept of Christ. This is no small task and perhaps the greatest source of contention in all of religion. And Zegula, I will of course have to make some assumptions for this version of the prophecy to congeal so please be patient with me. It's clear that your experiential knowledge is critical for us to be able to connect the dots and I would ask that you express those thoughts as we traverse the context of the actual events of the prophecy. For now, I'd prefer to finish establishing a foundation from which to have that conversation. Although we've already introduced many of the characters, I'm thinking that we must differentiate the parts that Jesus and the Christ contribute to the celestial prophecy found in the Book of Revelation before we can continue."

Dawa starts with briefly discussing Christ, "Notwithstanding disagreements amongst the many disparate religions on Gaia it does appear that based on an understanding of the symbolism found in the sacred texts that Christ, the Son of God, serves as the foundation for the second covenant, the promise. David writes, *'The LORD says to my Lord: Sit at My right hand Until I make your enemies a footstool for Your feet,' (Ps 110:1),* with scripture clearly claiming that from the beginning this world belongs to Christ as the only begotten Son of God. It's Christ that is blameless and without blemish and the perfector and author of salvation for mankind. This Son of God is of the Spirit and was sent by Father God; *'in the likeness of sinful flesh and as an offering for sin,' (Rom 8:3).* Coming in the likeness of Jesus, Christ, who was made for a little while lower than the angels, tasted death for everyone and condemned sin in the flesh so that the requirement of the law might be fulfilled in mankind, meeting the demands of the promise. *'Therefore, since the children share in flesh and blood, He Himself likewise also partook of the same, that through death He might render powerless him who had the power of death, that is, the devil, and might free those who through fear of death were subject to slavery all their lives,' (Heb 2:14,15). 'For since He Himself was tempted in that which He has suffered, He is able to come to the aid of those who are tempted,' (Heb 2:18).* Christ is the Lord of Lords, the first and the last and the living One; the Son of the Lord God Almighty."

Dawa briefly discusses Jesus, "Jesus was the fleshly vessel chosen by Christ; *'Therefore, holy brethren, partakers of a heavenly calling, consider Jesus, the Apostle and High Priest of our confession; He was faithful to Him who appointed Him, as Moses also was in all His house,' (Heb 3:1,2),* and *'but Christ was faithful as a Son over His house…whose house we are, if we hold fast our confidence and the boast of our hope firm until the end,' (Heb 3:6).* The prophecy tells us that those who hold to the testimony of Jesus will overcome as He did, *'But if the Spirit of Him who raised Jesus from the dead dwells in you, He who raised Christ Jesus from the dead will also give life to your mortal bodies through His Spirit who dwells in you,' (Rom 8:11). 'For all who are being led by the Spirit of God, these are sons of God,' (Rom 8:14). 'The Spirit Himself testifies with our spirit that we are children of God, and if children, heirs also, heirs of God and fellow heirs with Christ, if indeed we suffer with Him so that we may also be glorified with Him,' (Rom 8:17).* The testimony of Jesus is the spirit of prophecy in Revelation and the cornerstone message of salvation."

Dawa briefly discusses the symbolism of Jesus Christ, "Jesus Christ signifies the completion of the redemptive nature of the Christ in man. Jesus Christ is the firstborn of the dead and a brother of Christ and mankind becomes a son of God because Christ is God's Son. Many times, the Christ is presented as speaking first person through the vessel that is Jesus. The totality of the life of Jesus mirrors the reality of what it means to have a regenerate heart center and the spiritualized mind of man upon becoming a son of God; to fully reflect the nature of Christ. It signifies the behaviors that a redeemed human should aspire towards."

Dawa briefly discusses these natures as presented in the prophecy next, "Jesus Christ is presented as follows, *'and from Jesus Christ, the faithful witness, the firstborn of the dead, and the ruler of the kings of the earth. To Him who loves us and released us from our sins by His blood…and He has made us to be a kingdom, priests to His God and Father…to Him be the glory and the dominion forever and ever, Amen,' (Rev 1:5,6).* The Christ is introduced next; *'and in the middle of the lampstands I saw one like a son of man,' (Rev 1:13).* This generic reference to son of man suggests that the Spirit of Christ presented here is not Jesus Christ specifically, and that Christ was available to any son of man regarding the unfoldment of the prophecy. I say that noting that the revelation was given to an angel of Jesus Christ and delivered to John to record what he saw. It's evident that both would have immediately recognized if this was Jesus as they both knew Jesus intimately. Secondly, the prophecy, as it unfolds, simply doesn't work if it were Jesus Christ as the symbolism fails to connect. Furthermore, the symbolism of the Christ positioned in the middle of the lampstands is significant, for the middle of the seven lampstands is the fourth lampstand: the heart center. The regenerate heart center receives a new name; the new Jerusalem, and the Christ tells us that His name will become the 'new Jerusalem' for those that overcome. Next we have; *'a Lamb standing, as if slain,' (Rev 5:6),* once again signifying that this *Lamb* is the one who overcomes and applies to each human individually, for that's how the prophecy unfolds."

Dawa elaborates on the body tabernacle, "Next I think it's necessary to gain a greater understanding of what I mean by reference to the body tabernacle, as it is the kingdom of heaven and a central theme of the prophecy. Recall how the physical earthly sanctuary was constructed to include an outer court that included the lampstand plus other sacred items, while behind the second veil stood the inner court called the Holy of Holies holding the ark of the covenant, with the tabernacle of testimony in the ark. As reflected in the prophecy the outer court signifies the earth and the inner court signifies the heavens. The word *church* as used throughout the New Testament and in this prophecy symbolizes this body tabernacle suggesting that the letters to the churches of Asia are signifying conditions within the inner man psyche and that each church exhibits certain unique qualities. The seven churches also signify the seven Spirits before the throne which are further symbolized by the seven golden lampstands. The lampstands further signify the energy emanating from the seven primary spiritual centers located along the spine and reaching into the brain, with each of these spiritual centers correlating with a major nerve center and major glands of the endocrine system. Taken together these symbolize *the tree of life* as the working components of the mind in man; hence the meaning of the *kingdom of heaven is within* and the scripture proclaiming that man is *fearfully and wonderfully made*."

Dawa continues, "As we will see it revealed in the prophecy, the first three churches represent the earth, and the last three churches represent heaven. The fourth church in the center maintains a special designation as a kingdom like no other and initially belongs to the dominion of the earth; to the lower self or the *natural man* persona. So, the first of the four Spirits before the throne is the dominion of the beasts of Daniel. This prophecy is a detailed description of *the battle within* as the Spirit of man is raised from the dominion of the earth towards the dominion of heaven, symbolizing the crucifixion of the serpent persona or the image of the false prophet, leading to the resurrection of the divine nature in man;

referred to as the *Sonship* by Zegula. Based on what we've learned along the way I'd like to refine what the *Sonship* signifies. Alluding to an earlier discussion I'm leaning towards viewing the *Sonship* as the *Lamb,* with the *Lamb* symbolizing the life-giving spirit of the last Adam. It's here where the first man Adam, as a living soul, has been awakened and spiritualized by the Holy Spirit acting as the Helper and Spirit of Truth, worthy to take the book of the seven seals. Therefore, the Holy Spirit is synonymous with the *Lamb* in this prophecy, with the *Lamb* signifying a resurrected spiritualized Adam. Salvation is therefore represented by the marriage of the *Lamb* and his bride, the Christed regenerate heart center, or the *new Jerusalem,* with this marriage further signifying the reconciliation of mankind's dual natures. As I see it Zegula it's appropriate to refer to this renewed and awakened consciousness as the Christ consciousness."

Dawa continues, "This may be some helpful background regarding the symbolism incorporated related to the fourth Spirit before the throne. Jerusalem was destroyed by the Babylonian empire with the help of Egypt in 587 BCE and was later restored with Nehemiah rebuilding the wall in 444 BCE. Jerusalem symbolizes the heart center throughout all of scripture. This heart center is named Babylon while under the dominion of the serpent persona and is named the *new Jerusalem* when presented as the bride to the *Lamb.* The Apostle Paul addresses this by referring to the allegorical meaning of Abraham's two sons, with the first one being born unto a bondservant according to the flesh and with the second one being born unto a free woman according to the promise. *'This is allegorically speaking, for these women are two covenants: one proceeding from Mount Sinai bearing children who are to be slaves; she is Hagar. Now, this Hagar is Mount Sinai in Arabia and corresponds to the present Jerusalem, for she is in slavery with her children. But the Jerusalem above is free; she is our mother,'* (Gal 4:23-26). It's curious to note that the name *'Sinai'* is derived from the name of the Babylonian moon-god...*Sin.* The symbolism found here is like that of the city of Jericho, as Babylon in this prophecy is likewise under the dominion of the self-willed intellect granting licentiousness to Eve under the Hagar influence. Sodom and Egypt are two other mystical names given to this holy city while under the influence of the devil."

Dawa moves along without pause, "Now that may be a bit confusing, so I'm thinking that taking a brief look at eastern religious practices will be helpful before we revisit the seven churches. What follows those letters is a description or a visual of each of the seven Spirit centers opening and the awakening process moving on towards the battle of Armageddon which signifies the battle within for dominion over the fourth Spirit. Eastern philosophy proposes that the human body contains seven spiritual centers beginning at the base of the spine and moving upwards to the crown of the head. Each of these spiritual centers is represented by spinning wheels of energy called chakras, with the first chakra holding the kundalini divine feminine energy. Kundalini means circular or annular hence it's in the *spinning wheels* or *chakras* where the kundalini Spirit energy resides and is described as a coiled serpent sitting as 3½ coils at the base of the spine. This energy is likened to the Christ energy concept found in western religions and is clearly depicted in the Revelation prophecy as having a similar form and function. This first chakra is associated with red, with each chakra also being associated with variations of the lotus flower. It's here where the symbolism of the Red Dragon representing the lower chakras was birthed. Like all the chakras, when cleared and functioning properly, they represent positive attributes contributing to the unfoldment of the awakening process. When blocked and dysfunctional, they represent negative attributes and are hindrances to the enlightenment journey."

"Now there is an interesting corollary in regard to the spinning wheels of the chakras to the four living creatures guarding the throne in heaven," continues Dawa. "These four creatures are first noted in Genesis as cherubim guarding *the way to the tree of life (Gen 3:24)*. These living creatures appear again in Ezekiel and are elaborately described as being the same four living creatures guarding the throne in heaven found in the prophecy. In it, the cherubim had whirling wheels under them with *the spirit of these living beings being **in** the whirling wheels*. By all appearances, these cherubim represent the exiled Spirits of the lower four chakras, and they are before the throne of heaven, protecting the way to the tree of life from the four beasts of the lower self that are depicted as rising out of the sea in Daniel. Similarly, the lotus flower that is associated with each of the seven chakras is also used in the description of the Behemoth...one of the beasts associated with the lower chakras: *'Under the lotus plants he lies down, in the covert of the reeds and the marsh. The lotus plants cover him with the shade' (Job 40:21,22)*. Nevertheless, the similarities to eastern religious concepts are undeniable. It's curious to imagine how much more harmonious humanity would be if man focused on these spiritual similarities versus searching for ways to isolate and differentiate between eastern and western religious beliefs. Well, I digress back to the discussion at hand."

"The lower three chakras," Dawa continues, "govern the relationship that man has with his physical world. These include the condition of man's physical and emotional identity along with his self-image. The root chakra deals with the sense of self-preservation and man's survival instincts. Man's fight or flight is determined here, along with his ability to recognize and respond to danger. This chakra is associated with the **earth**. The sacral chakra is associated with the emotional senses and creativity. It is the center of man's emotions, relationships, and sensuality. It is associated with **water** as defined by the flow of emotions and sensual appetites running through man's bodies. Sexuality blossoms here, with all the joy and suffering that accompanies it. It's not uncommon for man to become a slave to his sexual desires, and when not controlled, these sexual energies are often sublimated into other destructive tendencies. A universally corrupted sacral chakra negatively affects the current state of mankind's civilization. The third lower chakra is the solar plexus chakra, or power chakra, and is associated with the ego, the source of personal power, self-belief, and self-worth. The chakra energy here is aggressive and concerned with power, the power to destroy or to create, and is associated with **fire**. The prophecy of Revelations addresses this third church, Pergamum, accordingly; *'I know where you dwell, where Satan's throne is where Satan dwells' (Rev 2:13)* where man's ego or false-self resides. It's here where the ruling power of the self-willed intellect sits and signifies the dominion of the Red Dragon. It's clear from my observations that men living at the levels of the lower chakras are mostly spiritually unaware and concerned with only the lowest forms of religious awareness. They seek health, wealth, and progeny, having little interest in higher spiritual attainment. Their petitions to God are mostly self-serving bargains for the fulfillment of the base desires of life."

Dawa returns to the prophecy, "Then there is a scene in heaven describing the throne as having a total of ten parties' present: three parties to the throne plus the seven Spirits appearing before the throne. This number ten will be relevant when describing the beasts of Daniel. But first, we need to better understand the key character of this vision as it breathes life into this prophecy. There was *'a' Lamb standing* between the throne with the four living creatures and the twenty-four elders **as if slain** the one worthy to open the book containing the seven seals. Who does this *Lamb* represent? Jesus Christ was the firstborn of the dead and *was slain* and is the *One* guiding the writer John through this prophecy. If this were to refer to Jesus, it would be consistent with every other reference and say **'the'** *Lamb*, not **'a'** *Lamb*. Secondly, those around the throne did not fall down before this Lamb until it took the book. Thirdly, after this Lamb took the book, those around the throne sang a **new** song, saying: *'Worthy are* **'You'** *to take the book and break its seals,' (Rev 5:9) for...' Blessed is he who reads and those who hear the words of the prophecy and heed the things which are written in it; for the time is near,' (Rev 1:3).* One of the elders around the throne tells the reader that Jesus as: *'the Lion that is from the tribe of Judah, the root of David, has overcome so as to open the book and its seven seals,' (Rev 5:5).* Jesus has already overcome, which verily serves to impart the power onto those who hold to His testimony to open the book and its seven seals regarding their own individual journeys towards salvation. Therefore, the remainder of the prophecy is pointed at the brethren set to follow Him being the second born, and thereafter through the authority of His Christ. Therefore, I'm suggesting that the *Lamb* here is not a direct representation of Jesus Christ, as most literal interpretations conclude, but presents to us instead *'a'* substitute Lamb, *standing as if slain*, representing the brethren who hold to the testimony of Jesus for He is the spirit of prophecy. The brethren are pseudo standing in the place Jesus Christ has prepared as they traverse through the prophecy."

Dawa continues, "The reason that I belabor this point, Zegula is that in applying the misplaced doctrine to the interpretation of *who is this Lamb* has once again served to rob man of the spiritual empowerment that was intended, for this Lamb becomes the full benefactor of being made perfect, like Jesus, the moment the *Lamb* **takes the book** with the seven seals. It appears that the Holy Spirit is the one that reveals the inner divine Truth and jump starts the process by taking the book. And as the prophecy depicts, it's through the power of the Holy Spirit that paves the way for the Christ to be birthed into consciousness. This may be a good time to make a distinction between the Christ energy that was revealed within Jesus and the nature of His Christ that slays the beasts. Recall where Paul tells us that *'faith comes from hearing, and hearing by the word of Christ (Rom 10:17)* while addressing the question concerning those who have not heard. Then Paul proclaims that they have indeed heard of Christ long before the manifestation of Jesus. It's here where Paul references the Torah as Paul didn't have any of the New Testament to reference, as his letters preceded the Gospels. One of these references says: *'I was found by those who did not seek Me, I became manifest to those who did not ask for me,'* *(Rom 10:20 & Is 65:1)* meaning that salvation has always been available for those who understood God's law of the inner man, even well before the life of Jesus. Likewise, the *Lamb* in this prophecy, the one who is to overcome, receives His Christ directly from *the one who is greater.* In truth, all of creation belongs to the body of Christ, and all are expressing this physical manifestation in many different forms to the honor and glory of *the one who is greater,* our *Creator God."*

THE SEVEN SPIRITS BEFORE THE THRONE

The Church at Ephesus & the Root Chakra

Dawa hurries along, "The prophecy then progresses through each of the seven Spirits, the seven chakras, until salvation is signified by the marriage of the *Lamb* and his bride. The opening of the first Spirit, *the root chakra*, begins upon the breaking of the first seal (beginning in Chapter 6) and continues through the breaking of the sixth seal. The letter to the church at Ephesus says: *'But I have this against you, that you have left your first love. Therefore, remember from where you have fallen…,' (Rev 2:4,5).* In order to become worthy to take the book and open the seals, the *Lamb* must come to some level of acknowledgment of his true spiritual nature believing that he has willingly *fallen* into a physical incarnation. This is also signifying the point at which Eve left her first love, Adam, in favor of the errant leadership provided by the serpent. This is where sense consciousness originated, leaving man functioning as if on unconscious autopilot, consciously unaware, and subject to the whims of the subconscious passions and desires. This Spirit in its unregenerate form is symbolized by Pharoah and mystically referred to as Egypt. Pharoah signifies the ruler of the ego-self and does so through his inherent power to impart fear, shame and humiliation. Recall that the Israelites were begging to go back to Egypt for fear they would die of hunger and thirst while in the wilderness, the essence of this first chakra's thriving and surviving characteristics. It's here where man becomes fearful and willingly subjugates his spiritual freedoms in return for slavery and perceived safety, whereby the familiar is more comfortable than the unknown. Ruling from Egypt is also suggesting that Pharoah does so in obscurity, serving to reinforce the *natural body* persona."

"Now Zegula," continued Dawa, "the church at Ephesus does have particular significance as the Apostle Paul spent three years at Ephesus and encountered *the wild beasts* when dealing with those in the church. The Ephesians were renowned for worshipping the heathen goddess Artemis, which symbolizes the fundamental carnal nature of man (Acts 19:24). Keep in mind that this church, the root chakra, is associated with the *earth* and it's here where man is concerned only with self-gratification, self-preservation, sustenance, and propagation. It's here where man also becomes attached to manmade belief systems. Collectively, this attachment to those things created by man, whether tangible or intangible, serving to satisfy man's carnal nature is of the beasts of the earth, the Behemoths of man."

Dawa continues, "This chakra's association with the *earth* is an important concept to understand as we go through the prophecy. The prophecy of Revelation begins with one of the four living creatures announcing, "Come" to the rider on the white horse. This horse represents the power of Christ being released to go out conquering and to conquer. Next, the second living creature announced to the rider on the red horse, "Come," and to him was granted to take peace from the *earth.* The next living creature made the same announcement to the rider on the black horse. This rider had a pair of scales in his hand, which represents the materialism of the earthy man. It's here where that carnal nature is to be starved of the trappings associated with thriving and surviving. Recall the story of Job and how he was stripped of his material wealth. When the *Lamb* broke the fourth seal, the fourth living creature announced, "Come" to the rider on the ashen horse. This rider was named Death and was followed by Hades. These four horsemen were given the authority over a fourth of the *earth,* meaning this first church, the root chakra, as it represents the first of the four earthy spiritual centers to be conquered or opened. This battle continued through the opening of the fifth and sixth seals."

Dawa continues, "At this point, there was an interlude where the four angels at the four corners of the earth, representing **earth**, **water**, **fire,** and **air**, were held back for a time. It's here where the remnant was introduced and marked. These represent those that remained true, protecting the heart chakra even though it was under captivity to the lower nature. This is symbolic of the remnant that remained after the Babylonian empire destroyed Jerusalem. The remnant was later credited with rebuilding the temple, fulfilling the prophecy. Nehemiah then led the effort to rebuild the wall around Jerusalem, signifying the restoration of the heart center. The Revelation prophecy refers to the heart chakra as Babylon until the battle of Armageddon has passed."

The Church at Smyrna & the Sacral Chakra

Dawa continues, "The breaking of the seventh seal (beginning in Rev 8) marks the beginning of the opening of the second Spirit, *the sacral chakra*, and starts with *'silence in heaven for about half an hour' (Rev 8:1),* representing the quieting of the mind through meditation. The tribulations related to the opening of the second Spirit end after the bottomless pit has been opened. The letter to the church at Smyrna says: *'I know your tribulation and your poverty (but you are rich), and the blasphemy by those who say they are Jews and are not but are a synagogue of Satan (Rev 2:9).* This is a reference to those who have disciplined themselves by controlling their sensual natures and admonishes those who believe themselves to be spiritualized and righteous, the symbolism of being *a Jew,* but remain slaves to their desires and passions of the flesh. This Spirit, in its unregenerate form, is mystically called Sodom and correlates to the necessary destruction of Sodom and Gomorrah as the Israelites made their way to the Promised Land. It's also important to note that this is a reference to the individual body as *'a'* synagogue of sense consciousness; the self-willed intellect…the carnal mind of man. The battle for this second chakra is centered on *water* and the destruction of the seas, rivers, and springs, turning them into wormwood. It also refers to the destruction of ships that were in the sea."

The Church at Pergamum & the Solar Plexus/Power Chakra

Dawa continues, "The third Spirit, the *power chakra* or the *solar plexus chakra*, begins to open at the sound of the sixth trumpet (Rev 9:13) and ends with the instruction to *'take the book which is open' (Rev 10:8)* and then eating it. While this is sweet as honey, the eating of the gospel of truth makes the stomach bitter signifying that the Gospel has been preached to the entire earth. This represents the location of the sacral chakra, which is the nerve center sitting just behind the stomach. Recall that the sacral chakra is the seat of man's personality, the ego-self. The letter to the church at Pergamum says: *'I know where you dwell, where Satan's throne is (Rev 2:13)* and *'But I have a few things against you because you have there some who hold the teaching of Balaam, who kept teaching Balak to put a stumbling block before the sons of Israel, to eat things sacrificed to idols and to commit acts of immorality,' (Rev 2:14)*. This is the power chakra and where the energy of the will is expressed. Symbolically this warning refers to the perils introduced as the stumbling blocks by the pursuit of power and control fueled by the misdirected practice of religion under the influence of sense consciousness, the *natural man* persona. This Spirit in its unregenerate form is first signified by the city of Jericho and later by Greece and Rome. This symbolizes the self-willed intellect taking control of the pseudo-spiritualization process and attempting to enter heaven illegitimately. It's here where man runs the risk of inadvertently misdirecting the ascension progress of those that are truly searching for authentic spiritual growth. These first three churches symbolically are referred to collectively as the *'earth'* in Revelations, the *earthy* lower self, the *natural body*. Riders having fire, smoke, and brimstone proceeding out of their mouths, waged the battle. Recall that this chakra is associated with *fire* and that fire was used for destructive purposes."

The Church at Thyatira & the Heart Chakra

Dawa continues, "The next Spirit, or chakra, that is unlike any of the others represents the seat of the subconscious mind and is associated with *air*. Much like Kalani moves without limitation over Gaia influencing all things and cannot be seen, so does the subconscious move, invisibly influencing the behaviors of man. Similarly, while Adam remains in his unconscious state, Eve remains under the influence of sense consciousness, just as Kalani moves without discipline while Gaia sleeps. The battle of Armageddon is to determine if the heart center remains under the dominion of the *earthly* nature, referred to as Babylon, or will the *heavenly* nature, referred to as the new Jerusalem, prevail. This fourth Spirit, *the heart chakra*, begins to open with the appearance of the two witnesses (Rev 11: 1-14). I believe that the two witnesses represent Divine Love and Wisdom, as these two attributes ultimately elevate consciousness to the heavenly realm with these two attributes also being attributed to David from the Old Testament texts. There is also reference made to the body tabernacle with a command to measure the temple of God and the alter with one exception: *'Leave out the court which is outside the temple and do not measure it, for it has been given to the nations; and they will tread under foot the holy city for forty-two months,' (Rev 11:2).* Recall that the outer court signifies the Spirits of the earth, the first three chakras. The dominion of these churches is not won until the battle of Armageddon is finished. The reference to nations refers to celestial geography and signifies the error thought emanating from spiritual strongholds of a corrupted earth."

Dawa continues, "The prophecy foretells of a process that man must experience, suggesting that the beast will kill these two witnesses, but their bodies will not be placed into a tomb. The desires of the ego-self will arise from the abyss from time to time to kill the influences coming from divine love and wisdom. This ongoing process is synonymous with Cain killing Able. The beast of the *natural man* rising from the abyss is never satisfied, truly leading to a bottomless pit of despair and enslavement. Thankfully, these two witnesses will never fully die and go away, returning as many times as it takes to slay the beasts within. And what is the fire that flows from the mouths of the two witnesses that is used to kill their enemies? In western religions, this fire refers to the Christ energy, while in eastern religions, it's referred to as kundalini energy. Recall when Moses raised the brazen serpent during the exodus so that the Israelites would be healed from the bites of the fiery serpents. This represents the rising of the lower self, suggesting that the life-giving energy from the serpent has a negative outcome when under the influence of the ego-self, while it is positive energy when under the dominion of the spiritualized man. It's curious to note

Zegula the use of the numbers 3½. It's used in reference to the forty-two months, or 3½ years, the holy city will be assaulted as well as how long the two witnesses remained dead, 3½ days. In eastern religions, this number refers to the 3½ coils of the serpent, or the Red Dragon, located at the base of the root chakra. This kundalini energy will ultimately rise through the seven chakras as a man becomes enlightened much in the same way His Christ resurrects the *earthly* into the *heavenly* in this prophecy."

Moving along, Dawa says, "This Spirit represents the center chakra located between the lower self and the higher self, and this *battle within* does not end until the Red Dragon, the serpent of old, comes up out of the abyss and is thrown into the lake of fire (Rev 20:10) marking the end of the battle of Armageddon. *'Thus says the Lord God, This is Jerusalem; I have set her at the center of the nations, with lands around her' (Ezek 5:5).* The letter to the church at Thyatira first acknowledges the love and faith and service and perseverance of this heart center. However, it does provide this warning: *'But I have this against you, that you tolerate the woman Jezebel, who calls herself a prophetess, and she teaches and leads My bond-servants astray so that they commit acts of immorality and eat things sacrificed to idols,' (Rev 2:20).* This warning is much like the last referring to the heart chakra as being under the influence of unbridled passions and under the dominion of the serpent mind. It's from the heart that man believes, and while under the dominion of the *earthly* nature, man cannot please God. And as signified by the heart center, the warning goes on to say: *'and all the churches will know that I am He who searches the minds and hearts, and I will give to each one of you according to your deeds (Rev 2:23).* This letter makes an interesting reference to Satan saying: *'But I say to you, the rest who are in Thyatira, who do not hold this teaching, who have not known the deep things of Satan, as they call them – I place no other burden on you,' (Rev 2:24).* The distinction being drawn here would seem to suggest that the *deep things of Satan* are abstract in nature; *as they call them;* and not a reference to an independent, thriving celestial being. This letter concludes that the one who overcomes till the end will receive *the morning star* and have *authority over the nations* meaning to receive the light of a spiritual awakening granting dominion over the earth. Once again, nations signify error thought rising up from the seven nations of Canaan and include the Canaanites, Hittites, Amorites, Hivites, Perizzites, Girgashites and the Jebusites. Each of these nations signify certain negative personality traits of the unregenerate natural man. For instance, the Amorites are associated with the undisciplined amorous thoughts coming from the sacral chakra."

The Church at Sardis & the Throat Chakra

"The battle for the fifth Spirit begins with the opening of the door to heaven," explains Dawa, "as the higher self Spirits in heaven must open in order to enable His Christ to be released to fight the battle of Armageddon. The opening of the first of these higher Spirits begins upon the sounding of the seventh trumpet; *'And the temple of God which is in heaven was opened, and the ark of His covenant appeared by His temple…' (Rev 11:19)* ushering in the beginning of the rein of His Christ *(Rev 11:15-17)*. The Apostle Paul says this about the last trumpet sounding, clearly depicting an event that happens while man is physically alive: *'Behold, I tell you a mystery; we will not all sleep, but we will all be changed, in a moment, in the twinkling of an eye, at the last trumpet; for the trumpet will sound, and the imperishable, and this mortal must put on immortality. For this perishable must put on the imperishable, and this mortal must put on immortality. But when this perishable has put on the imperishable, and this mortal will have put on immortality, then will come about the saying that is written, DEATH IS SWALLOWED UP IN VICTORY. O DEATH, WHERE IS YOUR VICTORY? O DEATH, WHERE IS YOUR STING?' (1 Cor 15:51-55; IS 25:8; HOS 13:14).* Another important symbolism is in reference to the ark of the covenant appearing by His temple. It may be helpful to recall that during the Exodus, the Israelites carried the tabernacle through the wilderness containing the ark of the covenant behind the veil of the Holy Place. God told the Israelites that he would reside there until the permanent temple was built in the Promised Land, meaning Jerusalem. This reference signifies the moment that the first Adam is transformed by the spiritualization process initiated by the last Adam, when the divine spark of God is revealed behind the veil and sitting on the throne. It's here where the *Lamb* is confirmed and where *'IT'* and the *Lamb* confront each other directly for the first time. This process is birthed by Sarah as the persona of Eve giving birth to the promise and initiating *the rising of the morning star in the hearts of men (2 Peter 1:19)*. The morning star is another name for His Christ. It's also here where the Red Dragon is thrown to the earth signifying that *'IT'* cannot battle with the Holy Spirit and hold up under the observation from the Holy Spirit that the *Lamb* represents. It's also here where it says, *'The serpent poured water like a river out of his mouth after the woman so that he might cause her to be swept away with the flood. But the earth helped the woman, and the earth opened its mouth and drank up the river which the dragon poured out of his mouth (Rev 12:15-16).* This signifies the tactics used by *'IT'* to create fear and trepidation to hijack the ascension process. Water represents the flow of error thoughts moving through man's mind, and flood signifies *'IT's* relentless assault. We will see another reference to this flow of water in a moment."

Dawa continues, "The letters to the churches in heaven take on an entirely different character than the earthly ones. The letter to the church at Sardis declares that: *'I know your deeds, that you have a name that you are alive, but you are dead. Wake up...' (Rev 3:1).* It's here where Jesus is acknowledging that through the law the individual man has become known by God, or that the individual man has come to know of God and is therefore alive with a name yet remains in the *natural man* condition... blind and naked needing to *Wake up.* Think of the imagery of the seventh and last trumpet as sounding loud enough to cause man's consciousness to awaken. It's here where spiritual progress is being acknowledged, but the risk remains that man's sense consciousness has not yet been overcome and continued spiritual ascension demands that his consciousness *Wake up: 'So remember what you have received and heard, and keep it, and repent. Therefore, if you do not wake up, I will come like a thief, and you will not know at what hour I will come to you' (Rev 3:3).* It finishes with an acknowledgment for the one who overcomes, the one who spiritually awakens with the sounding of the seventh and last trumpet, that his name will not be erased from the book of life and that Christ will confess his name before the Father."

The Church at Philadelphia & the 3rd Eye Chakra

Dawa continues, "The sixth Spirit, *the 3rd eye chakra*, opens next with *'...the temple of the tabernacle of the testimony in heaven was opened' (Rev*

15:5). This Spirit marks the arrival of His Christ with the marriage of the *Lamb* to follow. This also signifies the end of Armageddon and continues until Satan is thrown into the lake of fire with the other the beast and the false prophet (Rev 20). Recall that the tabernacle contained the Ten Commandments, God's laws, which are also referred to as the tabernacle of testimony. The opening of the sixth Spirit signifies the point at which God fulfills the covenant of the promise; *But this is the covenant which I will make with the house of Israel after those days," declares the LORD, "I will put My law within them, and on their heart, I will write it; and I will be their God, and they shall be My people." "They will not teach again, each man his neighbor and each man his brother, saying, 'Know the LORD,' for they will all know Me, from the least of them to the greatest of them," declares the LORD, "for I will forgive their iniquity, and their sin I will remember no more,' (Heb 8:10).'"* Dawa continues, "It's here where man's heart center has been restored with the Spirit of Truth and with the fullness of the knowledge of his divine nature. And perhaps the reference that it's no longer required to receive teaching from other men just may be the indicator as to why the practice of religion has been established to divert man's attention away from this event. The self-willed intellect that governs these institutions enjoys the control that the practice of religion affords and here God proclaims that this manner of religious practice will no longer be applicable."

"Back to the prophecy," continues Dawa, "this is where the Babylon the great is revealed as being a mystery and where she represents the heart chakra under the dominion of the *natural body* persona. Babylon is the great city in this state, and the name changes to the new Jerusalem after the battle of Armageddon. As I've stated, it's my suspicion that Babylon the great refers to Eve, in the Hagar persona, as she submitted to the serpent influence from the beginning and that her children are slaves as signified by the progeny of Ishmael and the seven nations of Canaan. It says the following of Babylon: *'To the degree that she glorified herself and lived sensuously, to the same degree give her torment and mourning; for she says in her heart, I sit as a Queen and I am not a widow, and will never see mourning,' (Rev 18:7).* This correlates directly to similar admonishments regarding Jerusalem symbolizing the heart center contained in earlier sacred texts. *'In the heart of the seas, You were in Eden, the garden of God on the day that you were created, You were blameless in your ways, From the day you were created Until unrighteousness was found in you. Therefore, I have brought fire from the midst of you; It has consumed you, And I will have turned you to ashes on the earth,' (Ezek 28).* In another reference, it says something similar: *'Yet you said, I'll be queen forever, I will not sit as a widow. For you have said in your heart, I am, and there is no one beside me. But evil will come on you, which you will not know how to charm away. And distress will fall on you for which you cannot atone, And destruction about which you do not know will come upon you suddenly (Is 47).* And yet another singular reframe: *'This is the exultant city which dwells securely, who says in her heart, "I am, and there is none beside me." How she has become a desolation, A resting place for beasts! Everyone who passes by her will hiss and waves a hand in contempt (Zeph 2).* The reference to her not sitting as a widow is an attempt to blame Adam for not being beside her while in his slumber. Adam is not dead but instead unconscious, waiting to awaken, which Eve, in the Hagar persona, is actively subverting. The reality of her situation is that she is not a widow, which makes her a harlot for defiling herself with the serpent persona and for becoming a hostess of the beasts."

Dawa elaborates regarding the nature of Hagar, Babylon the great, "The prophecy of Ezekiel addresses God's displeasure with Jerusalem under the influence of the harlot saying, *'Son of man, make known to Jerusalem her abominations and say, Thus says the Lord God to Jerusalem, Your origin and your birth are from the land of the Canaanite, your father was an Amorite and your mother a Hittite,' (Ezek 16:2,3).* The Hittite symbolizes those fearful and self-serving characteristics associated with the root chakra, while the Amorite symbolizes those uncontrolled sensual desires arising from an unregenerate sacral chakra. The prophecy goes on to claim that she played the harlot with the Egyptians as well as making references to her corrupted sisters, Samaria and Sodom. Here Samaria symbolizes errors in intellectual perception, while Sodom symbolizes uncontrolled passions and sexual promiscuity.

Dawa continues, "This part of the prophecy continues with reference to the stages of progression through the seven Spirits: *'Here is the mind which has wisdom. The seven heads are seven mountains on which the woman sits, and they are seven kings; five have fallen, one is, the other has yet to come…,' (Rev 17:9,10),* meaning that the heads, mountains, and kings all represent the same thing…the five chakras that have already opened or fallen at this point in the ascension, plus the seventh chakra that simply *is what it is*, for *He who overcomes* is either hot or cold, plus the heart chakra that has yet to come and remains the subject of the battle of Armageddon. The reference here to the seven mountains is clearly referring to Rome, the center of activity for the third Jewel of Gaia. Symbolically Rome signifies the pursuit of spirituality being sabotaged by the self-willed intellect, by the pretentious *natural man* persona. Recall that the Apostle Paul was imprisoned and executed in Rome while under the rule of Emperor Caesar Nero, signifying the self-willed intellect hindering the spiritual ascension process. In Revelation, anything aligned with Rome will be destroyed as politics and religion were inextricably linked during these times. In order to accentuate this connection, note that the sacred text says: *'Here is wisdom. Let him who has understanding calculate the number of the beast, for the number is that of a man; and his number is six hundred and sixty-six,' (Rev 13:18)*. This is the numerical equivalent to the name of the Emperor Caesar Nero, indicating that the beast of the sea was personified as the ruler of the self-willed intellect."

Dawa continues discussing the sixth church, "The letter to the church of Philadelphia says: *'He who is holy, who is true, who has the key of David, who opens, and no one will shut, and who shuts, and no one opens, says this: I know your deeds. Behold, I have put before you an open door which no one can shut because you have a little power, and have kept My word, and have not denied My name. Behold, I will cause those of the synagogue of Satan, who say that they are Jews and are not, but lie-I will make them come and bow down at your feet, and make them know that I have loved you,' (Rev 3:7-9)*. It's in this letter that Christ symbolizes the door that was opened, the 3rd Eye chakra, and cannot be shut. This serves to signify the completion of the ascension process of transitioning from the *natural body* nature into the *spiritual body* nature resulting in man's salvation/enlightenment. In it, Jesus once again makes the distinction between those that believe that they are spiritualized but unknowingly remain under the dominion of the serpent persona, meaning that their bodies remain a synagogue of Satan. Recall what Jesus says about the ascension by the wrong door; *'Truly, truly, I say to you, he who does not enter by the door into the fold of the sheep, but climbs up some other way, he is a thief and a robber. But he who enters by the door is a shepherd of the sheep,' (John 1:1-2)*, and because they did not understand what he was saying, Jesus continues with, *'So Jesus said to them again, Truly, truly, I say to you, I am the door of the sheep. All who came before Me are thieves and robbers, but the sheep did not hear them. I am the door; if anyone enters through Me, he will be saved, and I will go in and out and find pasture. The thief comes only to steal and kill destroy; I came that they may have life, and have it abundantly,' (John 10:7-10).* Here Jesus is specifically pointing out that the serpent persona's way to the throne is climbing up another way, through the wide gate, and not through His narrow gate."

Dawa continues, "Jesus cannot be clearer about how He feels concerning the risks that mistakenly believing that one is spiritualized and righteous introduces into the ascension process, repeatedly warning man against these perils. As we will see in the last letter, Jesus makes it clear that making this mistake disgusts Him. This brings me back to the story of Job when Job repents for his misguided self-righteousness and says: *'I have heard of You by the hearing of the ear; But now **my eye** sees You; therefore I retract, And repent in dust and ashes,' (Job 42:5).* This reference to a singular 3rd eye represents the activity of deep meditation when the Spirits in heaven have been opened, signifying Job's transition from the *natural body* into the *spiritual body,* and where Job can see his inner man adversary. It's also here the Lord's description of the Behemoth and Leviathan is relevant, for only the Lord, through the workings of His Christ, possesses the sword that can slay these two beasts of the inner man. It's also curious to consider that the descriptions of Pharoah and Egypt contained in Ezekiel 29 is the same kind of language that the Lord uses to describe Leviathan in Job, as they symbolize the same thing, the ego-self ruling in obscurity. Pharoah and Egypt are to Israel as Behemoth and Leviathan are to the unregenerate human psyche. It appears that the literal history of Jerusalem signifies the journey of the human soul. It's a story signifying that so long as one remains in the *natural body* persona, Cain was destined to kill Abel again and again, signified by Jerusalem being repeatedly captured by force and ruled by its enemies." Zegula briefly interrupts, "Dawa, this connection that your making sounds as if Pharoah is symbolically acting the part of the serpent persona within the *natural man.* This recalls another eastern-oriented thought. The name Pharoah means the sun and the ruler of the 3rd chakra, the solar plexus or the power chakra, pointing to Pharaoh as the ruler of the sun center in the subconscious mind. This situation suggests that Pharaoh is the force that rules the whole human body consciousness under the material-oriented regime. Pharaoh's being ruler of Egypt suggests that he rules the subjective mind in obscurity. This Pharaoh-influenced consciousness applies to the activities of the *natural man* only and only because the Adam consciousness is effectively unconscious. This also leads to another thought. Because of my abilities to discern the thoughts of mankind, my experiences have found that those who are undergoing the regenerative process, which, as you have suggested, are symbolically illustrated in the literal journey of the Israelites, that the offsetting forces signified by Pharaoh and Moses are constantly at work in man's consciousness. One is holding onto old ideas and striving to perpetuate them in form, and the other force is idealizing the new objectives and making every effort to break away from this material bondage and rise above its limitations." Dawa responds, "Zegula that is yet another way to look at it and I'm in agreement. The competing forces that you refer to are further exemplified by the first beast of the sea from Daniel's vision. These thoughts will be helpful for that discussion which will follow momentarily."

Dawa continues, "This sixth letter goes on to say: *'He who overcomes, I will make him a pillar in the temple of My God, and he will not go out from it anymore; and I will write on him the name of My God, and the name of the city of My God, the new Jerusalem, which comes down out of heaven from My God, and My new name,'* (Rev 3:12). This is referred to as the first resurrection as man was dead spiritually and has become spiritualized through the ascension process. The prophecy goes on to say blessed and holy is the one who has a part in the first resurrection, for the second death will have no power over them, and those who have not overcome will be thrown into the lake of fire, the second death. This suggests that upon death, the unregenerate man will be subject to a judgment process that will cause him anguish and consternation at some level, perhaps leading him back into a subsequent incarnation for him to complete his spiritual evolution. The Council has determined that the purpose of the Gaia journey is completed upon man being revealed as a son of God. What we don't know is what happens next for those ascended souls, the sons of God. Perhaps the sons of God have an option? The Council is hopeful that they come back to Gaia in order to participate in the creation of the

New Earth or, as this letter may suggest, that they will not go out from the presence of *the one who is greater* anymore. *This is certainly one of the greatest mysteries of all."*

The Seven Bowls of Wrath

Dawa proceeds, "The bowls of wrath mark the beginning of the opening of the temple of the tabernacle of testimony in heaven, this 3rd eye chakra. The first six of the bowls of wrath were poured out leading up to the battle of Armageddon. The first angel poured his bowl out upon the **earth**, representing wrath against the first chakra. The second angel poured his bowl of wrath into the sea. The third angel poured his bowl of wrath out into the rivers and springs of water. Then the angels of the **waters** praised the One who is holy. This represents wrath against the second chakra. The fourth angel poured out his bowl upon the sun, and it was given to it to scorch men with **fire**, representing wrath against the third chakra. Then the fifth angel poured his bowl on the throne of the beast suggesting this was poured out on the third chakra, as the third chakra is where Satan dwells. The sixth angel pouring his bowl of wrath on the great river Euphrates, causing it to symbolically dry up, making the way prepared for the kings from the east. It's curious to note that the previous references in the prophecy to kings of the earth represent those belonging to the nations of the lower chakras, while kings of the east refer to those belonging to the higher chakras. Anything referring to coming from the east symbolizes the rising sun or the spiritual ascension of the higher self. After these six bowls of wrath were poured, the armies gathered at Armageddon for battle. Then the seventh angel poured out his bowl upon the **air**, representing the heart chakra, and a loud voice came out of the temple from the throne, saying, *'It is done.'* Before the seventh bowl of wrath is poured the prophecy says, *'Behold, I am coming like a thief. Blessed is the one who stays awake and keeps his clothes so that he will not walk about naked and men will not see his shame,' (Rev (16:15).* We understand that to mean to be aware of your *natural body* nature and cover it with the knowledge of your awakening divine nature."

"One more thought before moving along," continues Dawa, "the reference to the river Euphrates is loaded with symbolism and perhaps something that may help us with *the happening*. Recall how the Garden of Eden had a river flowing out of it, and from there, it divided and became four rivers, *(Gen 2:10-14)*. There is also reference to a river coming from the throne of God in heaven. *'Then he showed me a river of the water of life, clear as crystal, coming from the throne of God and of the Lamb,' (Rev 22:1)*, and on either side was the tree of life. These are referencing the same river, with the first being in the unregenerate form and the second in the regenerate form. The listing of the four rivers goes from the lowest to the highest and corresponds to the four major sections of the spinal column. The first is the river Pishon in the land of Havilah, which correlates with the sacrum. Hagar's son Ishmael settled in the land of Havilah, and this corresponds to the first two chakras. The gold stone correlates to wealth and the need for the means to thrive and survive. The onyx signifies willpower, focus, strength, protection, and fortune, which are also characteristics of these two lower chakras. The bdellium is an aromatic gum like myrrh that is extracted from a tree and, when petrified, is correlated to being a pearl. Spiritually this 'stone' is believed to repel evil spirits and increase one's power to manifest desires and intentions. The second river is Gihon and flows in the land of Cush. This correlates to the lumbar region of the spinal column and is associated with the third chakra. The land of Cush is where Ham lived and symbolizes the material nature of man in his darkened thought. The third river is the Tigris which correlates with the thoracic area of the spinal column or the heart center. This river flows east out of Assyria, which symbolizes the reasonings, philosophical and psychical natures under the dominion of sense consciousness. The fourth river is the Euphrates and feeds the others. Practically speaking, Babylon sits at the bottom of the Euphrates and cannot sustain commerce without the steady flow of the Euphrates. Symbolically, it represents the means of carrying error thoughts from the lower chakras upwards through the unprotected heart center and into the throne of heaven. The drying up of the Euphrates signifies the need to abate the flow of error thoughts by quieting the mind through the process of meditation. Babylon fell in the battle of Armageddon, that lasted only one hour. This signifies that once a man's mind can be quieted for one hour in meditation, that the *Lamb* burns up the adversary *'IT'*, by denying *'IT'* the means to distract attention from itself."

The Church at Laodicea & the Crown Chakra

Dawa continues, "The final letter is most revealing and quite abrupt as this is the *'it is what it is'* notification. The Seventh Spirit, *the crown chakra*, begins with the revealing of the new heaven and the new earth (Rev 21), signifying the completion of the enlightenment journey. In it, the new Jerusalem is presented as the *wife of the Lamb*. God pronounces…*'He who overcomes will inherit these things, and I will be his God, and he will be My son,' (Rev 21:7)*. This reference also confirms that the *Lamb* is not Jesus as He has already overcome and is the firstborn of the dead, *the spirit of the prophecy*. Furthermore, the reference here to the one who overcomes connects all the events associated with the *Lamb* to be the same *'He who overcomes,' (Rev 2:7,11,17,26; 3:5,12,21)* referenced in each of the letters written to the seven churches."

Dawa continues, "The prophecy ends with references to the river and the tree of life, *'Then he showed me a river of the water of life, clear as crystal, coming from the throne of God and of the Lamb, in the middle of its streets. On either side of the river was the tree of life…,' (Rev 22:1,2)*. As we've already explored, the river coming down from the throne represents the spinal cord running down the middle of the body, and inside is the spinal fluid, the water of life. This is the same *'living water'* that is often referred to by Jesus, as it's alive through the power of His Christ. The tree of life here represents the components of the nervous system that feed directly into the spinal column sending information up to the throne in heaven or into the brain of man. The seven spiritual centers are located along the entirety of the spinal column with the crystal-clear water, or spinal fluid, suggesting that the chakras have been opened and are functioning in a spiritualized state. The 24 elders are the 12 pairs of cranial nerves that come out of the brain. These nerves do not travel down the spinal cord but instead flow outward directly into the body controlling the five senses and bodily functions. It's at this point man has awakened into a new state of consciousness, and the body and mind are working harmoniously as he has put to death the enmity between his dual natures. Man, is truly *fearfully and wonderfully* made Zegula, and now we see that *the kingdom of heaven is within*."

Dawa continues, "The letter to the church at Laodicea says: *'I know your deeds, that you are neither hot nor cold; I wish that you were cold or hot.*

So, because you are lukewarm, neither hot nor cold, I will spit you out of My mouth,' (Rev 3:15,16). This serves as the final warning for those that have been deceived by the serpent persona while in pursuit of spirituality or the practice of religion. He describes those remaining under the influence of sense consciousness, those that have not awakened into their true authentic divine nature, as being lukewarm, irrespective of how sincere their efforts may be, for *it is what it is.* He goes on to describe a sort of perverted contentment that these practitioners risk adopting due to the deceptions inherent in a self-righteous mind. The letter goes on to say: *'Those whom I love, I reprove and discipline; therefore be zealous and repent. Behold, I stand at the door and knock; if anyone hears My voice and opens the door, I will come into him and will dine with him, and he with Me. He who overcomes, I will grant to him to sit down with Me on My throne, as I overcame and sat down with My Father on His throne,' (Rev 3:19-21).* Once again, this is a clear message that there is a knowing that comes with an awakening, *it is what it is,* for it's an enlightening experience when man has spiritually ascended through the seven churches. It's also here whereby the humanity of Jesus is seen to be absolute, for without making any other qualifying distinction, all of mankind can become the *Lamb* in the story. It's here in the prophecy that the *Lamb* overcame, just as Jesus also overcame, becoming the enabling spirit of the prophecy."

THE WILD BEASTS OF
THE NATURAL MAN

Daniel's Vision of the Four Beasts

Dawa continues, "I think that we will be looking into this salvation process in greater detail as it relates to our interactions with man individually. For now, I'm simply seeking to gain a comprehensive understanding of the overall condition of mankind and how the situation has devolved into such an abysmal state. So back to the beasts of Daniel…," Saffron interjects, "Dawa, this is certainly revealing especially considering the way the practice of faiths between the eastern philosophies and western doctrines contrast with each other. It appears that there are more similarities than there are differences, however, they seem to have set up competing ideologies. Was this a misunderstanding, or could it be with intention? I only ask that as I'm beginning to see how the motivations of mankind are not always in their best interests, yet I still can't understand why. Why would mankind sabotage his own spiritual ascension?" Dawa answers, "Saffron, the *natural man* is inherently fearful. Fear and love cannot coexist, which is why the Spirit of the heart center remains under the domain of the lower self until the higher self or the three Spirits of heaven are opened. This fear leads to all manners of attachment, which cannot happen without expectations. It's these expectations that drive the need for control, and invariably the need for control gives birth to the insatiable desire to have power and the need for these competing ideologies. Saffron, man will seek power and become consumed by it even though it moves him further away from the awareness of their true spiritual nature. It's the nature of Pharaoh and the influence of Rome. Saffron, they do not remember where they have fallen, and in their ignorance, they do not know what they do. *IT's* inherently fearful nature is the source of man's suffering."

Dawa picks back up with Daniel's visions as Saffron looks on with a sad countenance, "The first vision is of the four beasts that arise from the sea. Recall that the sea represents the astral body and its influence on the subconscious mind in man. This imagery depicts four beasts that have dominion over the four lower Spirits or chakras, whichever way you want to think of it. This happens due to man being asleep consciously so that man functions mostly out of the impulses and desires of this lower nature signifying Pharoah ruling in obscurity. The first beast correlates with the first Spirit and has the appearance of a lion. *'The first was like a lion and had the wings of an eagle. I kept looking until its wings were plucked, and it was lifted up from the earth and made to stand on two feet like a man; a human heart also was given to it' (Dan 7:4)*. Recall that the first chakra is associated with the earth hence he was lifted from the ground but essentially ruled by the subconscious mind. This represents the subconscious projection of the material man. Going back to our earlier discussion, we suggested that the root chakra is symbolized by Pharaoh and Egypt. Holding to this concept, the characteristics of this beast rising out of the sea are remarkably like the Egyptian goddess Sekhmet and her son, the Egyptian solar war god Maahes. Sekhmet was depicted with the body of a woman and with the head of a lion wearing a sun disk. Recall that Pharoah means sun, and she was seen as the protector of the Pharoah's and led them in warfare. Maahes was considered to be the patron of Pharaoh and could take the form of a lion. The lion held a privileged status in Egypt and was regarded as the fiercest warrior in the wild. The lion symbolizes both danger and protection, both key characteristics of the root chakra. The visual of this beast having the wings of an eagle suggests that it could move about and perhaps even fly into the heavens, pretentiously sitting on the throne and why the cherubim are guarding it. Recall that when the 5th chakra opened, the ark of the covenant appeared, initiating the birth of the promise of the Holy Spirit by the woman Sarah resulting in the removal of Satan from heaven. In this visual, Sarah was clothed in the sun, symbolizing the Spirit with her feet on the moon, symbolizing the submission of the self-willed intellect or the Rome/Pharoah persona to the power of the Holy Spirit at work. This signifies the power of the sun transitioning away from Pharoah and marking the end of the self-willed intellect's rule of the higher self. The visual continues with Sarah scurrying to the wilderness to escape the wrath of the Red Dragon that was thrown out of heaven and down to earth. Recall that Sarah was helped by the earth, as it swallowed up the flood coming from the mouth of Satan and was given the wings of an eagle that were perhaps symbolically plucked from this first beast as a means to flee from the devil's pursuit. It's curious to note that upon having its wings plucked, the first beast was given the heart of a man signifying the opening and redemption of the first of the seven Spirits."

Dawa continues, "Next up' *And behold, another beast, a second one, resembling a bear. And it raised up itself on one side, and three ribs were in its mouth between its teeth; and thus they said to it, Arise, devour much flesh!'* (Dan 7:5). The sacral chakra is identified with emotions and sensuality. This energy can be transmuted into all manners of unhealthy machinations represented by the bear being sensually aroused and raising up itself on one side, satisfying this sexual desire through the devouring of his prey. The three ribs further suggest that instead of taking only a single rib from Adam to form Eve, the bear has taken a larger bite out of consciousness rendering Adam helplessly unconscious and unable to maintain dominion over his astral body. Recall that before David slayed Goliath, he had previously killed a lion and a bear with both being beasts of the unregenerate lower self. Next David killed Goliath which symbolizes a characteristic of the ego-self and affiliated with the third chakra."

Dawa continues, "Next up' *After this, I kept looking, and behold, another one, like a leopard, which had on its back four wings of a bird; the beast also had four heads, and dominion was given to it,'* (Dan 7:6). The power chakra or the solar plexus chakra is associated with man's carnal personality and personal power. Once again, this is where the ego-self resides, and as we saw earlier, it's where Satan dwells. Dominion was given to it, suggesting that this is the home of the *natural man* persona and personal will. The four heads are also indicative of the Spirits of the chakras located in heaven, which are closed to the unregenerate man having relinquished their pseudo authority to the beast of the power chakra, as the additional three heads symbolizes the three higher Spirits in subjugation to the lower nature. These four heads can also correlate with the nations that had previously conquered Jerusalem. These were Babylon, Persia, Greece, and Rome. The significance of looking at it from this view is to consider what followed. The progression is indicative of the growing influence of the intellect interfering with spiritual ascension. The influence of Rome intermingled the pursuit of political or Roman empire goals with the incorporation of the influence of the Roman church. From this point forward, it's not a battle between nations for control of territory but instead a battle for the control of the mind of man. Reducing the pursuit of spirituality into the practices of man-made religious doctrines has been the primary difference maker in maintaining control of the mind of mankind and perpetuating the *natural man* persona. It's also curious to note the primary characteristics of a leopard. First and perhaps most relevant is they are nocturnal predators. They hunt in obscurity and ambush their prey. They are also solitary and very adaptive. Sure, sounds like the devil doesn't it?"

"Now we come to the most terrifying beast of them all," Dawa elaborates, "as it is in control of the heart center. As we will investigate in more detail later, this beast has rendered the heart chakra into the dominion of the *natural man* persona. The Apostle Paul also refers to the serpent influence within the heart center pronouncing to those who are alive in Christ: '*...you formerly walked according to the course of this world, according to the prince of the power of the **air**, of the spirit that is now working in the sons of disobedience*', *(Eph 2:2)* the subconscious under the obscure dominion of Pharaoh's sense consciousness. This beast had ten horns, and during the vision, a little horn came up among the first three. Next, those first three horns were pulled out by the roots, which left eight horns. This little horn possessed eyes like a man and a mouth uttering great boasts. This boastful horn became powerful but not of his own power representing the projected false-self image coming from the subconscious. This little horn grew to be larger than the others and waged war until the Christ regained dominion. This little horn represents the serpent's influence claiming the pseudo authority of the throne of heaven by displacing the prior three horns reflected as the One sitting on the throne, the twenty-four elders, and the four living creatures. This beast was slain as part of the vision, with the dominion of the other three beasts being taken away for an appointed time."

The Beast of the Sea

Dawa continues, "This takes us back to the Beast of the Sea that rises from the sea after the Red Dragon was thrown to the earth upon the opening of the fifth Spirit. The Beast of the Sea was a conglomerate of all four of the beasts rising out of the sea in Daniel, with one having evidence of a fatal wound that had healed. This represents the point when the *Lamb*, during meditation, sees the Red Dragon pretentiously in control of heaven for the first time and is immediately hurled down to the earth. At this point, the lower three chakras have already been opened, and those beasts no longer have dominion. We are told: *'As for the rest of the beasts, their dominion was taken away, but an extension of life was granted to them for an appointed period of time' (Dan 7:12)*. The purpose of this extension was for them to coalesce into one for the battle of Armageddon and this appointed time was one hour. The fatal wound that healed was that of the fourth beast enduring the ripping out of the little horn when Satan was flung to the earth as when it rises as the Beast of the Sea in Revelation; it now has the original ten horns back in their place. This signifies the awakening awareness of the *Lamb* leading to the serpent's loss of dominion over the subconscious and of the three parties to the throne in heaven. Having said that, pseudo dominion over the seven Spirits and the throne represented by the ten horns remained under the Red Dragon's *dominion for one hour (Rev 17:12)*, until the battle of Armageddon was finished: *'The ten horns which you saw are ten kings who have not yet received a kingdom, but they receive authority as kings with the beast for one hour,' (Rev 17:12)*."

Zegula chimes in, "Wow, Dawa, that's a profound interpretation of the visions of the prophecy. I'm looking forward to hearing more from you on this. I will say, though, that this explains much of what I have experienced as I travail through man and discern his thoughts. The negative and frenetic energy emanating from these spiritual centers is certainly the most frightening. The lightning and thunder coming from the twenty-four elders are terrifying and highly charged. Sometimes this energy simply gets blocked in one of the seven Spirits and randomly redirected, being released without intention, causing it to angrily radiate throughout the mind and body of man. The intensity of this misdirected energy can cause all kinds of damaging physical manifestations for humans and is surely the source of most diseases. I now understand the contrast of energies between what I experienced with the thoughts of Jesus Christ and other men, the peace and love of Jesus versus the fear and suffering of the others. What does this mean, Dawa? How do we use this knowledge?" Dawa responds, "Zegula, I haven't yet determined what this means…we will have to figure that out together and somehow merge the process of redeeming the seven Jewels of Gaia with the stimulation of man's seven spiritual centers."

The Ram & the Goat

Dawa continues, "These discoveries regarding how man is made certainly lead me to thoughts regarding the seven Jewels of Gaia and those similarities. The first of the seven Jewels is the largest and most populated on Gaia. Interestingly, this Jewel is characterized by the Red Dragon itself and will require much effort to transform. Not to be distracted, I would like to address the next vision of Daniel, *the Ram, and the Goat,* as it reveals the nature of man's sleeping consciousness; the first Adam. But before I continue, I would like to make another observation from the sacred texts as it relates to the first three beasts of the lower nature. In the Book of Hosea, the Lord was expressing His continued frustration with His people. He had brought them out of Egypt, however, they continued to rebel, desiring to go back into the comfort of the familiar. The sacred text says this: *'I cared for you in the wilderness, in the land of drought. As they had their pasture, they become satisfied, And being satisfied, their heart became proud; Therefore they forgot Me. So I will be like a lion to them; Like a leopard, I will lie in wait by the wayside. I will encounter them like a bear robbed of her cubs, And I will tear open their chests; There I will also devour them like a lioness, As a* **wild beast** *would tear them' (Hos 13:5-8).* You can see here that the three beasts rising from the sea are specifically referenced and suggesting that the Lord uses these beasts to reprove and discipline mankind if only man can see their own self-destructive ways and the source of their suffering. There's also a curious reference to these wild beasts related to Jesus: *'And He was in the wilderness forty days being tempted by Satan; He was with the wild beasts, and the angels were ministering to Him' (Mark 1:13).* Once again western religion positions this experience as Satan being the third-party source of evil soliciting the temptation to Jesus. But we've already seen that temptation is from within; *'one who is greater does not tempt anyone, but each one is tempted when he is carried away and enticed by his own lust,'* *(James 1:14)*. It's also clear that the reference to the wild beasts that Jesus was with corresponds to the beasts of the lower self as pictured by Daniel. Paul makes a similar reference to these wild beasts: *'If from human motives I fought with wild beasts at Ephesus, what does that profit me? If the dead are not raised, LET US EAT AND DRINK, FOR TOMORROW WE DIE. Do not be deceived: Bad company corrupts good morals' (1 Cor 15:32-33)*. It's here where Paul is suggesting that he encountered those under the influence of the *natural man* persona while engaging with those at the church of Ephesus. And finally, Elihu makes a curious reference to these beasts while admonishing Job. Recall that Elihu symbolizes the Holy Spirit, and he says, *'Who teaches us more than the beasts of the earth,' (Job 35:11)*, clearly indicating that these beasts are simply part of the God designed nature of the *natural man* and necessary to know both good and evil."

Dawa plows forward, "The ram had two horns, with one growing longer and coming up faster than the other. The ram was *butting to and fro with no apparent discipline or agenda while it was also doing as it pleases and magnifying itself exceedingly. No other beasts could stand before him, nor was there anyone to rescue from his power (Dan 8:4)*. The ram here represents the unity consciousness of Adam before being rendered unconscious by the fall into the physical realm and before the serpent had aligned with Eve. The male goat had a conspicuous horn coming up from between his eyes, and he was enraged at the ram; perhaps this signifies jealousy on the serpent's part. The goat struck the ram and shattered his two horns trampling the ram to the ground, and there was none to rescue the ram from the power of the goat marking the point when Eve betrayed Adam. Then the male goat magnified himself exceedingly, but as soon as he was mighty, his large horn was broken and in its place, there came up four conspicuous horns growing towards the four winds of heaven, towards the dominion of the higher self. Out of one of them came forth a rather small horn, which grew exceedingly great toward the south, *towards the lower chakras;* toward the east, *towards the rising sun representing the rising sun or the resurrection;* and, toward the Beautiful Land, *towards the Promised Land or the heart center.* It magnified itself to be equal to the Commander of the host, and the place of the Commander's sanctuary was thrown down. The host will be given over to the horn, and it will fling truth to the ground and perform its will and prosper. This is where the authority of the heavens was thrown down to the earth to be subject to the rule of Satan's pretentious throne."

Dawa continues with the interpretation, "The ram represents the psychic aspect of man's consciousness that has yet to take dominion and remains in a vulnerable condition. The large horn of the goat represents the serpent persona that subdues man's consciousness. The four horns represent four kingdoms, which will arise from his nation but not from his power. These four kingdoms are the first four of the seven Spirits and reflect the overpowering impact of the sense consciousness of the serpent over man's consciousness, the subconscious, and the Commander of the host. The small horn represents the false prophet or ego-self that is projected outward from the influence of the serpent mind as sense consciousness. This is indicative of Adam's consciousness that has been supplanted by the serpent, rendering Adam *'unconscious'* and unable to defend his dominion. The power of the ego-self is illusory and temporary and will be broken without human agency. This process happens through the power of the Holy Spirit and the authority of His Christ reflected in the prophecy of Revelation. The shaggy male goat is the Behemoth, and the unconscious consciousness is reflected as Pharaoh being the responsible party for all of man's creations under the influence of *the Thinker* persona. Recall that the tent of the tabernacle is made from goats' hair. The serpent's sense consciousness rules both the conscious and the subconscious and is *'IT.'* The subconscious aspect of the lower chakras that is under the dominion of the four beasts represents *the Wanter* subject to the influence of the serpent persona. Think of Leviathan when these four beasts coalesce to become the Beast of the Sea. This sense of consciousness functions as man's autopilot consciousness, and as such, man remains unaware that it's even there. Because of the testimony of Jesus, the *Lamb* initiates the ascension process the moment the *Lamb takes the book* of the seven seals from the One who sits on the throne. At this point, the hosts in heaven then sing a *new song (Rev 5:9)* honoring the *Lamb 'standing as if slain' (Rev 5:6)* as if he were perfected in Christ and standing in the de facto position to be the second-born of the brethren; having dominion over his own body temple. There is an important distinction being made here: the *Lamb* must *take the book* from our Father God, accentuating that our Father God isn't going to simply hand it to the *Lamb*, for it's the responsibility of the *Lamb* to open the seven seals. It's here that the *Lamb* adopts the belief *from the heart* that his true nature is divine and that he is a son of God *worthy to take the book."*

Dawa continues, "This is also the point that man moves into the position of following the *'Way'* as modelled by the crucifixion and resurrection of Jesus which is the testimony of Jesus. This is reflected by the declaration, *'And they overcame him,'* meaning the beast, *'because of the blood of the Lamb and because of the word of their testimony, and they did not love their life,'* meaning the false-self persona, *'even when faced with death,'* meaning the death of the ego-self', *(Rev 12:11).* After the *Lamb* takes the book the subsequent references to the blood of the *Lamb* represents the *Lamb's* willingness to crucify the false prophet within. Once the heavens are opened, meaning the higher Self has engaged and the process cannot be stopped, the devil is cast to the earth. It's curious to note here that the letter to the fifth church, Sardis, specifically implores the recipients to *'Wake up, and strengthen the things that remain'* and *if you do not wake up, I will come like a thief, and you will not know at what hour I will come to you,* (Rev 3:2,3) for the *Lamb* must be awakened to open the temple of God setting into motion the power of the Christ in heaven."

The Beast of the Earth

Dawa continues, "At this point, the Behemoth, the shaggy male goat with the four horns, is slain, leaving the Beast of Earth to rise with two horns as that of a lamb but speaking like a Dragon. The Ram is now reflected as a naïve double-minded consciousness still unable to wrestle away from the control of the Red Dragon as this beast continues to project the voice of the serpent persona, meaning the sense consciousness still rules. This sense consciousness is ultimately supplanted by the rising Christ consciousness (Rev 19:11-19) as reflected by the marriage of the *Lamb* to his bride, the *new Jerusalem,* the seat of consciousness where *'there is no longer any sea' (Rev 21:1).* The meaning of *'there is no longer any sea'* suggests that the unbridled negative influences flowing from unchecked passions and desires of the astral body, that up to this point has been ruled by sense consciousness, is no longer present. It's here where the enmity between the two natures has been reconciled into one body, meaning the seven Spirits are now opened and fully connecting the lower and higher natures and under the dominion of the throne in heaven. It's here where the last Adam is reunited with Eve, and they become one flesh."

THE PERILS OF BLIND FAITH & NAKED HOPE

Salvation by Declaration – Truth or Myth

Zegula interjects, "Dawa, I'm now beginning to understand the concepts from the sacred texts concerning the heart center and how this wisdom has not been fully developed in man's practice of religion. From what you've described, it's clear that the eyes of the heart must be enlightened for Christ to dwell there, for it's with the heart that man believes (Rom 10:9). The confusion stems from yet another doctrine that misdirects this process into one of being saved by the mere pronouncement of belief. This action may serve to initiate the process of salvation but isn't the same as the *Lamb taking the book*. The *Lamb* must first believe in his divine nature, establishing his worthiness to take the book, signifying that the *Lamb* is prepared to crucify his false ego-self. The implication here is the *Lamb* must be aware of awareness to see the serpent persona running his life in the *natural body* sense, just as Job experienced. I'm afraid that for man to assume this mere pronouncement of faith is sufficient for salvation dismisses the entire experience related to winning the battle within the inner man. This effectively leaves man in his *natural man* persona and vulnerable to his sense consciousness. The self-willed intellect under *the influence of Rome* ceaselessly deceives man into trusting that he believes from the heart, avoiding Armageddon completely. It's here where man has relinquished the power of his own intuition and objectivity in favor of a reliance on a man-made belief system construct. There's another pseudo doctrine that speaks to this dynamic that Paul repeatedly references. Religion has posited that Paul frequently warns the churches from the perils of *falling away*, while I've come to see those warnings from the perspective of the failure of not *following through*. And speaking of falling away I can now see the meaning of the scales falling away from Paul's eyes upon regaining his sight. This signifies the moment the serpent is thrown out of heaven and down to the earth. The scales belong to Leviathan symbolizing the extinguishment of the Leviathan influence."

"Dawa," Zegula inquires, "when I think of Paul prior to his conversion he was a Pharisee and was one of only ten sitting on the Sanhedrin Council. You know that he must have had a front row seat in understanding the stark contrast between the practices surrounding the law of Moses, matters related to the preservation of the soul, with those related to salvation ushered in by Jesus Christ, those matters related to the spiritualization of the soul. I'm thinking that dilemma is also being referenced by Paul when he draws distinctions between the priesthood of Melchizedek, a Levite, and His Christ saying, *'And this is clearer still, if another priest arises according to the likeness of Melchizedek, who has become such not on the basis of a law of physical requirement, but according to the power of an indestructible life,'* *(Heb 7:15,16)*; and, *'For, on the one hand, there is a setting aside of a former commandment because of its weakness and uselessness (for the law made nothing perfect), and on the other hand there is a bringing in of a better hope, through which we draw near to God,'* *(Heb 7:18,19)*. Paul goes on to say, *'For the law appoints man as high priests who are weak, but the word of the oath, which came after the law, appoints a Son, made perfect forever,'* *(Heb 7:28)*. This is a stark distinction as well as a warning. Paul refers to the *law of physical requirement* when describing an attribute of the law which is administered by Levites, the order of the priests. I'm now beginning to imagine that's where the name Leviathan originated, as *'IT'* represents the slavery to things physical in the *natural man; the first of the ways of God.*"

Dawa continues, "Zegula that's an appropriate perspective of the symbolism found there. The depth of deception related to imbedded religious belief systems were just as real then as they are today. Perhaps this is what Jesus meant when He said, *'For I say to you that unless your righteousness surpasses that of the scribes and Pharisees, you will not enter the kingdom of heaven (Matt 5:20)* and then later instructed His followers to; *'Enter through the narrow gate; for the gate is wide and the way is broad that leads to destruction, and there are many who enter through it. For the gate is small and the way is narrow that leads to life, and there are few who find it (Matt 7:13-14).* In the very next verse, He once again warns His followers to; *'Beware of the false prophets, who come to you in sheep's clothing, but inwardly are ravenous wolves (Matt 7:15).* Within the same teaching, Jesus goes on to say; *'Not everyone who says to Me, "Lord, Lord" will enter the kingdom of heaven, but he who does the will of My Father who is in heaven will enter. Many will say to Me on that day, "Lord, Lord, did we not prophesy in Your name, and in Your name cast out demons, and in Your name perform many miracles?" And I will declare to them, "I never knew you; Depart from Me, you who practice lawlessness (Matt 7:21-23).* These teachings correlate directly back to the letter to the church at Laodicea, where it says that you are either hot or cold; *it is what it is,* with being lukewarm as the worst place to be symbolizing the perils of being blind yet say that *'You see'* and being naked to your shame. This is where the man says that he is a Jew but is lying, for he remains a synagogue of Satan; he remains a *natural man* and not a spiritualized man."

Moving Into 'the happening.'

Dawa interjects, "Unfortunately, trusting a belief system that originates from the intellectual mind is just what the serpent persona is seeking to accomplish from establishing an unyielding reliance on these ideological belief system constructs serving to keep man from understanding God's law of the inner man. Understanding the imagery of the various beasts along with the progression of the opening of the seven Spirits may be the key towards the development of a comprehensive strategy for *the happening.*"
"Dawa," Zegula begins, "I'm beginning to picture a connection between the Journey of Saffron, the energy of the Glow, and the redemption of the seven Jewels of Gaia as it relates to the Councils goal of assisting *the one who is greater.* As we suggested, I believe there may be merit in considering a methodology designed to help move mankind towards his salvation by helping *the one who is greater* make the water in the tree of life

alive. From what I have experienced, the power of the Glow should not be underestimated and could be effective in clearing the blocked neural pathways of these energy centers helping to heal the tree of life. Now that we have this understanding of the condition of the collective, we can approach the redemption of the individual inner man in a manner like how we approach the redemption of the seven Jewels of Gaia. What is clear is that the unregenerate man's nervous system is systemically dysregulated and can only be accomplished as he sleeps. But to do that, we must reach the tipping point whereby most of the drops have the Glow, for that is the energy that will flow through mankind towards that end. It's only when the man sleeps, letting down his defenses, can the spiritual centers be restored. It's much too tumultuous when the man is on guard, preparing to react to even the slightest of incursions. Saffron, do you think that this is what *the one who is greater* is asking of the Council? For this kind of solution for this kind of effort?"

"Zegula; Dawa," Saffron begins, "what I believe is that *the one who is greater* has been guiding us through this challenging process all along. Man's tendency to gravitate towards reliance on belief systems and the defense thereof causes me to conclude, as you two already have, our only option is to approach the solution by focusing our efforts on the inner man. It's clear that man will reject any effort that is physically forceful, coercive, or even destructive, as that would only serve to perpetuate the problem by triggering man to react. It's almost amusing to consider that it's in this triggering effect, this agitation, that man seems to be immediately compelled to besmirch a competing belief system versus making any attempt to reevaluate his own. And I do see the intrinsic synergies with your strategy Zegula. I agree with a process that accentuates the inherent strength of the drops while facilitating the fundamental objectives of the Journey of Saffron. In this way, the Council is simply seeking to influence the situation naturally versus making any attempt to overtly manipulate man's behavior through reliance on manufactured external physical events. Once *the happening* begins, all we can do is execute the plan trusting that the ultimate success of the strategy is in the hands of *the one who is greater.* Only our Father God knows how much human suffering is enough."

Dawa responds, "Well, speaking of executing the plan, I think that Zegula has the right thought on how to approach the individual man. Now

Zegula, we've learned that there's a progression of sorts as you consider the strategy on how to approach the seven Spirits. First, we know that man must become aware that he has a dual nature and that he begins in his *natural body* persona. As we've noted, it's possible for a man to remain in his first Spirit, his root chakra, for his entire life, provided that he finds himself quite content with what he needs to survive and thrive. His entire life can be quite absorbed with consuming all manners of self-gratification and pleasures. My guidance would be that your efforts focus exclusively on the first four spiritual centers of the lower self, as *'all the beasts of the field play there' (Job 40:20)*. The Council has determined that it will direct all its resources towards the redemption of the seven Jewels of Gaia with particular emphasis on the first four. The first will be the continent of Asia, as it's characterized by the Red Dragon and is aggressively influencing others. The second will be Africa, as it's characterized by the exploitation of its vast natural resources, including the enslavement of its own people for profit. The third will be Europe, as it's where I see the synagogue of Satan to have originated. The influence of Rome, where political goals and objectives have infiltrated spiritual pursuits in order to maintain power and control. It is the only way to explain why this knowledge has remained hidden. The fourth will be North America, as it serves as the pseudo-heart center of the world, and much like the Babylonian empire brought destruction to Jerusalem, it too has lost its way and become corrupted from influences arising from the first three. The Red Dragon has sought to undermine the political stability of the fourth Jewel while also serving to corrupt its capitalistic-oriented economy. The second Jewel and its relationship with the fourth Jewel have served to create untold amounts of civil unrest and discord that continues into these modern times. The third Jewel has heavily influenced the religious institutions that the fourth Jewel was founded upon with hopes of separating the activities of the church from those of the State. But as we'll see, something has gone terribly awry in this regard. What is clear is that each seeks its own influences over the heart center of Gaia, and now the walls around the fourth Jewel have all but collapsed, allowing these forces to affect their respective manners of chaos from within. It seems that these outside negative forces affecting the fourth Jewel have effectively aligned as a multiplicity of ideologies that are at war with this Jewel's original nature. It has turned into a zero-sum game

Zegula, as there is no longer any room for conversation, for conversation has become meaningless. Instead of a conversation, it seems that both sides of these competing ideologies are seeking power and control, disregarding the art of listening and reconciliation, instead choosing to ramp up the volume and rhetoric. It does appear that man is moving post haste towards creating humanity's own Armageddon. So Zegula, your plan will be our approach to *the happening*, as it appears to be a great inside-out strategy. So long as Mother Gaia sleeps, the Ethereal Council will not rest."

A perplexed Zegula responds, "Dawa, I realize that we must confront these realities in order to affect *the happening*, but I do have a question... how did the fourth Jewel become the heart center of Mother Gaia in such a very short window of time? I mean, it's only been a country for 250 years. I know much has happened with population expansion, the Industrial Revolution, and the Information Revolution all during that timeline, but it does seem to be a bit surreal, don't you think? How did so much change happen so rapidly?" Dawa answers, "Zegula, the fourth Jewel, is specially located on Mother Gaia with two of the largest of Mira's seven seas separating the fourth Jewel from the first Jewel on the western side and from the third Jewel on the eastern side. There were back-to-back World Wars that took place during this time frame. These two wars directly involved most of the humanity located on the first and third Jewel, with each basically representing competing political ideologies. This battle eventually spilt over to include the northern regions of the second Jewel and threatened to eventually engulf the other Jewels if they didn't intervene. The fourth Jewel initially responded by building out an enormous industrial complex to build the war machines necessary for those battling for humanity's freedoms to prevail. Ultimately, even it had to get involved after the first Jewel attacked it. The war ended with the detonation of a new weapon by the fourth Jewel that eerily had the potential to destroy even Mother Gaia. The ensuing period of restoration saw the fourth Jewel obtain a place of dominance and leadership, initiating the period of extremely rapid globalization. This advent of globalization required cooperation amongst the Jewels even though the competing ideologies persisted. This period is only 75 years in the making, but the war between these ideologies has never ceased Zegula; it merely changed in its design. You see, the Information Revolution has practically levelled the battlefield, resulting in the incessant creation of new competing ideologies that are corrupting the fourth Jewel from the inside out. It used to be that humanity would endeavor to act in its best interest, while today, it focused only on retaining power camouflaged as benevolence."

Dawa continues, "Zegula, much has happened in your absence. Government regimes in these times are tenuous at best. Invariably we've seen corrupted governments overthrown by those seeking to deliver more equitable lives for those it serves. Many of these revolutionaries began their quests with noble intentions desiring to create environments that redistributed wealth through these new governments, generally referred to as socialist's philosophies. In order to accomplish this, these new revolutionary leaders would entice the population with promises that if elected, the party in power would continue redistributing the country's wealth to their benefit. Upon learning that they had the power to vote the country's treasury in their favor, the population would become dependent upon this largess, resulting in ever-increasing expectations. The flip side of this equation was the de facto application of increasing financial burdens on those producing the income that was being redistributed. Invariably, the overall production would be downwardly impacted, resulting in fewer resources available for the satisfaction of these increasing expectations. Unmet expectations will always lead to civil unrest, causing those in power to maintain control only through the exercising of that power. Initially, those in power may have had those noble intentions, but they quickly deteriorate in order to maintain them. This quickly digresses into authoritarian-type structures leading to even dictatorships where almost all lose their freedoms. This will ultimately trigger a new revolution of sorts starting the cycle all over again. But with globalization, it's looking like a different outcome is on the horizon. Even though these first four Jewels continue to possess differing ideologies, there does appear to be alignment amongst them to enable the governments in place to remain in control with promises of a new level of global cooperation. The fourth Jewel is moving down this path very quickly, but there's one big departure from historical precedents. The ruling parties are very aware that this is a power play, and they're making very little effort to pretend otherwise. This gets back to the phenomenon of cognitive dissonance. It seems that the barrage of these numerous ideologies has deadened the senses and distracted the population so completely with infighting that the unfoldment of this effort is inevitable. I'm afraid that by the time humanity wakes up to what is going on that the only recourse will be a wholesale revolution, or worse, civil war, and that Zegula will only serve as an opportunity for those in power to take away even more freedoms. Humanity, it seems, is determined to experience its own Armageddon and by its own creation. The *natural man's* attraction to power and control is that blinding."

Dawa continues, "Zegula…we began with asking the question, what has happened with mankind since your encounter with Jesus Christ? What kind of impact has he made on humanity, and why? What we've learned is that His Christ, chose Jesus as His human vessel with which to manifest leaving Jesus Christ as the divine mechanism to show man the *'Way'* to his salvation. This salvation is a journey to the enlightenment of the eyes of the heart, beginning with the *natural body* nature and transitioning into the *spiritual body* nature much in the same way the Buddha taught. What we have chronicled is how far the *natural man* will go to mute and even misdirect the intent of His Christ, compressing the testimony of Jesus into maligned doctrines that serve to steer all of mankind away from understanding God's law of the inner man. We have seen how the kingdom of heaven is truly found within, as reflected in the seven Spirits and the throne in heaven. Man does not remember from where he has fallen and has forgotten that he is fearfully and wonderfully made. In their ignorance, mankind has left its first love and knows not what they do. For now, more than ever, we understand the meaning of the Ethereal Council's creed: *'For the anxious longing of the creation waits eagerly for the revealing of the sons of God. For the creation was subjected to futility, not willingly, but because of Him who subjected it, in the hope that the creation itself also will be set free from its slavery to corruption into the freedom of the glory of the children of God. For we know that the whole creation groans and suffers the pains of childbirth together until now, (Rom 8:19-22).'"

———————————

THE STORY BEHIND THE STORY

The Story You Find Yourself In is devoted to the exploration of the inconvenient questions that arise when we view our stories objectively. Much of whom we see ourselves to be, has been manifested in the stories that ceaselessly ruminate about within our minds and has been arrived at without a great deal of unprejudiced introspection. We really don't know how to do it; how to be honest with ourselves; for the liberation from the emotional burden arising from self-deception is so very sweet and addictive. And admit it, we're lazy. It's not easy to analyze something that you don't understand and to look for something that you can't see. It's much more convenient to stuff such matters into a belief system and forget about it. Align with those doing the same, and there you have peace and harmony in the world of the *natural man,* avoiding the inconvenient questions altogether. But to accept this as your fate as enough is to also accept the oblivion of your ignorance. My hope is that you will expect more from yourself; to challenge yourself; to love yourself enough to *move.*

From Genesis to Revelation is an effort to build a visual bridge from where the pursuit of spirituality and the practice of religion tend to leave you, leading you to a place where you remember from where you've fallen. This bridge serves to deliver you over the abyss and into the *spiritual body* persona to where you are revealed as a son of God, your authentic divine Self as the *Lamb.* For most of us, it's the avoidance of those pesky inconvenient questions and a willingness to challenge your inherited belief systems that are keeping us from the prize. To say it more accurately would be to call out the attachments to the belief systems (politically, religiously, socially, spiritually, culturally, etc.) you adhere to; to recognize the attachments you have to the stories bouncing around in your mind about who you are; to reflect on the attachments related to your conditioning and early programming; and, to acknowledge that you're fearful of feeling the shame and humiliation that surely flows from such introspection. I get it. I know. It's simply how we are made. There's no avoiding the pain.

The Story You Find Yourself In is the name of my first book. It's a harsh unedited documentary of my awakening story where I discovered *'IT'...the Beast within...* working in the shadows of my psyche and where I FOUND my SELF. The mere act of posting it up on Amazon wasn't at all financially motivated as I began that effort targeted solely for the consumption of my three sons. It was designed to be their father's confession of sorts. Upon completion, I arrived at the realization that my early conditioning had created an intense aversion to humiliation and the associated fear response. I became desperate to eradicate that emotional handicap for good and determined that if I could hit that button, causing my book to go live for all to see, well then, there was nothing left to fear. That the deconstruction of my ego-self would be complete. It was the most courageous thing that I've ever done, hitting that *go-live* button. The experience was so thoroughly and profoundly spiritual that I became determined to find the Biblical corollary explanation believing in my heart that it had to be in there. *Genesis to Revelation* is a documentary of what I found, and I must admit that there is always the risk that my level of determination can lead to bias, which can distort one's own objectivity. I get that and have struggled to accept that no matter how diligent I've been in that regard, many will disagree, concluding that I was, in fact, biased in my analysis.

Much of what you see in here developed as I wrote it and reflects a process of investigation and revelatory discovery. For perspective, I had written over 40,000 words before I had the inclination to seriously venture into the Book of Revelation for it's just that intimidating. I did not have any prior experience with this book of the Bible, nor did I adhere to the traditional approach taken by mainstream Christianity regarding its literal meaning. But I was compelled to go there, and there I went, resulting in a substantial rewrite and adding months to the project. Given the variety of interpretations being bantered about, I had no idea that I would discover a thread that would connect so completely with my personal experience.

Irrespective of the pain and vulnerability that's on full display in *The Story You Find Yourself In*, I realize that what I've written will be met with vitriol and venom from mainstream religion. All I can say about that is to hope that in the process of defending doctrines and belief systems, some of those folks will welcome the opportunity to be introspective before they respond. I can make the above comments from a place of honesty, as I was once a fervent religious practitioner. As a Deacon for a very conservative Christian denomination, I taught an adult Bible class and was approached to become an Elder at 41 years of age. I was in deep, and then my life imploded and I self-destructed. If I put myself back into that mindset while reading these two books, I don't know how I would react. I use the word *react* with intention, as that's what I would expect from most religious-minded folks and probably what I would expect from my younger Self. So just know that I've done my best with this effort and that we have the latitude to disagree civilly.

To that end, I've decided to lift out key moments from The Story You Find Yourself In and include them here in The Story Behind the Story, recognizing that there are those without the means or motivation to make an additional purchase. What you're going to see first are the first few pages of the book marking the moment that I saw my *'IT.'* I had determined to chronicle every step of this experience and determined to drop in the actual unedited journal entries that I wrote while practicing my meditation. These experiences are intense and profound, serving to guide me through the process of writing *From Genesis to Revelation*. It's very difficult to describe the feeling of being awakened in the middle of the night by a dream or out of deep meditation, feeling absolutely compelled to write down what you've just witnessed, and then experiencing the feeling of awe and inspiration as you pick-up that thought and follow it through to a revelation that was totally out of the left field. I promised God that if he were to show me something, anything, I would track it down with doggedness and determination until the purpose was revealed. Although I stand emotionally exhausted from this process, I have never been left empty-handed. The answer is always there, at least the answer designed for me and my search.

This first segment signifies the opening of the fifth chakra, or the fifth Spirit, before the throne. It's here where the *'other'* and *'IT'* are forced to acknowledge their mutual existence with this *'other'* symbolized as the *Lamb* from the prophecy. This event is further symbolized by what Jesus said to the blind man; *'Both of You have seen Me,'* as it's also the moment that *'IT'* realizes that its time is short, becoming the overt destructive adversary. It's at this point where *'IT'* stops the pretense that it is acting in your best interest and determines that going nuclear is warranted, as mutual destruction is better than facing the humiliation of being crucified alone. This is where The Story You Find Yourself In begins, after the opening of the first four chakras. Part Two of The Story You Find Yourself In will look at the carnage that ensued during my mid-life leading me to this place. I can't help but think of Job as my mind goes back to the stubbornness of those days. That will surely be a difficult book to write.

------------ ⁃⊷⊶⁃ ------------

(from pages 1-5 in The Story You Find Yourself In)

My Personal Story: What's happening to ME?

Suicide consumed my thoughts" *to die would be welcomed,"* I said to Tom to begin the phone conversation. After briefly explaining what had happened over the weekend, we agreed to meet the usual the next day. We both knew that this conversation would be different from the others we've had over the last 18 years working together. These one-on-one lunch meetings were traditionally entirely personal; as my corporate attorney and business partner, we avoided business talk at these lunches. Although the topic was somewhat familiar, the situation had evolved to a level of seriousness neither had anticipated.

These lunches have become just about the only guy time I get with a man close to the same age group, much less with the same spiritual orientation. I'm thankful for Tom; he's a rock for me, and I have cherished these conversations. These impromptu meetings began around the time of the failure of my 30-year marriage and intensified after the costly cessation of one of the business initiatives we were both involved with. Unfortunately, they've become very heavy, crisis-oriented, and one-sided. I was troubled, very troubledly, and we couldn't quite agree on the totality of what was happening. Over the last several years, Tom had been using the analogy that I may leave God no choice but to whack me with a 2x4 to get my attention. I would then kind of laugh it off and counter with, "I'm doing a fine enough job of whacking myself; don't think I need God to be whacking any deeper." I had been experiencing an intense struggle within, and while I felt it was with something within my own psyche, Tom would suggest that it may be Satan, a spiritual attack of sorts to keep me from becoming the "Godly Kingdom" kind of influential person Tom believed was my potential. We would joist around with that thought, but I just could not bring myself to accept that the "Satan" philosophy applied here, nor was it consistent with what it felt like I had been fighting against. This struggle was personal; it was deep, dug in, and emanated from a part of me.

(The events serving as the catalyst for the 2012 ending of my first marriage represented an absolute moral failure on my part. No one deserves to experience that kind of betrayal and to feel that kind of pain, especially her. I've struggled to make sense of my behavior. Perhaps then it was a bit of a karmic backlash when in October 2014, a business partner that I was related to through my second marriage made a malevolent decision that would kill the business initiative that we were partners in and contribute to the loss of my full investment in another related venture. I recall telling Tom on that Monday evening call when I learned of it that it felt like something broke in me. My source of income would completely disappear, along with much of my net worth. So, I'm here now visiting with Tom realizing that my second marriage most likely cannot be sustained, and I'm financially devastated. In a rebound effort, I started a new business venture in 2016 that has consumed all my remaining resources. My back is against the wall, and I'm facing a realization that was totally out of the left field. I'm seeing the source of my confusing nature for the first time, and it's connected to everything that has caused others and my pain and suffering. The depth of the devastation makes me feel like a deadbeat loser. All my credit cards are toast when just several years earlier, they were unused. Additionally, I've borrowed money from my sis and Tom to keep me in the game and this initiative alive. I've become a burden to those I love. Forget any kind of vacation; he has not seen one in years. I'm tired of hearing my own story and have difficulty trusting myself. Fuck it! There's no respite from this

torment. No dignity in sight, I've become what I've feared most; how did I get here? How did I let this happen???)

I finished journaling just in time to hit print and head out. I was teary-eyed all the way there and sat in the parking lot for a bit to gain my composure. As I enter, I look over to our table and see Tom looking down, not at his phone or anything, in particular, just looking down. As I approached the table and started to sit down without looking up, he said," Talk to me; what happened?" I felt my entire torso constrict as I pushed back the tears, and I simply could not talk. My heart hurt, and I was holding my breath to fight back the sob that was desperate to explode out of my chest. I made a slight squeaking sound as I struggled to hold it back. I was too embarrassed to say anything, so I handed Tom the journal entry I had spontaneously and furiously typed out earlier that morning.

Tom nodded his head in a slight manner as he finished reading the entry, and without looking up, he asked, " Tell me what happened over the weekend." I had regained my composure and began explaining that I had another episode while at an out-of-town Mardi Gras event. The group was mostly unfamiliar and, per the usual, much younger. I had once again found myself feeling alone, isolated irrelevant causing the now somewhat familiar switch to "observer" mode. There I become overwhelmed with the awkward feeling that "I don't belong here, I'm not wanted here, I don't want to be here; how do I get out of here." It was only 9:00, but I had to exit. Where *was* she? I made it out to the car and waited for a bit. I said, "Tom, as the feeling of disappointment with myself increased, so did my anger towards the situation that was making me feel this insecurity. It overwhelms me."

We made it back to the house, and once upstairs, the switch was in full swing. It's this feeling that there's the "you" inside watching this other takeover, leaving the "you" inside to become the spectator of your own self-destructive behavior. This time it was as if this "other" in me wanted me to die to get it over with. "What about the boys? How are they going to come to grips with you killing yourself?" The "other" I am mocking her with is "they don't give a shit what happens to me; I'm just an embarrassment to them." I was looking to leave the house, and as I moved around her towards the door to leave, I stumble and fell just outside the opened bedroom door, landing on my left elbow, sending a stinger through my already injured left shoulder (I've already have had six surgeries on this one shoulder needing a seventh…16 orthopedic surgeries overall) that thankfully shut-down the episode. The following morning it felt like I had shattered into a million pieces, wondering what remained of me to work with and whether I and "we" could recover from this experience. Based on what I had recently discovered, we discussed the merits of whether I should even try to make it work. Tom put his head in his hands, rubbed over his entire face a couple of times, and just shook his head.

It's a hard thing to peg, which of the last six years has been the most difficult. They each have presented a uniqueness that can trump the other. But 2018 took me through an emotional tornado. One of the business partners involved in the venture that began in 2016, a 20-plus year friendly relationship, made a move to take control of the initiative and sell it to a party affiliated with one of his fellow political connections. The drama ended in his resignation in October 2018 after I threatened to serve up a 16-page 60 Exhibit Injunction against him and his cohorts. During this six-month-long battle, I saw a behavior emanating from my long-time buddy that I could not have imagined. My other partners were insistent that the man was a narcissist and pathological. These were terms that I was vaguely familiar with but had never truly studied or understood. But now I needed to know what I was up against and went in for a deep dive on these topics, for I had been experiencing an entirely different person than I had known for 20-plus years. Sure enough, my buddy fit almost every aspect of a narcissist's false facade, and yes, I had been experiencing each of the tactics associated with how they interact. That's when I learned what gas lighting, projection, triangulation, dog-whistling, crazy-making, the discard, and yes, those damned ol' "flying monkeys" meant. It's a relentless onslaught of energy that refuses to yield, combined with a complete lack of empathy for the carnage that's being caused.

On the other hand, I rarely found a forum for discussion on narcissism that didn't also reference codependency. The findings from this exploration seemed to suggest that both forms of dysfunction originate from very similar family dynamics. The descriptions eerily seemed to fit with my life. I became enthralled with the Quora forum about narcissism and was drawn to "@the.holistic.psychologist" on Instagram as it related to understanding codependency. It appeared as if Dr. LePera was living through a similar story that I had unexpectedly found myself in. Going into 2019, I'm learning that I'm suffering from one or the other of these personality disorders. My biggest hint that I'm not a narcissist is that I've attracted several of them into my life, which would suggest that I'm codependent. Following this lunch meeting with Tom, I would pursue a new suspicion regarding my current relationship. I asked that, given the challenges that she faced in her childhood, what would be the most notable takeaway regarding how she had been impacted? The response was, "I don't have empathy, and I don't want to have to feel what you're feeling." This was the game changer, the realization that I was in the classic, now intimately, give-and-take relationship between the narcissist and the codependent. I took the journal entry that I had presented to Tom and modified it to fit this new revelation.

Journal entry January 30, 2019:

"I began research on EGO Death after the MG Ball on the 19th. My thoughts began with "Deconstructing the Beast," and it led me there. I've now begun to focus on the Ego and what happens when you begin to observe "IT's" behavior. I'm experiencing this internal conflict between "IT" and something else, the "other" part of me that's observing "IT." This is new and unsettling as I'm not sure who the "other" really is. I want to begin to learn how to define what this Beast is, what triggers "IT", and to be able to recognize its behaviors when "IT" shows up." I've also learned that the "other" is real and needs to be defined.

What is the Beast?

"Until recently, I wasn't sure what the Beast represented. I was starting to think of it as a sort of personality disorder that was worsening. For most of my life, I wasn't aware that there was such a thing as a Beast or that I was afflicted in any way by some obscure subconscious issue. However, two distinct patterns have emerged, and they are absolutely related. First are my "episodes" that occur when I've been drinking heavily combined with some trigger that makes me aware of my insecurities. Second is the recently increasing noise/static in my mind and this feeling of a presence just beneath the surface raging, yes

raging, around my thoughts; whatever it is, it's pissed off. It's always hovering around these days, whereas I was completely oblivious to it before."

What triggers the Beast?

- *"The Beast needs to be fed. I've been removed from my sphere of influence and comfort, and IT's hungry. There was a definitive point at which my career began to spiral downward, and that's the trigger that set things in motion.*
- *The Beast resents that I've entertained the idea that I may be codependent. It views that as a weakness. It has been protecting me from those feelings of inadequacy.*
- *In my mentally sober times, meaning the lack of distractions, I'm excited about the changes that are occurring and shocked at my behavior when I lose control. I like who I am becoming and abhor many of the characteristics I have and continue to shed.*
- *This Beast is further being starved by the lack of the other sources of fuel that were commonplace for me. The abundance of friends that appreciated me, career success that seemed to come easily, a model family unit that it could be proud of, the joy of winning, financial freedom, etc.*
- *The Beast demands that I stop observing IT. That's the biggest trigger when I'm trying to find and observe IT. Becoming conscious of what I'm doing and how I react to other triggers.*
- *It knows that I've been getting closer to figuring out its pattern and behavior's and has ramped up the efforts to "win" because that's what we used to do frequently. It is begging me to let it take us back to a place of success and winning if I'd only let it. It could start winning again, and Stu would go back to being oblivious and content. It promises me that those things will happen once again."*

"The second condition mentioned above is this IT is constantly hovering around now. It's the Beast willing to be revealed out of desperation. Because of my need to be loved, I failed to sabotage the relationship in a covert style. Now its intention is, or was, to convince me that I had some sort of personality disorder originating from my childhood and that I needed to focus on trying to unwind all of that. The Beast is pulling out all the stops in order to distract me away from IT.

Actually, IT doesn't really want me to commit suicide if there's even a vestige of hope that these efforts could be successful because IT doesn't want to die. It wants to hang around because it can do more destructive things with me if I'd only let it have control back. It is petrified that I could somehow become successful without IT getting the credit and the glory. IT wants me to become successful and allow it to parade us around together and feel good again without me recognizing the systemic dysfunction in my psyche. It is like saying you're okay let me take control."

"I can see IT now. I know what IT feels like and smells like. My number one goal is to remove all sources of fuel required for IT to exist. It has already shrunk from this four-legged Rhinoceros-sized mangy Beast to nothing more than a distant shriek as it tries to hide from me. But IT will be back again and again and again. IT will never disappear because under my control, with God's foot on its throat, I know that I need my ego. I like who I am, and with proper care and nurturing, my ego will become compliant and helpful. I don't mind being a winner; in fact, I kind of prefer that to thrash about. It's just very different when it's not the Beast running the show. I must learn a new way of thinking this through."

Music has always been a refuge for me, particularly when I'm attempting to reconcile matters of the heart with that pesky thing we call reality. The song "One Last Breath" by Creed fits the heaviness of the moment: https://www.youtube.com/watch?v=5vNJwR2vVOk: The first verse is as follows:

"Please come now. I think I'm falling
I'm holding on to all I think is safe
It seems I found the road to nowhere
And I'm trying to escape
I yelled back when I heard thunder
But I'm down to one last breath
And with it, let me say
Let me say

Hold me now
I'm six feet from the edge, and I'm thinking
Maybe six feet
Ain't so far down."

Suicidal thoughts? As I described in this vision there was something within me that wanted something in me to die, and I thought that *'IT' was me*. Why did this *'other'* presence want me to die? I've struggled with that thought mightily and it is what partly drove me to write this book, for I found the answer as I wrote it. I now know what was taking place front and center in my frenetic mind. The *Lamb* appeared and most certainly intended to kill the false prophet of my psyche and in this noise the battle of Armageddon was raging. In not being aware for what was taking place I sincerely thought that I was losing my mind. As it turns out, I was. *'IT'* must die to make way for the *Lamb* to ascend the throne displacing the false prophet from his pretentious claim that the spiritualization process is complete. There's a curious reference to this dynamic in Revelation as the torment raged. *'And in those days men will seek death and will not find it; they will long to die, and death flees them,' (Rev 9:6)*. I felt that.

The consequence of this scene is further magnified in the second chapter of 2 Thessalonians with the warning that even though *the day of the Lord has come* those in the faith must comprehend the truth regarding the process of being saved from this imposter. *'Let no one in any way deceive you, for **it will not come** unless the apostasy comes first, and the man of lawlessness is revealed, the son of destruction, who opposes and exalts himself above every so-called god or object of worship, so that he takes his seat in the temple of God, displaying himself as being God,' (2 Thess 2:3-4)*. Once again this is an affair of the inner man as your body tabernacle is the temple of God. We are alerted that to project this to be an event to occur outside of yourself is the ultimate deception of the evil one and what keeps you in darkness. It's here where the form of the world as you've been conditioned to see it will fall away, releasing you from bondage to the illusion that it is. Our Father God created us for this purpose and designed this experience with miraculous precision towards this end. Trust the process and you'll resurrect into your true divine nature, for that is *the promise*.

Perhaps it would be helpful to circle back around to the concepts of the tree of the knowledge of good and evil and the tree of life for a visual of the demarcation line when your body tabernacle transitions into you body temple. Recall that both trees are in the midst of the garden suggesting that they are referencing two natures of the same tree as only one tree can be in the middle. Think of the one that we experience first correlating with our time immersed in our natural body persona's. It's here where we learn that our knowledge of good and evil unfolds from our lower selves while our divinity is veiled and protected within the internal ark of the covenant. This represents our *Cain* nature's. Upon our awakening we transition into the body temple laying claim to the tree of life which is second and the fulfillment of *the promise*. This represents our *Able* nature's.

This next segment will be from the middle of my awakening story and will center on the practice of meditation. Just for reference's sake, the time period for this experience lasted about four to six months, beginning in January 2019. During this period, I became hyper-vigilant about documenting my thoughts and visions. Although I attribute much of this progress to meditation, I honestly have trouble fully discerning what revelations appeared through *working through a thought process* or just letting them come to me. Meditation was a tricky thing to navigate at the beginning, and now I've come to realize that much of what was revealed was a byproduct of my abject isolation. I wanted to be alone, and I was all alone. So, there were periods when I felt that I was in constant meditation as I had nothing to distract me. But it didn't start out like that, nor is it practical for most people to check out as I did, for to do so does come at a price.

I've never studied meditation. I'd also never given the concepts of awakening or enlightenment a second thought. My first attempt at meditating was one out of desperation, with me screaming into my mind wishing for the noise to stop. I recall the first time that I made a sincere effort to observe my thoughts; it may have endured for 5 to 10 seconds with that brief moment feeling like a long time. It was as if my mind would switch off while the thoughts would come flooding back in. I'd sort of snap back and give it another go. It would feel as if the window shades would be pulled down suddenly, and the lights would go out like a switch. It took me quite some time to learn how to push the thoughts out far enough to get that space to even begin observing. Even after I had gained some level of mastery of clearing my mind there were those days that it would all cave in and thoughts of death would return. My breakthrough would come on the evening of April 8th when the wall first appeared, and *'IT'* was finally exiled to the periphery.

(from pages 44-47 in The Story You Find Yourself In)

My Dad was my Touchstone: Working through the Confusion

Over the weekend, most of my thoughts and journaling centered on trying to find a proper perspective on my relationship with my father. Reconciling these early childhood experiences with my adult behavior seemed to be yet another form of rationalization and deflection. This was not how I would characterize our "adult" relationship. Was I unjustly abdicating responsibility for these unpleasant outcomes by acknowledging these feelings? As an adult, the opinion of my dad was the only third-party figure that mattered to me. He was clearly my touchstone where I would go to get validation. I knew it and recognized it. However, in hindsight, I now realize that I've never had that independent internal mechanism that would permit me to measure myself against my own goals and expectations. Conversely, this helped to explain why I did not have that internal compass that could regulate my instinctive, impulsive, and risky decision-making. *Right? If I'm unaware that I'm subconsciously looking to satisfy the expectations of another,* **not even knowing what that expressly looks like,** *then it only stands to reason that I'm not adhering to a methodical decision-making process regarding what I'm going to do secure that validation.* Was this yet another manifestation of my newly realized codependent nature? When I overlay this revelation on top of my life's progression, a pattern begins to emerge. I can see now that there were opportunities to learn some very powerful lessons in more friendly, productive environments that would not have led to this much pain. Missing those earlier opportunities led me down a path of having to repeat the lesson in more hostile predicaments, resulting in experiencing more fear, which led to more resistance, which led to self-destructive outcomes ***if only I had been paying attention.***

That thought right there is the paradox for many of us. ***If only I had been paying attention,*** then I could've made better decisions. However, the reality is that many of us aren't even aware that we're functioning out of this pre-programmed ego-self mindset, which could be analogous to an embedded software subroutine that you forget is even there. Confronting that deep feeling of shame after you've disappointed yourself or others, without fully understanding the origin of this deep shame, leaves you bouncing back and forth between beating yourself up and looking to blame somebody else. So much of this struggle is baked into our psyche through our conditioning, and until you've fully worked through it, your ego-self will go into extreme modes. It's bizarre to visualize how *"IT"* can sit high on a throne in your psyche, and it either dispenses blame in a defensive tirade towards a third party or sidesteps responsibility for the consequences of self-destructive behaviors. There is that internal component in each of us that will make you a slave to your mistakes while *"IT"* avoids detection.

My dad did not have a substantial relationship with any of my other three brothers; at least, I never witnessed them. Our relationship had always been a bit different as he allowed me latitude and freedoms that he didn't the others. For instance, pretty much the day that I got my driver's license, he allowed me to trailer the boat and take it out into Lake Huron unsupervised, and I was on the lake with every free moment I had. As an adult, he was always interested in the progression of my business career, and we would sit for hours discussing the business world. My dad was also a golfer, and I was the only son that took up the game in earnest. One of my favorite times of the year was Thanksgiving. We had a standing golf match the Wednesday before. My mom would always have a big pot of red beans, Andouille sausage, and rice ready, and after scarfing down a bowl or two, dad and I would head down to the course loaded up with an ample supply of cold beers. Those are great memories, for sure.

My mom passed in 2006 in the aftermath of Hurricane Rita; the eye came right over our Orange, TX, childhood home. She was in poor health and deteriorated from there. The change in my dad was quite remarkable. He relaxed. His intensity dropped a few octaves, and he seemed to enjoy his time alone. He ended up with several "girlfriends" (I say that amusingly as he was, I guess, around 75 at the time), and he looked forward to my visits. However, my work life took a turn for the worse during the mortgage crisis of the Great Recession. Sadly, the frequency of my visits faded. For other more personal reasons, my marriage was also in peril (Part 2 story). So, when I met the ambulance at St Luke's in July 2011, in Houston, after my dad suffered a massive stroke, I felt something give. He ended up living in an assisted living facility until his passing in early 2016. The last time that I had visited dad, three weeks prior to his stroke, we played 18 holes on a Thursday afternoon and 36 the following day, which was quite an accomplishment for an elderly man. We headed over to the casinos in Lake Charles that night and had a grand time. I recall him getting upset during that final round on Friday, and I said to him jokingly," Hey, dad, just chill, drink a beer and enjoy watching your son kick your ass; you never know when or if we're going to have a chance to play again." I ended up playing the best round ever, with him scoring a 72 with a birdie on the par five 18th. He was so proud. It would be the last time we would play. I recall him tearing up as I left that Saturday, and that made me tear up as well. We hugged, and we never had another comprehensible conversation. Didn't realize then how much I was going to miss him.

I became an emotional wreck with every trip to visit him in assisted living; he couldn't have a conversation, and I could tell how frustrated he was with not being able to visit with me. I would cry just about the entire way back as I drove west down I10. As my sister told me just the other day, Stu, you really started to spin out when dad had his stroke. I agreed almost to the day. I had lost my touchstone, the person whose opinion was the only one that mattered. Unwinding from this, it turns out it would take me almost 10 years to understand.

5:30 am Monday, April 8th:

Woke up & decided to lie back down to meditate. I was able to quickly push out all my thoughts to a considerable periphery making space.

I then focused on just me w/o the illusory self-baggage & noticed that she was not within the periphery where I had always allowed her to stay. This time she was outside of the periphery & not even in a significant way & it was as if she were moving away further and further out

The "discussion" that ensued was, "she's not in here, Stu; this is only you with all else in the universe connected to the Father as you are of the Father. You don't have to feel that pain unless you choose to. It was necessary for you to arrive here. She's not ready for this journey; she can't be a part of your next chapter. You two are moving in different directions

8:17 pm Monday, April 8ᵗʰ:

Started looking back over the January 23ʳᵈ Journal entry. I read the last paragraph of page 1 and the first paragraph of page 2 = IT didn't reconcile with what I've come to know to be true. In one instance, it confirmed the lie that I had bought into & why IT was exhibiting aggressive behavior. I was actually being pulled into an abyss where my identity was being consumed. That's the codependent nature when matched up with the narcissist counter partner. It's why I was becoming suicidal & that's where this process wanted to take me. Helps to explain why she refused to talk about my subsequent efforts to work thru it & instead cast indifference and invalidation on it. Suggesting that I was "making up" my own narrative to justify these episodes = making me feel even crazier," yet I persisted" through it, and I get to declare that I am not crazy

Whew, glad getting that out is behind me. I've been stuck here for several weeks, trying to get the courage to sit down and deal with it. It goes without saying that I had never experienced anything like this. If a person does ever experience something like this, it will only happen once and will always be something they haven't been through before. As difficult as it is for me to reveal these private moments, there's still so much that's being left unsaid. The truth of the matter is that even though I had experienced a breakthrough and had gained some clarity, I was still very much a broken man. I still didn't fully understand codependency and how that could possibly be me; it sounds so weak, right? I felt embarrassed about it. I wasn't finished reconciling how all of this happened and remained quite bitter at some deep level. Then the reality check, I'm living in my buddy's home; my startup company remains unfunded and tenuous; I have yet to move out fully; I'm alone, needing to still get through a divorce, and I'm flat-busted. How do I do this? Can I do this? Do I even want to deal with this? I'm in full humiliation management mode, and in the midst of a full-grown emotional meltdown, death still sounds like an easy way out. Those harmful thoughts alarmed me, and I immediately gave Tom a call. Tom would remind me of the need to observe my thoughts and, through discernment, determine the source. Monday the 8ᵗʰ ended with me going back into meditation to attempt to corral these thoughts and find perspective. The song "Child of Mine" by Jaci Velasquez has been a go-to for me for a number of years: https://www.youtube.com/watch?v=eN-i7u1QVmg: The key verse follows:

"You were made
In a beautiful way
Born to be holy
And sure of your faith
Something inside you
Has led you astray
Now you're locked in a struggle
And it won't go away

I know you have been
Down on your knees
I saw you cryin' for mercy
Well, how can I help
When you're still holdin' on
To somethin' more precious than me."

(from pages 69-70 of The Story You Find Yourself In)

My Personal Story: Learning to Trust Yourself

It's strange being a grown man living in someone else's home. I have been living inside the 610 Loop for the last 6+ years, but I am very familiar with the area where Larry has his home. I used to live a little further north and worked in this area. Two of my previous businesses are located within 3 miles of his home, and at one point, I had my TPP office around the corner from here. The area has declined quite a bit since he built the house almost 30 years ago. My truck was broken into four separate times before I left the area after the sale of one of these companies in December 2014. At the time, it was THE place to live in the northwest part of Houston. You can easily walk to Champions Golf Club from his house, one of the highest-rated courses in the state, with the most recent LPGA Women's Open played there. It's a nice place with the back of the kitchen looking out on a comfortable courtyard-styled backyard. The kitchen has a large island with a window bar facing into the game room. The game room set-up is pretty sweet, with a first-rate pool table, dartboard, big screen, and 10 guitars lining the walls. I've occupied the back left upstairs bedroom with an on-suite bathroom. It's a nice size and more than adequate. There's a small desk with wheels and a stool next to the window that I use for my journal writing. Larry's office is set up in the bedroom next to mine, and he's routinely working in there until midnight when he's in town. It's not unusual for us to carry on conversations through the wall.

Larry's family business is a bakery that was started by his daughter while attending UT in Austin. It's named after his daughter, and all of Larry's family is involved. His wife, Rhonda, handles purchasing, and his two boys help out in a number of capacities. Larry's an easygoing guy with a "Hey Man" greeting for everyone he meets. That's his nickname amongst his oilfield buddies "Hey Man." I met Larry back in 2002 when I was putting together the second of my TPP oilfield buy-and-build initiatives. We ended up making four purchases, and he was one of those companies. I was the CEO for a time, and Larry ended up as the President when the company sold to another larger oilfield consolidator, which is also located nearby. He's always been an entrepreneur and independent. Like many of us, he's had some great years mixed with lean ones. So, it's an odd combination now to see him running a bakery in Austin. He has quite the story that you'll see more of as mine develops.

I'm looking forward to seeing him later this week. This isolation and alone time are not my jam. He's coming back into town to help me move my stuff out on Thursday. Crazy for me to even attempt to imagine how fast this is happening. Thankful for Tom, I don't need anybody else to know just how close I am to spinning out. My mind is fried in need of some peace. As I get ready to go down for the night, I enter into a moment of meditation, and this was my journal entry from that evening.

11:35 pm Monday 8ᵗʰ:

Visual of the gate around my mind w/ heavenly hosts warriors guarding the periphery

Satan futilely works to get over the Sentries/wall & they all take one unified step forward & it shakes the Heavens = Satan <u>exits</u>

Notes from the following morning's Tuesday 9th journal entry:

I had become fairly efficient at pushing out my thoughts far enough to become an observer of those thoughts that appeared. I'd even started to identify my ego part the noisemaker named him Peter even. I had learned to exile him to the right side of my mind during meditation, never forcing him outside, for I had attempted to befriend him as part of reintegration. But I had asked for protection the soldiers were massive and stretched out endlessly from horizon to horizon, standing shoulder to shoulder with shields covering from the neck to the ground touching the shields to the right and to the left, holding a massive spear in on hand and the shield in the other. Dressed in Roman soldier-style armor. When they stepped forward, they raised the shields in precise unison and slammed them to the ground with a flash like lightning and the sound of thunder. It was amazing. And my nemesis Satan, standing outside of the perimeter, looked familiar, like it may have been my Peter, my "IT?"

(NOTE: This visual has stayed with me ever since and reappears from time to time during my meditations. It would, however, take on an expanded meaning a year and a half later once I started connecting the dots.)

Over the week, my journal reflects one big, conflicted conversation with myself. I was learning that my friends had missed me and expressed how concerned they've been for me. It hurt to hear the honesty of how each observed the confident Stu wilting as our interactions faded to nothing. It happened gradually, but there came a moment when I realized that I had become dependent solely upon her friend group. In hindsight, it's not hard to see what and how it happened. That's where my newly discovered codependent nature revealed itself most abruptly and how I had been progressively giving up control of my life. It had been an unhealthy, mutually parasitic relationship destined to end with me experiencing this kind of confusion. That "trauma bond" stuff is for real. It's like I was being pulled apart inside out. Conflicted or not, healing was priority number one, and it couldn't have happened to stay there. I had to find Stu and get him back. Larry drove in from Austin on Wednesday, and we made it over to my place Thursday morning with movers. We moved my things into his garage, believing that it was going to be a short-lived stay. We wrapped up the move, enjoying an awkward laugh about it, and then went out for a couple of beers.

(from page 92 in The Story You Find Yourself In)

(Back to the beginning of the chapter and from my journal – **11:35 pm Monday 8ᵗʰ***)*

"In my moment of despair, I retreated into meditation and simply could not create any space. My thoughts were crashing into other thoughts, with those breaking into even more thoughts endlessly, ricocheting about. All I could pray for was space, some quiet. I started by trying to visualize a line, kind of like the edges to clouds, to serve as a target of sorts, to then push these thoughts one by one to the other side. Then the wall appeared, and then the soldiers beyond the wall formed. As the line formed, these massive soldiers stretched from horizon to horizon. And when they moved in unison pushing back the thoughts, the lightning and the thunder shook the heavens, and all became quiet."

That's your heart center, the wall that guards your heart. That's Nehemiah's rebuilt wall around Jerusalem. That's where you meet with God, and he meets with you. It's in meditation; contemplative meditation. He will meet you there without fail. But there is that nemesis always. We will get to him next because we can't have this extraordinary experience without *"IT."*

The Story You Find Yourself In finished with a visual that I had regarding my *Dark Night of the Soul* experience. For the record, finishing this effort marks the end of my three plus-yearlong sojourns through that *Dark Night*, as it does take some time to reorient yourself as you emerge from the illusion and learn how to trust yourself again. What's peculiar here is that the Apostle Paul took a three-yearlong sojourn after his miraculous conversion, and I imagine that its symbolism reflects Paul's own version of the Dark Night of the Soul. This period of adjustment and reorientation is difficult when you emerge transformed. I imagine that's the symbolism found in the post resurrection appearances of Jesus as well, when His own disciples knew it was Him but didn't recognize Him.

(from pages 131-133 in The Story You Find Yourself In)

My Personal Story (cont.): Dark Night of the Soul: Seeking Closure

The evolution of the soul, even though liberating and necessary for realizing the ultimate goal of salvation, is a disruptive process requiring a transformation of the mind. During this period of adjustment, the psyche will continue to seek the familiar and resist this new state of awareness. There are times that are downright euphoric when you get to catch your breath with thoughts of "I've made it through." Then there are those times of abject feelings of depression where all you want is to be alone and for it to be over. It truly is the *Dark Night of the Soul* that simply requires perseverance on your part and understanding from those that love and care about you. The song "Dark Night of the Soul" by Van Morrison captures that *feeling* for me. https://www.youtube.com/watch?v=1GqszEwXPlc. One set of lyrics goes like this:

> *"Sitting here, but I didn't plan it this way*
> *Well, the plans of mice and men have gone astray*
> *Now I'm standing on the landing*
> *I'm looking for a brand-new day."*

The Holiday Seasons have been especially challenging since 2013. Much of this history will be covered in Part 2 to follow but approaching the end of 2020, and I'm in the midst of perhaps the most difficult of them all. I'm still living in LC's place and head out when his family congregates for their holiday celebrations. It's awkward even though they've been exceptionally loving and mindful of my situation. Most times, I trade places and stay in their Austin apartment while they are in Houston. I'll be moving out after the New Year. As Thanksgiving approached, I was nearing the end of writing "The Story You Find Yourself In – Part 1" and felt a sense of anxiousness to complete it so I could deliver it to my boys before Christmas…that was my original goal. It's been a strange year for everybody considering the resurgent COVID – 19 restrictions and our politically polarized environment. There hasn't been a great deal of communication with anyone, as I'm feeling numbed by it all, and I found myself with no Thanksgiving Day plans. I've been nonresponsive to those that do reach out and find myself avoiding any socially interactive setting, totally protecting my own energy. This was telling me that I was still navigating through my *Dark Night of the Soul* even though I felt like I was close to the end. It's a strange feeling, for sure, considering how socially active I once was. I'm just not ready, but I understand that I must learn how to exist in this world, seeing things so differently.

It's not yet comfortable moving about and feeling the things that I'm observing. The clarity of seeing how superficially my former self moved through life has caused me to unintentionally pick up on the pain others are experiencing as they deal with reality. I wished it weren't so. On the other hand, it's very rare to find someone that can comprehend what I'm going through without sounding like I've lost my mind. Perhaps I have only time that will tell. What is true for me is I see things through another lens…one that has expanded my periphery view of what's going on around me like I'm looking through a magnifying glass. I can "*not*" see it. It's another form of torment to see and feel the pain and anguish that this society has produced, so I avoid it for now.

So now I find myself driving west to Austin on the Wednesday before Thanksgiving 2020 while thinking that I sure do miss the traditional drive east to Orange for red beans and a golf match with my dad. I'm wiping the tears from my face as I listen to Van Morrison's *"Dark Night of the Soul"* and check out my phone. I noticed a new Instagram posting from Dr. Nicole LePera (@the.holistic.psychologist) about her *Dark Night of the Soul* experience. It was a surreal moment as this was going to be the last section of Part 1, and what I had planned on penning while in Austin over Thanksgiving synchronicity. Her work has been instrumental in helping with my own healing process. One of the objectives of this effort is to unwind my own religious conditioning while homing in on what my reconstructed belief system was going to look like. It's a dicey proposition for a licensed psychologist to venture into this area, and I wanted to find that interconnect that may help others answer their own questions regarding the Bible and "spirituality." As I've said earlier, I'm not viewing this as an exercise that's made me more spiritual, but instead a process of unlearning the conditioning that has hidden from me the true nature of *Who I Am*. The weather was beautiful on Thanksgiving Day, and I headed down to my favorite spot-on, Lake Travis, to write this section. What follows is some of what came to me as I was sitting on my tailgate listening to Spotify's Van Morrison Radio station, drinking some cold beverages while looking out over a serene Lake Travis. I start to ponder and write the following:

"*Have you ever seen a turtle flipped over on the back side of its shell? Its long neck outstretched and those stubby legs flailing about looking for the familiar ground? Just looking for something to connect with to get the right side up? Observing that predicament, you wonder about the futility of how that little buddy could ever flip over without some help. All the while, you're thinking, how did you get like this in the first place? Then you reach down and give it a slight nudge expecting it to scurry off right away. But it doesn't nope; it just stays there for a long moment gaining its bearings, I suppose. You can imagine it sitting there contemplating the same thing as you; what just happened? How did I end up on my back? How can I see to it to never being that vulnerable again? I reckon how long that moment can last depends on just how disoriented you are. How long was that little guy on his back? Then it takes that first step not sure if it can trust if you're not going to flip it back over. Then it starts to move on, never to forget that experience.*"

"*Losing your own narrative is like that. It's unsettling. Relearning how to trust yourself in relationships when you were conditioned that love was conditional and directly connected to accomplishment and your ability to excel. Even your love for self was a conditional failure, resulting in the form of self-hate. Coming to a resolution on how to reconcile those failures and the struggle to rebuild a reliable foundation when you don't know what that should look or feel like is a confusion that haunts you. It includes some embarrassment, some shame, and some fear. For whom of those that know me can come along aside and truly understand what you're going through? Who can you share this with? Then deep down, you're realizing that your life has fundamentally changed. You see things upside down from where you once were. You realize that it's not all that safe to share it. It's lonely. It's a quiet journey other than what's going on inside your mind. It's flipped over on its back, fighting for that something familiar. You wish*" *for it to stop, but you know that's not what you want. You want the truth, and that's painful. "Stop…but don't stop" is oscillating between my ears."*

*"Well, Stu, that's awfully dramatic, don't you think? Well, I guess it could be, but boy, oh boy, I was in it deep and am bewildered at how efficiently I was operating, totally unconscious of the workings of these conditioned characteristics. It's like having behind-the-scenes software subroutines running that you've built to never need maintenance. They just keep on processing in a do-loop over and over and over. I've had an onion to peel back, akin to hunting down these many interrelated toxic subroutines embedded behind firewalls. **"IT"** had locked them under layers of coping mechanisms and didn't want me to find them initially for helpful motives and now for selfish reasons. There were lots of internally generated fears and anxieties to contend with along the way. That vulnerability feels so much like humiliation, fumbling around in the dark, trying to run away from it, and that's the fear that manifested and led me to this place. I've come to realize that the purpose of our learning and evolving is designed to address these false fears originating from the natural body and for us to move beyond them.*

*As we are told by Paul, we are sons of God, that there is no place for fear, and that fear is the mechanism the natural body uses to maintain control and keep us from recognizing our true nature, our divine sonship. It's in this context that Paul is telling us that we haven't "adopted a spirit of slavery leading to fear again." I'm emotionally exhausted because of **"IT,"** my natural body's negative energy, and **"IT's"** need for control; the need for the familiar is relentless. Yet the process, once it starts, is unstoppable. You cannot un-see what you've seen. Suppose that's the pursuit of the "Helper," as it's also relentless. It has been intense this internal war. But the "Helper" wins always. That's a truth that I can trust. It will make sure that I don't get flipped back over on my back. That's the Dark Night of the Soul for me. My story, my timing, my journey. Like that turtle, I'm thankful for the help I received from those that love me, for those who helped to get me flipped back over the right side. It couldn't have happened without them. There were those that vanished from sight when the troubles started. I forgive them, knowing that we all got what we bargained for and that we are all right where we are supposed to be or else we would be somewhere else."*

As the song above says, there will be *a brand-new day*. Writing all of this down has been a cathartic experience, and hopefully, there's a nugget or two that a reader can hold onto. **We are all in multiple stories, and there is always someone else who needs you in *theirs*.** The last song I listened to this Thanksgiving Day was an odd one for sure. I must have listened to it 6-8 times back-to-back as the sun was fading. It reminded me of my High School days, living in Canada, at the southern tip of Lake Huron, where it feeds into the St Claire River between Port Huron, Michigan, and Sarnia, Ontario. The big ships would pass through on the way to Detroit and beyond. Edmond Fitzgerald was one of those, and it was bigger than most. While I was living there in Sarnia, it went down on Lake Superior on its way to Cleveland in 1975. Gordon Lightfoot, a Canadian, wrote a song about it. Interestingly, I picked up on an esoteric message in it; imagine that I had to laugh as I was listening to it on repeat. The song describes it as the "pride of the American side," and it was confronted with an unexpected November storm. It was being battered about as the song went on and eventually went under. I could feel that. Here's the link: https://www.youtube.com/watch?v=FA_LR7PgRCk

There's a reframe in it that goes like this:

> **"Does anyone know where the love of God goes**
> **when the waves turn the minutes to hours;**
> **The searchers all say they'd made Whitefish Bay if**
> **they'd put fifteen more miles behind her"**

The message of hope in these lyrics that became my takeaway was that no matter the storm you're in and your situation in life, you can always find a way to make 15 more miles as you have no choice; it's simply *The Story You Find Yourself In*.

Going back to the opening paragraph of *My Story,* I suggested that "suicide" was an option that consumed my thoughts. While we all know that's not the answer, I honestly can't say for certain if it was a mere *passive* thought or an actual potential *action* thought. It was most definitely an unhealthy thought that could only lead to ruin.

"Did you really want to die?" *"No one commits*
suicide because they want to die."
"Then why do they do it?" *"Because they want to stop the pain."*

---- Tiffanie DeBartolo, "How to Kill a Rock Star" ----

Truth be told, after fully reflecting on it, I've concluded that I did actually commit a form of suicide. My self-exiled isolation was my way of exiting. Abject, absolute, extended isolation, an escape to heal to reconstitute a new me. Something had to go to be carved out of me for good, forever. The journey reflected in Part One of The Story You Find Yourself In served to formulate a spiritual foundation as I navigated through the Dark Night of the Soul. The word "enlighten" tends to suggest that this process is a euphoric one, like what the word "nirvana" would suggest. It is not like that.

As I've alluded to above, The Dark Night of the Soul is a process a person will typically experience on the back end of the awakening process, and it can take some time to pass through it. It has been a particularly uncomfortable period for me, and I'm going to attempt to provide some context as to why that has been so. I mentioned that there was a point where my life imploded with much of that strictly of my own doing. I self-destructed largely through the process of self-sabotage. It's in the healing process of deep introspection that a person experiences the Dark Night as it is an attempt to rationalize one's behavior and find the significance behind the pain. When this process happens later in life, society tends to shrug it off as a man recklessly having a mid-life crisis, and from the outside looking in, it is almost stereotypically comical. But no man wants this kind of destruction in his life and the associated collateral damage, as the ones that get hurt are the ones you love the most. It's a very difficult thing to reconcile into and come to peace with. *Part Two* of *The Story You Find Yourself In* will focus on this concept of the mid-life crisis using the second half of my life and the events leading up to my awakening as the foundation. That period of my life is synonymous with opening the first four Spirits before the throne, the lower Self chakras. For now, I think it would be helpful to home in on one thought coming out of my Dark Night that syncs up nicely with *From Genesis to Revelation.*

Ernest Hemingway was asked, *"How did you go bankrupt?"* He responded, *"Two ways. Gradually then suddenly."* The patterns in my life that led to my destruction began decades ago, and they were missed until they weren't. Like playing a game of Jenga, the tower of wooden blocks will eventually crash, spreading out all over the ground, and causing those playing with you to jump out of the way. The *universe* is unrelenting that way, especially for those that sincerely desire to become better humans. To evolve means to learn and grow with lessons placed on repeat until they're learned. I was fortunate enough to have a very dear friend and business partner that witnessed most of the carnage, and thankfully he never left my side. He knew my heart and lamented in my angst. I wouldn't be here but for him. Even though I didn't understand where it was taking me, I stayed on the bus. So, here's the point: I now know who the driver was and is. Some would say it was God, and I'm not dismissing that conceptually, as I do believe that everything ultimately begins and ends there. To put a finer point on it, however, I truly believe that it originated with the *Lamb* within. I wanted to change and the divine within guided me to this place. This has been my personal Job journey, and, in my stubbornness, I needed to be crushed. Now obviously, there's more to it than just that, for I had to first circumnavigate through layers and layers of conditioning and programming that originated from the environment that I was raised in order to find myself and awaken to my true nature. I'm so thankful for the guidance provided from afar by the selfless work of Dr. LePera. I cannot overstate how important it was for me to have found her and the guidance I was unknowingly desperate for.

I had no concept of what awakening, or enlightenment meant when this journey began, and that ignorance cost me dearly, for I literally had to take the beat down, all the way down, before I could see what was going on. It doesn't have to be that painful; at least, I don't think it does. I wrote *From Genesis to Revelation* as the book that I wished I would've had access to before beginning that journey. This book was written in hopes that it will ease the pain of your journey, for having even a tiny bit of awareness of your objective would help to establish healthy expectations. *Genesis to Revelation* was written to address the inconvenient questions that none of us want to ask, especially those of us who have been immersed into an institutionalized religious practice, for it's there that I got stuck. I thought that I was where I was supposed to be, only to discover that I had climbed up the other way and had not opened the narrow gate. So, what's next, you ask? Well, it's the inner work, and it begins with learning how to quiet the mind and observing your thoughts. And if it goes down the same way for you as it did for me, the next thing you'll see is *'IT,'* the source of those thoughts and of the ego-self, the false prophet of the inner man. It's the façade that you project out as the illusory Self into the illusory world that you've unknowingly constructed as your reality. At some point, you'll see these two illusions for what they are. It's both parts kind of cool to see for the first time and yet equally terrifying. It's the beginning of your Dark Night of the Soul, leading you on toward the prize, which is your spiritual salvation. But here's a warning, you really must want this and must be willing to work for it, for it doesn't manifest without effort and some pain.

"There is no coming to consciousness without pain."
C.G. Jung

CLOSING THOUGHTS

Pain? Why is pain necessary and how does it manifest? What does this pain look like? Well, I suppose that depends on you don't you think? But for reference let's take a final look at the story of Job, for in his stubborn patience he certainly endured much pain. Why is that you think? Like most of humanity that is involved with the practice of religion or the pursuit of spirituality we are easily deceived by the enemy within, which is precisely what the story of Job signifies. Job clearly possessed a fertile heart but had unknowingly ascended the throne by climbing up some other way, bypassing the door of the shepherd that Jesus animates for us in John 10. Job relied on his self-willed intellect, loving from the mind while being deceived that he was loving from a regenerate heart. It's so very easy to do as it's precisely how our religious institutions approach salvation, but that is to be expected, as it's also how we're made and nothing to be ashamed of. It's why you see the Lord's admonishment of Job feature the detailed descriptions of the Behemoth and Leviathan immediately preceding Job's admission of his error and repentance, for the Lord reminds Job that He made them and that only He can subdue the beasts of the inner man. Job responds, *'I have heard of You by the hearing of the ear; But now my eye sees You; Therefore I retract And I repent in dust and ashes,' (Job 42:5,6)*. It's here where Job also sees his Behemoth and his Leviathan, and for the eye to see, you must enter through the narrow gate, the door of the shepherd swung open by the power of His Christ. Job is now the *Lamb* that has slain the false prophet within.

So, let's get back to the pain discussion. Job signifies the blind man that says, 'I See' and must become blind again so that he can find the proper 'Way' to the throne in heaven. How far will the Lord go once He determines that your heart is ready? As far as He must. I attribute Job's patience more to a display of sheer stubbornness. Job was deep into the illusion, but he did persevere, and that's enough. However, through the process he felt abject isolation; he felt debilitating shame; he felt total humiliation; he questioned everything that he thought he was as did those around him. It's painful to recognize the truth that who you believed yourself to be was illusory. It's painful to look out on the world knowing that it's a mere simulation designed for the illusory self to explore what it is to know good and evil, knowing that you must find a way to survive and thrive in what's now hostile territory. It's painful when you see the destructive nature of mankind's belief systems and ideologies knowing that even the religious institutions will not accept your new narrative. You've become the alien and sojourner that Peter speaks of. The isolation can be crippling as even those that you love the most are troubled that you no longer fit their personal narrative that they so desperately need you to be for them to feel complete. But there is the prize on the other side of that door, and it does not have a price. I've had my Job experience and for that I am thankful. My heart is restored and there is no noise in my mind. The conflict within is over, and it is now time to reintegrate into the simulation that the world now appears to be, while seeking to protect my energy from its corruption. For the moment I must accept that the world may consider me to have lost my mind, but in my heart I'm convinced that to God I am a brother of Jesus, for it was His testimony that got me through. I would like to wrap this up from the perspective of C.G. Jung, a giant in the study of human psychology, for that is what the Bible reveals to those participating in this truly extraordinary spiritual experience. The Bible must be the greatest book written on the psyche of man.

"Your vision will become clear only when you can look into your heart. Who looks outside, dreams, who looks inside, awakes."
C.G. Jung

If we are masterful by nature to do one thing it's this…to unknowingly deceive ourselves throughout this process.

> *"Through pride we are deceiving ourselves. But deep down below the surface of the average conscience a still, small voice says to us, something is out of tune."*
> **C.G. Jung**

But until we become aware of awareness we believe that much of what we endure is happening *to us* and not a byproduct of our own ignorance.

> *"Until you make the unconscious conscious, it will direct your life and you will call it fate."*
> **C.G. Jung**

Now read the above quote substituting *'IT'* as the one directing your life. This dynamic is reflected in the collective psyche and serves to provide cover for *'IT'*, as one is the mirror of the other.

> *"We shall probably get nearest to the truth if we think of the conscious and personal psyche as resting upon the broad basis of an inherited and universal psychic disposition which is as such unconsciousness, and that our personal psyche bears the same relation to the collective psyche as the individual to society."*
> **C.G. Jung**

The primary influencer from the collective consciousness is the unconscious attachment to ideologies and errant belief systems.

> *"Every form of addiction is bad, no matter whether the narcotic be alcohol, morphine or idealism."*
> **C.G. Jung**

While in the *natural body* persona we see ourselves as separated from God and the world around us as real versus the illusion that it is.

"Man's task is to become conscious of the contents
that press from the unconscious."
C.G. Jung

We all suffer from a form of psychosis that needs to be proactively confronted.

"A psychoneurosis must be understood, ultimately, as the
suffering of a soul which has not discovered it's meaning."
C.G. Jung

However, *'IT'* knows that it's not real and will do whatever it takes to keep you from looking at the inner man using fear as its primary tool.

"People will do anything, no matter how absurd,
to avoid facing their own souls."
C.G. Jung

The instruction provided in the Bible fully recognizes this dynamic and through His Christ provides for a *'Way'* through. Having said that, the practice of western religions does not recognize the substance of *'IT'* and instead places the emphasis on modifying *'IT's* moralistic behavior.

"The Christ symbol is of the greatest importance for psychology in
so far as it is perhaps the most highly developed and differentiated
symbol of the self, apart, from the figure of the Buddha."
C.G. Jung

The pursuit of spirituality has similar challenges.

"One does not become enlightened by imagining figures
of light, but by making the darkness conscious."
C.G. Jung

But the prize is worth the effort and the pain.

"The privilege of a lifetime is to become who you truly are," even if, *"The most terrifying thing is to accept oneself completely."*
C.G. Jung

The practice of religion is at a crossroads and needs to take a hard turn in order to return to the truth of how we are made. Even though it appears that I'm coming down hard on the practice of religion, those perceptions don't compare to the actual warnings peppered throughout scripture regarding the inherent perils that religiosity represents. Religion didn't work for me, and I would personally suggest that I'm an omniest, believing that there is a thread of truth running through all religions, for deep in our hearts we all must believe that there is ultimately only one truth. The divisions that we see today are a byproduct of the various doctrines inherent in every man-made belief system, religious or otherwise, that serve to justify one through the denigration of the other. Humanity can do better than this; it must if we are to reflect what that one truth signifies. I can't for a second suggest that the ultimate truth is reflected in this effort, but I can say that focusing on matters that we can all agree on will get us much closer to the truth than the practice of focusing on the differences. It's a choice that each of us must make, for it's the journey of your soul and:

The Story You Find Yourself In

ARTISTS DESCRIPTION OF BOOK COVER PAINTING

Front Cover Artist: Becca Tindol

The painting on the cover is titled "Journey Into the All-Knowing Eye". The original was painted with acrylic paints on a 18x24 inch canvas. The meaning of this painting is as follows:

"This painting is the physical expression of the journey from suffering, trauma, self destruction, overwhelming fear and depression to discovering connection, truth, and love through a spiritual awakening. I painted this to illustrate my experience with the dark night of the soul, a painful but necessary catalyst to growth, and as I grew through this experience I reconnected with the spirit within me, as well as the source of infinite love and wisdom that underlies all things. Seeing life through the eyes of this infinite loving spirit has shown me the truth and brought me peace unlike anything I've ever experienced before. Although I am human and this peace can be clouded by stresses and life events, if I turn inwards I can always find it as it is a part of me. I hope this painting serves as a reminder than anyone can overcome any trial and tribulation in this life and come out the other side as a new person."

Becca is a painter and mother from Alabama. She focuses on painting visions that she sees in her minds eye when meditating. She started focusing on painting mid-2018 after having an experience while painting where she felt she was a conduit for the universe who was expressing itself through her. Themes of her artwork include consciousness, spirituality, duality, the infinite nature of the soul, beauty of nature, and the human experience.

You can find more of Becca's artwork on her website www.alteredmoonart.com or contact her through email at alteredmoonart@gmail.com

Lightning Source UK Ltd.
Milton Keynes UK
UKHW010732130123
415295UK00001B/51

9 798765 236840